Political Competition, Innovation and Growth in the History of Asian Civilizations

Political Competition, Innovation and Growth in the History of Asian Civilizations

Edited by

Peter Bernholz

Professor Emeritus of Economics, Center for Economics and Business (WWZ), University of Basle, Switzerland

Roland Vaubel

Professor of Economics, University of Mannheim, Germany

With a foreword by Eric Jones

Edward Elgar
Cheltenham, UK • Northampton, MA, USA

Published by
Edward Elgar Publishing Limited
Glensanda House
Montpellier Parade
Cheltenham
Glos GL50 1UA
UK

Edward Elgar Publishing, Inc.
136 West Street
Suite 202
Northampton
Massachusetts 01060
USA

A catalogue record for this book
is available from the British Library

Library of Congress Cataloguing in Publication Data

Political competition, innovation and growth in the history of Asian civilizations /
    edited by Peter Bernholz and Roland Vaubel.
        p. cm.
    Includes bibliographical references
        1. Competition—Asia—History. 2. Asia—Economic policy. 3. Asia—Politics
    and government. 4. Technological innovations—Asia—History. I. Bernholz, Peter.
    II. Vaubel, Roland.

    HD41.P642 2004
    950'.072—dc22

                                                                            2004053038

ISBN 1 84376 919 0

Typeset by Cambrian Typesetters, Frimley, Surrey
Printed and bound in Great Britain by MPG Books Ltd, Bodmin, Cornwall

Contents

About the authors

Jean Baechler is Professor of Sociology at Sorbonne University, Paris. His books include *Les phénomènes révolutionnaires* (Presses Universitaires, 1970), *Les origines du capitalisme* (Gallimard, 1971), *La solution indienne* (Presses Universitaires, 1988), *Le capitalisme* (Gallimard, 1995) and *Esquisse d'une histoire universelle* (Fayard, 2002).

Peter Bernholz is Professor of Economics, Emeritus, at Universität Basel, Switzerland. He is Research Fellow of the Center of Public Choice, George Mason University, and a corresponding member of the Bavarian Academy of Sciences. He has been President of the European Public Choice Society. He is author of *The International Game of Power* (Mouton, 1985), *Democracy and Capitalism* (Journal of Evolutionary Economics, 2000) and co-editor of *Political Competition, Innovation and Growth: A Historical Analysis* (Springer, 1998) which focuses on European experiences.

Michael Cook is Cleveland E. Dodge Professor of Near Eastern Studies at Princeton University. Prior to his move to Princeton in 1986, he taught at the School of Oriental and African Studies in the University of London. His publications include *Population Pressure in Rural Anatolia, 1450–1600* (Oxford University Press, 1972), *The Koran*, in the Very Short Introductions series (Oxford University Press, 2000) and *Commanding Right and Forbidding Wrong in Islamic Thought* (Cambridge University Press, 2000).

Günther Distelrath is Privatdozent at Forschungsstelle Modernes Japan, Universität Bonn, Germany. His main research subjects are the social and economic history of Japan and the development of the social sciences in the twentieth century. He is author of the book *Die japanische Produktionsweise: Zur wissenschaftlichen Genese einer stereotypen Sicht der japanischen Wirtschaft* (Iudicium, 1996).

Mark Elvin is Professor of Chinese History at the Research School of Pacific and Asian Studies in the Australian National University. His doctorate is from Cambridge University, and he was Harkness-Commonwealth Fellow at Harvard University. He is an Emeritus Fellow of St Anthony's College Oxford and a Fellow of the Academy of the Humanities of Australia. He is best known for *The Pattern of the Chinese Past* (Stanford University Press, 1975) and as the co-author of the *Cultural Atlas of China* (Facts on File, 1983/1998).

Toby E. Huff is Chancellor Professor of Sociology at the University of Massachusetts Dartmouth. He is author of *The Rise of Early Modern Science: Islam, China and the West* (Cambridge University Press, 1993) and co-editor of *Max Weber and Islam* (Transaction Books, 1999). A revised second edition of *The Rise of Modern Science* is published in 2003 with a new epilogue.

R. Stephen Humphreys is Professor of History and King Abdul Azis Al Saud Professor of Islamic Studies at the University of California, Santa Barbara. He received his doctorate from the University of Michigan. His books include *Islamic History: A Framework for Inquiry* (Princeton University Press, 1991) and *Between Memory and Desire: The Middle East in a Troubled Age* (University of California Press, 1999).

Eric Jones is Emeritus Professor of La Trobe University, Professorial Fellow at Melbourne Business School, University of Melbourne, and Visiting Professor, Graduate Centre of International Business, University of Reading. His books include *The European Miracle: Environments, Economies and Geopolitics in the History of Europe and Asia* (Cambridge University Press, 3rd edn 2003), *Growth Recurring: Economic Change in World History* (University of Michigan Press, 2nd edn 2000), and *The Record of Global Economic Development* (Edward Elgar Publishing, 2002).

Timur Kuran is Professor of Economics and Law, and King Faisal Professor of Islamic Thought and Culture at the University of Southern California. Among his published works is *Private Truths, Public Lies: The Social Consequences of Preference Falsification* (Harvard University Press, 1995), which has also appeared in German, Swedish and Turkish. He edits an interdisciplinary book series for the University of Michigan Press. He has been a member of the Institute of Advanced Study in Princeton and has held the John Ohlin Visiting Professorship at the Graduate School of Business, University of Chicago.

Deepak Lal is James S. Coleman Professor of International Development Studies at the University of California, Los Angeles, and Professor Emeritus of Political Economy at University College, London. He was educated in India and at Jesus College, Oxford. He has been Lecturer at Jesus College and Christ Church College as well as Research Fellow at Nuffield College, Oxford. During 1983–87 he was an Economic Advisor and then Research Administrator at the World Bank, on leave from University College, London. His books include *The Hindu Equilibrium* (2 vols, Clarendon Press, 1988/89), *Unintended Consequences* (MIT Press, 1998) and *Unfinished Business* (Oxford University Press, 1999).

Pak Hung Mo is Professor of Economics at Hongkong Baptist University. His doctorate is from the University of Washington. He has published, *inter alia*, on Chinese economic history and development (for example in *Kyklos*, 1995) and on consumer theory.

John Powelson is Professor of Economics, Emeritus, at the University of Colorado. He has also taught at the universities of Pittsburgh, Johns Hopkins, Pennsylvania, George Washington and Harvard. He is author of *Centuries of Economic Endeavour* (1992) and *The Moral Economy* (1998), both University of Michigan Press.

Dietmar Rothermund is Professor of South Asian History, Emeritus, at Universität Heidelberg. He studied history and philosophy at the Universities of Marburg and Munich and received his doctorate from the University of Pennsylvania. He is chairman of the European Association of South Asian Studies. His books include *Government, Landlord and Peasant in India* (Steiner, 1978), *India and the Great Depression, 1929–1939* (Manohar, 1992) and *A History of India* (with H. Kulke, 3rd edn, Routledge, 1998).

Dean Keith Simonton is Professor of Psychology at the University of California, Davis. He received his PhD in Social Psychology from Harvard University. He has authored eight books, including *Genius, Creativity, and Leadership* (Harvard University Press, 1984), *Scientific Genius* (Cambridge University Press, 1988), *Psychology, Science and History* (Yale University Press, 1990) and *Origins of Genius* (Oxford University Press, 1999).

Ken'ichi Tomobe is Professor of Japanese Economic History at Keio University, Graduate School of Economics, Tokyo.

Roland Vaubel is Professor of Economics at Universität Mannheim, Germany. He received a BA in Philosophy, Politics and Economics from the University of Oxford and an MA from Columbia University, New York. He has been Visiting Professor in International Economics at the Graduate School of Business, University of Chicago. He is author of *The Centralization of Western Europe* (Institute of Economic Affairs, 1995) and co-editor of *The Political Economy of International Organization* (with Thomas D. Willett, Westview Press, 1991) and *Political Competition, Innovation and Growth: A Historical Analysis* (Springer, 1998).

Erich Weede is Professor of Sociology at Universität Bonn, Germany. Previously, he was professor at Universität Köln and Visiting Professor of International Relations at the Bologna Center of Johns Hopkins University. His two most recent books are *Economic Development, Social Order and World Politics* (Lynne Rienner, 1996) and *Asien und der Westen* (Nomos, 2002).

Foreword

Eric Jones

A new phase of scholarship starts when an accepted generalization is placed under serious review. The specialists may then confirm some of its applications but they also start to point out anomalies, the instances when the evidence does not fit very well. In its broadest sense the proposition scrutinized in this volume is that spells of political fragmentation in the pre-modern world had very large consequences indeed. The suggestion is that they were accompanied by, and in some measure actually occasioned, a broad range of episodes of cultural creativity, innovation both technological and commercial, and economic growth. This hypothesis, originally drawn from the European case, is examined here by scholars whose careers have become virtually synonymous with the interpretation of historical experience in China, Japan, India and the Islamic world. The volume nevertheless carries on beyond mere second-phase work. The comparative histories that it contains clarify a number of issues and enable us to derive a programme for the next stage of research.

The volume's central notion is labelled by its editors, the Hume–Kant hypothesis. The writings of Hume and Kant, taken together, urge that competition among countries is not only economically beneficial but vital to preserve liberty. However those of us who started to argue along these lines a generation ago seldom referred to predecessors like Hume or Kant. Certainly I never came across the relevant passages in their works, let alone those in Gibbon's *Decline and Fall*. We rediscovered the wheel for ourselves, so to speak. What we added – the sidelight we thought illuminated the core idea – was the suggestion that political systems in Asia were too centralized to reap the benefits secured in Europe.

This extrapolation outside Europe took as its reference point Western writings that portrayed Asian histories as sagas of empire. Perhaps we did not understand that by the 1980s traditional European and American scholarship about the non-Western world was wearing out; old stereotypes were on the brink of being replaced by more generous and complex visions. Asian specialists were soon highlighting phases when unitary empires were absent from that continent and identifying the spells of political fragmentation that had occurred there. The original hypothesis implied that such periods would have been marked by creativity as in Europe, though in reality perhaps less continuously or cumulatively. This extension of Hume–Kant is what the present volume uses modern research to test.

The founding generalization invokes a competitive model of cultural, political and economic change. The notion that fragmentation and innovation are connected was of course never meant to account for every historical detail. Those of us who employed the concept always intended it as a sketch rather than a portrait. It is obviously an ideal type of explanation that seeks primarily to indicate the direction of change. In order to fit the complexities even of European experience, the central notion requires various modifications. We also noted that interstate competition by itself did not fully explain economic development. For instance, a technological threshold probably had to be crossed to bring about economic advance on the scale seen in Western Europe by the start of the nineteenth century.

'Test' is the appropriate word for the exercise presented here: interesting quantitative data on cultural creativity are offered and considered. In the event, scholars do not always agree about either the facts of the Asian record or the validity of the argument. While some find the hypothesis useful, others read the histories of their chosen regions more sceptically. Individual Asian histories seem set on divergent paths. As a result, the story seems to blur and this appears to render the link between political fragmentation and innovation indeterminate. On the face of it, we are plunged back into a familiar but unexciting type of history where precision supersedes inspiration, much is contingent, and little by way of an underlying logic can be detected.

At this point it may seem that the message of the volume is negative, leaving us uncertain about the generality of the original idea yet at the same time without a clear alternative. Nevertheless beneath the surface disagreements and the caveats advanced by students of one country or another, a pattern does begin to emerge that suggests amending rather than abandoning the hypothesis. This new notion is more qualified than before, which is only to be expected when so much additional knowledge about intricate, historically ill-recorded circumstances is brought to bear. But the possibility of a new relationship between fragmentation and creativity should inspire the next round of investigation.

Consider what emerges. It is that the creativity and innovation expected of periods of fragmentation, and clearly to be found in many of them, can sometimes be suppressed, so that the relationship as a whole threatens to become misty. In Japan, the workings of Hume–Kant may have been denied for long periods by internal warfare. In India (accounts differ) a blanketing cosmological choice may have brought Hume–Kant forth stillborn. In the Islamic world the relationship may have been prevented from flowering by a homogeneous legal system.

What does this imply? It implies that political fragmentation *tout court* was not sufficient to induce growth; the historical pattern of Hume–Kant operated only within an 'optimality band'. When a political system veered outside the band in one direction, towards overmuch central control, creativity was restricted. This much may be deduced from the original proposition and is documented here. On the other hand, where political fragmentation corresponded with the opposite circumstances of instability and warfare, creativity may have been unable to flourish – or if it did, it may not have ripened into full innovation. The histories of the political systems under review (five of them if we include Europe) exhibit from time to time and place to place every kind of disturbance and repression, every disability as far as innovation is concerned.

Nevertheless when there was relative stability among competing states, there were often creative bursts in Asia as there were in Europe. What one author refers to as the 'barely adolescent state of our knowledge' means that there is more to do before the Hume–Kant thesis can be fully defined in an Asian context. How long the effects typically take before revealing themselves is one aspect that needs more investigation. In the event, this volume offers a fruitful way forward. It helps to specify more precisely the range of conditions under which decentralized political arrangements conduce to economic development.

1. Introduction and overview

Peter Bernholz and Roland Vaubel

In 1742, David Hume notes in his essay 'Of the rise and progress of the arts and sciences':

> That it is impossible for the arts and sciences to arise, at first, among any people unless that people enjoy the blessing of a free government . . . (61) . . .
>
> That nothing is more favourable to the rise of politeness and learning than a number of neighbouring and independent states, connected together by commerce and policy (64).
>
> Where a number of neighbouring states have great intercourse of arts and commerce, their mutual jealousy keeps them from receiving too lightly the law from each other, in matters of taste and of reasoning, and makes them examine every work of art with the greatest care and accuracy (65).

Immanuel Kant, who always took much of his inspiration from David Hume, elaborated on this theory and suggested that freedom itself rests on the existence of a number of neighbouring and independent states, connected by commerce and jealous of each other:

> Now the States are already in the present day involved in such close relations with each other that none of them can pause or slacken in its internal civilization without losing power and influence in relation to the rest . . . Civil liberty cannot now be easily assailed without inflicting such damage as will be felt in all trades and industries, and especially in commerce; and this would entail a diminution of the powers of the State in external relations . . . And thus it is that, notwithstanding the intrusion of many a delusion and caprice, the spirit of enlightenment gradually arises as a great good which the human race must derive even from the selfish purposes of aggrandizement on the part of its rulers, if they understand what is for their own advantage (1784/1959: 31).

The idea was taken up by Edward Gibbon (1787)[1] and Max Weber (1923)[2] and developed into a full-blown theory in two books by Jean Baechler (1975) and Eric Jones (1981). Since then, many eminent historians, social scientists and legal scholars have commented on what might be called the Hume–Kant hypothesis.[3] At the same time, controversy continues as to whether competition among neighbouring and independent states favours innovation in the arts and sciences primarily because it provides diversity and facilitates comparisons (Hume) or rather because it restrains the rulers and promotes civil liberty (Kant). This volume testifies to the liveliness of this debate.

The title of Eric Jones's path-breaking book is *The European Miracle*, thus suggesting that the beneficial effects of interstate competition were largely confined to European history. By contrast, China, India and the Islamic Middle East, which around AD 1500 were at a similar level of development, tend to be regarded as inherently imperial and overcentralized. All of them, it is true, fell behind after 1500. The enlightenment, the scientific breakthrough and the industrial revolution took place in Europe – not in Asia. But China, India and the Islamic Middle East have not always been unified. In their history, there have been long spells of decentralized rule or interstate competition. The same is true for Japan. If the Hume–Kant hypothesis is correct, it should also apply to those periods. It has to be tested against additional evidence. That is the purpose of this book.

The volume contains the papers and comments prepared for an interdisciplinary conference which took place in Heidelberg, Germany, in September 2002. The contributors are historians, sociologists, a socio-psychologist and economists.

While we are primarily interested in the Hume–Kant hypothesis, we also have to allow for competing explanations. If, in some instance, decentralization and interstate competition did not have the predicted effect, how can this be explained? Is the hypothesis conditional on certain other factors which failed to be present? Or was the predicted effect offset by other influences on innovation and growth? We present an overview of the results.

This Introduction is followed by two general chapters – one theoretical and deductive, the other empirical and quantitative. Four case studies ensue.

In Chapter 2, Jean Baechler argues that the most important factor explaining surges of human creativity is a political pattern of fragmentation in which a unified cultural area is divided among a plurality of competing polities. Such a fractal pattern is an organizational structure consisting of multiple levels, each allowed and able to deal with all the problems raised at that level without interference from above or below, and all integrated from level to level so that a problem which cannot be solved at a lower level, can be at a higher level. The fractal pattern optimizes exploration because implementation of innovation requires political freedom, and a plurality of polities is a precondition of political freedom. While the supply of talent is a random variable in society at large, demand for it is larger if no individual or coalition can block new entrants – especially disruptive talents – indefinitely. All histories of political unification are stories of the enlargement of both the polities and political power. By contrast, if political power is fragmented, each ruler needs, in order not to be vanquished, the support of the social elites and has to buy their support by concessions of power, wealth and prestige. The elites obtain from these concessions the opportunity to build strong coalitions among themselves against the central power. When a limited number of polities have been shaped by chance and by history in such a way that none is strong enough to crush a coalition of all the others, imperialization can be prevented indefinitely.

This was the case in Europe, but the best example of a fractal pattern was the tribal world. China appears to be the perfect model of an empire but it has also experienced two long periods of the fractal pattern. Its predynastic and interdynastic periods have been the most creative and innovative. Japan, having tried during the Nara period to follow the Chinese path to a monopolistic kingdom, failed entirely and began a long journey through the fractal pattern. This evolution culminated in a feudal system which was a perfect example of the highest achievements in innovation and development. In the Middle East, the interdynastic periods are long enough to make empires the exception. But the area becomes divided into mutually exclusive entities, each developing a monopolistic pattern, so that the result is entirely different from what can be observed in Europe.

There are three comments on Baechler's chapter. Michael Cook argues that turning Baechler's insight into a testable hypothesis requires much more specification. Is the fractal or federal pattern a sufficient condition or a necessary condition for cultural creativity, or neither of these? What is to count as cultural creativity? What is to count as a federal pattern? Over what time scale must the effects of interstate competition register?

Mark Elvin in his comment recalls the distinction between stimulus on the one hand and facilitation or inhibition on the other. Without stimulus there is no creativity, but creative response to stimulus requires appropriate conceptual and physical tools as well as physical and organizational resources. The most important single facilitation mechanism for creativity is the intensity per unit of space of interactions between people, that is the exchange of commodities, techniques, ideas, beliefs, fashions and so on. In some respects, empires can be extremely good for creativity because they create a large zone of peace and, at times, free trade. In other respects, the problems of control created by vast political size can lead to the use of techniques that suppress creativity, or creativity of certain types.

Erich Weede suggests that in order to arrive at clearly testable hypotheses, the explanandum should not be cultural creativity but scientific, technological or economic development; the explanans should be defined as political fragmentation rather than a federal pattern; and the side condition is not only a unified cultural area but also a fairly integrated economic area. Political fragmentation is an effective way of dealing with human fallibility because it minimizes the risk of big errors and maximizes the likelihood of detecting and correcting errors. Political fragmentation also forces rulers to recognize private property rights because confiscatory policies would weaken the economy and reduce tax revenue. The recognition of private property permits economic development, the overcoming of mass poverty and ultimately democracy.

In Chapter 3, Dean Keith Simonton surveys the quantitative evidence on the sources of creativity in different civilizations. Starting from the observation that creative genius is not randomly distributed over the history of any civilization but tends to fall into temporal clusters, he notes several potential causal factors which have been investigated in the literature, finally focusing on political fragmentation and cultural heterogeneity. He recalls the finding of Naroll et al. (1971) that political fragmentation was the only factor significantly associated with the appearance of creative geniuses in the Chinese, Indian, Middle Eastern and European civilizations. The analysis of Schaefer et al. (1977) confirmed that political fragmentation is positively and significantly correlated with the number of creative geniuses in the history of India from 500 BC to AD 1800 (r = 0.73). The raw data of Naroll et al. and Schaefer et al. are attached to Simonton's chapter.

In China, however, in the field of literature the correlation between the number of outstanding authors and political fragmentation was strongly negative (Ting 1986). Simonton considers two explanations. First, Chinese literature may have been a special case because all Chinese languages are written in the same way, so that any tendencies of political disintegration could not take voice in a corresponding literary movement. In philosophy, by contrast, the Golden Age occurred when China had disintegrated into numerous independent states. (We shall see that Pak Hung Mo in Chapter 4 offers another reason for considering Chinese literature a special case.) Second, Simonton suggests that cultural heterogeneity may be a more important cause of creativity than political fragmentation (with which it is closely related). He also argues that political fragmentation in China usually did not contribute to cultural heterogeneity because the emergence of new states would represent the conquest of Chinese peoples by invading non-Chinese barbarians. In the civilizations of India or Islam, by contrast, imperial expansion often meant the oppression of cultures quite different from those of the conquerors. Simonton also notes that, according to Armajani (1970), the high point of creativity in the Islamic civilization did not appear until after the disintegration of the caliphate, and that creativity in the history of Japan has been shown to be positively affected by the degree of exposure to foreign influences, that is cultural heterogeneity. But political unification will not be a detriment to creativity where concentrated funds are necessary to finance the achievements, for example, monumental architecture.

In Chapter 4, Pak Hung Mo analyses the varying degrees of inter-jurisdictional competition and their effects on innovation and growth in the history of China. During the Chou dynasty (1122–221 BC), especially from 722 BC onwards, a well-established feudal system generated fierce competition among a considerable number, at times hundreds, of rulers and forced them to design institutions favourable to economic development and military strength. After the unification of China in 221 BC, political competition was weak. Sometimes, centralized rule was interrupted between the dynasties, for example in AD 222–261 and AD 311–580, but development was hampered by anarchy, barbarian invasion and political instability. The renewal of the unified empires of Sui and T'ang in AD 589 led to counterproductive policies of confiscation and government control and an underutilization of technology. But since bureaucrats were recruited according to their poetic ability, there were remarkable accomplishments in poetry. Under the Sung dynasty (960–1275), which faced severe international competition and had to pay tribute to neighbouring 'barbarians' for most of its reign, China advanced to the threshold of a systematic experimental investigation of nature and created the world's earliest mechanized industry. Private printing was popular, and water-powered machines for spinning hemp thread appeared. The government promoted education, irrigation and trade, including maritime and foreign trade. Military technology was at a high level. The Sung period was both the climax and the end of scientific and technological progress. After the rule of the Mongols from 1276 to 1367, the Chinese Ming dynasty was characterized by the complete centralization of all power in the hands of the emperor and a powerful secret police. It adopted policies of reducing contacts between Chinese and foreigners and of stopping private ventures overseas because this would lead to centrifugal coastal centres of power. As the dominant recruitment subject, the Ming introduced a special type of essay which was rigid in form and elegant in style, but indoctrinating in substance and hostile to innovation in effect. Mo attributes the striking literary and cultural unity of China primarily to the pictorial nature of the Chinese characters, which meant that they could be understood and used by people of very different languages or dialects. In the Appendix, he presents a formal mathematical model to show how interstate competition induces utility-maximizing rulers to adopt more growth-oriented policies even though they risk increasing the power of potential opponents at home by doing so.

In the first comment, Mark Elvin emphasizes that China has also benefited from competition between religions, a highly competitive examination system, the prevalence of a personally free legal status, the trend towards the privatization of land holding and the rise of free markets. Religious competition seems to have been the motive force behind the invention and spread of woodblock printing more than 1000 years ago, with Buddhism in the lead role. The rise of relatively free markets began under a weakened empire in the ninth century, continuing with the political fragmentation of the Five Dynasties and Ten Kingdoms and then again under the Sung dynasty. Elvin broadly agrees with Mo that the Chou and Sung eras were economically highly creative, but he doubts that interstate competition at the time of the Sung can be legitimately described within a framework of overarching cultural unity. The period of fragmentation after the break-up of the Han empire was much less creative in economic terms; however it was very creative in cultural respects. The Ming and Quing empires also had their innovations but these were of a collective nature: the quality of seawalls was improved with the help of a new technology, and the Quing merchant guilds secured regular trading relationships.

Toby Huff agrees that the Sung period was one of considerable creativity and innovation. There were major changes in land ownership, a state and educational reorganization and, above all, a great upsurge in commercial activity. Some have suggested that the levels of economic output (as measured by tons of iron produced) achieved an all-time high during this period, from which they dropped by 50 per cent during the next three centuries. But some of these institutional changes which lasted all the way to the end of China in 1911 proved to be a fatal block on intellectual progress, civil autonomy and economic development. Most notably, it was the Sung officials who put the civil service examination firmly in place and made the Confucian classics the main subject of study. The examinations were based almost entirely on memorization and discouraged any independent thinking. The system was run by bureaucrats who themselves had mastered the examinations. No independent body of professors could emerge, as the whole system was embedded in the state bureaucracy. Without appropriate institutional foundations, science could not flourish as in Europe.

Erich Weede emphasizes that the political system of imperial China was patrimonial rather than feudal. While feudalism nurtures ideas of reciprocity and rights, including property rights, patrimonialism permits much more arbitrary rule. The ideas of law and of equality under the law never grew roots in imperial China. Moreover, China lacked independent cities which could defend themselves. Weede suggests that China's fast growth since 1979 is to some extent due to devolution and interstate competition. Local and regional governments have to act as if they respected private property rights in order to gain and maintain the favour of investors from inside and outside China.

Finally, the chapter contains several tables which offer quantitative evidence on China. The tables and graphs indicating the number of innovations in the Chinese history of science, which have been extracted from Needham, confirm that innovation was at a very high level in the fourth to second century BC and in the eleventh century AD. Without chemistry, which dominates the total, this was no longer true for the second century BC (Early Han), but the sixth century AD (six dynasties) stands out. The two peaks in the fourteenth and the seventeenth centuries are entirely due to the outliers in the field of mechanical engineering (mainly milling and pumping).

If the number of innovations is computed not per century but per dynasty, and if it is normalized for the duration of each dynasty, the Northern Sung take second rank after the Yuan and before the Earlier Han. Moreover, the number of innovations rises steeply under the Warring States and the Six Dynasties (diverse states 1). The sharpest decline occurs under the Later Han and the Ching.

The results for the Early Han and Yuan may be due to the fact that many innovations had to be assigned to the dynasty in which they were first reported rather than the dynasty during which they were actually made. Moreover, initially, a new empire may still benefit from the innovative thrust of the earlier competitive environment, and the market integration that goes with political unification strengthens the incentive to innovate. But as time goes by, the centralized system degenerates and innovation suffers.[4]

Table 3.1 in the Appendix to Simonton's paper reports the data of Naroll et al. (1971). The number of eminent creators in China is at a peak in the eleventh century when the number of independent states is large. Both numbers drop thereafter. Obviously, these raw data have to be adjusted for population size and the increasing availability of historical data. The quantitative studies quoted in this volume take this problem into account.

The last piece of evidence is in Table 1.1 below. Real GDP per capita in China is estimated to have increased by about one-third between 1000 and 1500. It then stagnated until 1820 while in Western Europe it rose by about 60 per cent. After 1820, Chinese per capita GDP even declined (by 27 per cent until 1950).

In Chapter 5, Günter Distelrath explains how centralizing and decentralizing tendencies alternated in the history of Japan and how these changes affected political stability, legal security and economic prosperity. Before

Table 1.1   Real GDP per capita* in selected years (0–1950 AD)

	0	1000	1500	1600	1700	1820	1870	1913	1950
China	450	450	600	600	600	600	530	552	439
Japan	400	425	500	520	570	669	737	1387	1926
India	450	450	550	550	550	533	533	673	619
Asia excluding Japan	450	450	572	575	571	575	543	640	635
Total Western Europe	450	400	774	894	1024	1232	1974	3473	4594
World	444	435	565	593	615	667	867	1510	2114

Note: *1990 international US dollars.

Source: Angus Maddison (2002: 264).

AD 645, Japan was completely decentralized and divided among a large number of local rulers. In 645, Japan was unified and a strongly centralized system was set up following the Chinese model. Legal security, the currency and the irrigation system benefited, but this order disintegrated when local positions became heritable, landownership spread and tax sovereignties were set up. Towards the end of the Japanese Age of Antiquity, the local power-holders attacked the imperial government as well as each other. In 1185, the position of supreme military commander (shogun) and a system of vassals and retainership were introduced. This feudal structure of the Japanese Middle Ages was very different from the Chinese model and is commonly regarded as an essential step forward, enabling private ownership and the law of contract. But it ended in a century of civil war (1467–1568) which resulted in social and economic collapse. In 1603, the beginning of the Edo period or the Tokugawa shogunate, a new system was established which finely balanced centralizing and decentralizing elements. While the direct rule of the shogun was confined to a limited area, the families of the feudal lords were forced to reside permanently in the national capital (Edo). This hostage system enabled the central government to maintain peace and legal security but at the same time to increasingly delegate administration, including the power to tax. From the mid-eighteenth to the mid-nineteenth century, more than 250 fiscally independent and state-like units (*han*) competed with each other in matters of economic and trade policy, and many had their own (paper) currencies. Less-developed jurisdictions at the periphery could catch up with the most-developed regions or even surpass them by offering good governance and adopting new economic strategies. This 'proto-interstate competition' promoted economic prosperity and urbanization. During the Edo period, Japan was isolated from the rest of the world. Its re-emergence as a centralized state in 1867/68 was a reaction to external threats and pressures. However, the Meiji Restoration opened Japan for international political and market competition.

Ken'ichi Tomobe points out that in the Edo period each feudal domain had dominant power not only over the production of local goods and foods, but also over their distribution and circulation. The freedom of economic activity in each domain was basically undisturbed from the eighteenth century onwards. Nor did the central government interfere with local culture, which each domain had developed independently for a long time. While the central government kept Japan united as a nation by centralizing diplomacy and military power, decentralization of economic, social and cultural affairs allowed much progress to occur. Interjurisdictional competition in this period prepared the basis for modern Japanese capitalism in the late nineteenth century.

John Powelson argues that Japan – relative to other countries – has been decentralized from the beginning of history, but because of internal wars and other civil disturbances, decentralization did not lead to significant economic development until approximately the thirteenth century. Thereafter, lower levels of society – farmers and merchants – formed village organizations that were favourable to freedom, innovation and growth. The most significant push towards these institutions occurred during the Edo period, with the development of modern farming, free merchants, new transportation, financial institutions, insurance companies and other instruments such as forward contracts. All this occurred because the Tokugawa shogunate was too weak to stop it. Japan remained decentralized after the end of the Tokugawa shogunate, but Japan's isolation from the rest of the world during the 1920s and 1930s led to new power for the Japanese army and a recentralization of government. At the end of the Second World War, the army was destroyed, and decentralized Japan was reinvigorated. This was the period when Japan became a world economic power.

Quantitative evidence is provided by Simonton's table on creativity in the history of Japan, and the Table 1.1 on real GDP per capita in this Introduction. The total number of eminent creative individuals began to rise remarkably at the beginning of the Edo Period, with a peak in the middle of the eighteenth century when decentralization reached its highest level. (This is also true for medicine, the only field in the sample that is close to science.) Creativity seems to have increased even more after the Meiji Restoration (1867/68). Real per capita GDP rose by 42 per cent from 1600 to 1870, while it dropped by 6 per cent in the rest of Asia. In Western Europe however it more than doubled in this period.

Chapter 6 is devoted to India. Depak Lal suggests that, in the case of India, political and military competition among states and decentralization did not promote institutions conducive to economic freedom, innovation and growth. He argues that this was due to cosmological beliefs, notably the caste system. The nomadic Indo-European tribes who entered India from the north-west used the prevailing caste system to tie labour down to land when it was scarce relative to land. The caste system enabled them to secure a stable rural labour supply for the relatively labour-intensive plough agriculture. It established a decentralized system of control, and ensured that any attempt to start new settlements outside its framework would be difficult if not impossible. Any oppressed group planning to leave a particular village to set up on its own would find – if it were confined to a single caste group – that it did not have the necessary complementary skills to start a new settlement. Vertical mobility was dependent on the whole caste moving up the social hierarchy by adopting a different occupation, possibly migrating to a new region and demanding a higher ritual status. The other decentralized element of the Hindu sociopolitical system were the relatively autarchic village communities which had the tradition of paying a certain customary share of the village output as revenue to the current overlord. Like Europe, India was characterized – most of the time – by political disunity but cultural unity and a disjunction of state and society. One of the few things on which Indian historians agree is that the periods of dynastic imperial rule and political stability – sometimes, though fairly rarely, extending over the whole of the subcontinent – were also the most prosperous and glorious periods of Indian history, and the periods when innovation and growth took place. The basic reason was that the empires provided the subcontinental law and order that allowed long-distance trade to develop.

Dietmar Rothermund in his comment is less inclined to stress cosmological beliefs or the caste system in explaining the impediments to Indian development. He tends to agree with Pomeranz (2000) that the 'Great Divergence' between Europe and India originated in the eighteenth century under the oppressive weight of the Mughal empire. Until about 1200, medieval India was probably at least as stable as medieval Europe. Competition among the medieval kingdoms led to cultural innovation in the styles of literature, sculpture, construction of temples and so on. There was considerable interregional trade carried on by guilds of traders. There was also a fairly free international maritime trade. This system was upset when conquerors from Western Asia swept through Northern India and established the Delhi sultanate. The kingpin of this system was the man on horseback, usually a slave. Earlier institutions of local government were wiped out. The Mughal empire did not change this style very much. The massive expenditure on warfare pre-empted development in other spheres. Rothermund objects to the notion of a disjunction of state and society in the Indian context. On the contrary, the Brahmins were agents of state formation and legitimized the king with their rituals.

Erich Weede argues that interstate competition constrains the natural predatory tendencies of the state only where polity and dynastic persistence is the rule. In India, the survival of the political units was much more precarious than in Europe, where many states lasted for centuries even though their frontiers may have shifted. Rational Indian rulers did not have the same incentive to limit their confiscatory inclinations and recognize the property rights of some of their subjects. Moreover, where the mass of the population is excluded from war-fighting, there is little reason for rulers to grant rights, including property rights, to the disarmed population. Since India was ruled by Muslims for centuries, the political system was patrimonial and 'sultanistic' (Max Weber). The sultan recruited his staff largely from foreigners and slaves who were extremely dependent upon him, and reliable tools of arbitrary rule. Moreover, polygyny among the ruling Muslim classes meant that reproduction at the top of society was much faster than below, so that the prospects of upward mobility were reduced. This contributed to political instability. The pressure for conformity within the castes hampered the introduction of new working techniques. Finally, the caste system came close to preventing individual mobility so that a wealth-maximizing division of labour became impossible.

As the editors have pointed out, the caste system, by hampering not only vertical but also horizontal mobility, also protected local Indian rulers against interstate competition. The exit option was hardly available to an individual or family, and their local caste found it rather difficult to move to a neighbouring state. By tying down labour to the land, the rulers had restricted interstate competition for labour and human capital. Thus in India political fragmentation did not necessarily entail interstate competition as in Europe.

Quantitative evidence on India is provided in Table 3.2 of Simonton's chapter and Table 1.1 in this Introduction. Table 3.2 is taken from the study of Schaefer et al. (1977) which finds a very high correlation between creativity and political fragmentation in the history of India. The number of eminent creative persons peaks in the fourth and the twelfth century, the competitive medieval period discussed by Rothermund. The table also reveals that the twelfth century had the largest number of independent states (56). Table 1.1 shows a 22 per cent increase of real GDP per capita between AD 1000 and 1500, stagnation until 1700 and decline thereafter (until 1820).

The last chapter deals with the Islamic civilization in the Middle East and the Mediterranean. Timur Kuran, in his extensive chapter, argues that there is no systematic relationship between the degree of Islamic political unity and the Middle East's economic success. Its political centralization varied over time in ways that correlate poorly with the observed institutional creativity. The Ottoman state was highly centralized during the period considered its Golden Age. But all versions of the 'absolutist Islamic state' make the mistake of projecting state control in the modern sense to distant periods when social control techniques were still primitive. The critical difference between Europe and the Islamic world was not that one of these civilizations was more fragmented than the other in a political sense, but that laws critical to organizational development were relatively less flexible, and therefore more homogeneous, in the Islamic world. Greater homogeneity implied less institutional experimentation and fewer opportunities for starting down the path to modern capitalism. Islamic states allowed legal pluralism only to the non-Muslim minorities. Two elements of Islamic law, in particular, hindered the emergence of social pressures capable of inducing changes from within: the inheritance system, which kept commercial enterprises small and ephemeral, and the individualization of Islamic law, which precluded corporations. They also weakened the merchant class and limited the growth of civil society, thus restraining the demand for legal reforms. Moreover, Islamic states harmed economic growth through predatory policies inimical to private wealth accumulation. Thus the economically productive class gradually lost political influence to the state bureaucracy.

There are six comments to this chapter. Peter Bernholz draws attention to the beneficial consequences of political and ideological competition in

Muslim Spain. With the decline and fall of the Umayyad dynasty (756–1031), many small kingdoms (*ta'ifas*) developed in Islamic Spain. The dispersion of political power did not mean the end, but a greater extension, of cultural life: Seville, Granada, Valencia and other cities became political and cultural centres besides the old Cordoba. Indeed, the Spanish–Islamic culture gained real independence and discovered itself during the eleventh century. The sciences and medicine also flourished during this period. When the King of Castile conquered Toledo in 1085, the princes of Seville, Granada and so on felt threatened and asked the Almoravids (Morocco) for help. This help was granted but the Almoravids used the opportunity to subjugate all Spanish Muslim kingdoms except Valencia. The Almoravids (1086–1144) – after another, very short period of competing small kingdoms – were followed by the Almohads (1155–1212). Both the Almoravids and the Almohads were religious fundamentalists and quite intolerant, but they had to compete for citizens and human capital with the Christian rulers of Spain. After the decline of Almohad rule, the kingdom of Granada remained as the last Muslim state on the Iberian peninsula. It was able to maintain a highly developed culture, of which the Alhambra still bears evidence. Thus the zenith of Arab civilization on the peninsula, and perhaps of Arab–Islamic culture in general, occurred at a time of political decline when the rule of small states was self-evident. Bernholz also shows that Muslim Spain flourished economically. But it seems impossible to distinguish economic performance in these sub-periods as most of them were fairly short.

Michael Cook gives a picture significantly different from Kuran's. He argues that Islamic history provides quite a varied terrain on which to try out the Hume–Kant hypothesis. He distinguishes four periods:

(A)   a unitary period (from the time of the Prophet down to the later ninth century)
(B)   a plural period (from the later ninth to the early sixteenth century)
(C)   another unitary period (the Ottoman empire of the sixteenth century)
(D)   a crypto-plural period (the Ottoman empire of the seventeenth and eighteenth centuries).

Cook argues that the hypothesis is in trouble in period (A), which was one of remarkable cultural creativity. But Islamic law developed outside the context of state patronage, in places far from the political centre. In such a case it may be irrelevant whether there is one state or many. The disunity of period (B) did not deliver a good economic performance but produced some kinds of cultural creativity, for example the re-emergence of Persian as a literary language. Political instability may have been a problem. The hypothesis performs fairly well in the high Ottoman period (C): the absence of interjurisdictional competition dampened pressures for raising the sophistication and efficiency of the law. The late Ottoman period (D) of formal unity and effective disunity was definitely not one of vibrant and sustained economic growth. Once more, political instability may have been the explanation.

In Mark Elvin's view, Islam as a cultural phenomenon must not be considered a historical constant. Initially, the process of Islamic jurisprudence was quite responsive to the needs of key economic players. The early Islamic polities – the Umayyad and Abbasid caliphs, for example, were much more open to change than their successors. Gradually, this flexibility was lost. Elvin questions the decisiveness of the Islamic laws of inheritance which made it hard to accumulate enduring concentrations of wealth in private hands. Other great pre-modern societies, including China, also had laws or conventions of partible inheritance. The example of China also shows that the predominance of the state bureaucracy does not explain why the Ottoman rulers were absolutely indifferent to fostering the economic well-being of their subjects in a proactive fashion. For the Chinese empire, the people's livelihood was a well-understood Confucian responsibility.

Toby Huff agrees with Kuran that Islamic law blocked the way to continuous economic development. Although after the demise of the Abbasid empire the Islamic lands were divided up into potentially competitive rivals, the institutional structure that was derived from Islamic law negated the creative potential of the rivalrous context. Even the Ottoman empire fell far short of including all the major Islamic lands: there were three additional great Muslim empires (the Safavid centred in Iran, the Uzbek or Timurid, and the Mughal empire) – not to mention the Mamluk empire (Cairo), the Malaccan sultanate (Morocco), the Maghreb and the Songhay empire (Timbuktu). Even the competition with Europe did not result in enhanced economic development for the Ottomans. The break-up of the cultural and political unity of the Abbasid empire had not brought about a flowering of scientific creativity either. Instead, from the thirteenth century onwards, scientific culture in the Islamic lands continued to deteriorate. Most of the major philosophers and scientists required royal patronage, and when they lost it, suffered at the hands of local religious opposition groups. A major impediment to the development of modern science in the Muslim world has been the lack of legal autonomy, as enjoyed by European universities, cities, professional guilds and corporations.

Stephen Humphreys suggests that the most useful way of thinking about the relationship between polities, economics and cultural dynamism is to assess the capacity of a given regime to assure order and stability without becoming predatory. The causal direction however is often far from clear: should we ascribe the grandeur of ninth-century Baghdad or sixteenth-century Istanbul to the power of the Abbasid and Ottoman states, or should we say that these states owed their grandeur to economic vitality which was quite independent of them? What is certain is that large states which spent themselves into fiscal crisis (as the Abbasids did) or which spun into fiscal crisis for reasons beyond their control (as with the Ottomans at the turn of the seventeenth century) rapidly became predatory regimes, with disastrous economic (though not always cultural) results. As for the detrimental effects of Islamic commercial law, Kuran's argument is weakened by the barely adolescent state of our knowledge about the concrete historical development of Islamic legal doctrine over the centuries, and about the internal trade of the Ottoman empire.

Erich Weede identifies three reasons for the legal stagnation in Muslim civilization. First, legal competition was too weak, and obviously one background condition for legal competition and evolution is political fragmentation. Second, the common roots of Muslim law in the *Shari'a* further mitigated legal competition. And third, legal stagnation followed from the traditionalism inescapably linked to the ideas of God as law-giver, the Prophet as the mouthpiece of God, and the closing of the gates of interpretation at about 1000. Political fragmentation could not lead to the usual results because the revealed divine law represented the unchanging will of God. However, Weede insists that kleptocracy was a more fundamental problem than the Islamic law. The insecurity of property rights under sultanism discouraged capital formation by the merchants and market augmentation.

The editors would like to add that in most cases Islamic law seems to have prevented the Islamic states from competing effectively with regard to property rights. Large parts of Islamic law were binding in all Islamic states – even at the time of political disunity. As in the case of India, political fragmentation was not a sufficient condition for political competition because religious rules suppressed such competition.

Quantitative empirical evidence is provided by Table 3.1 attached to Simonton's chapter. The data of Naroll et al. (1971) reveal that in the Middle East, both the number of eminent creators and the number of states peaked in the tenth century.

The editors draw the following conclusions from these chapters and comments:

1. Political fragmentation is not a sufficient condition for political competition, innovation and growth but it is a necessary condition for interstate competition and for a high probability of sustained innovation and growth, at least in the private sector.
2. Political fragmentation will not lead to interstate competition unless there is considerable mobility among jurisdictions. This may have been lacking in India because of the caste system, and to some extent in the Islamic Middle East.
3. Political fragmentation will not lead to interstate competition if the rules

of a common religion effectively prevent the states from competing, for example in the field of property rights, as under Islam.

4. Interstate competition will not bring about widespread and sustained innovation and growth unless there is a minimum of political stability. The rulers must be sufficiently confident to keep their jurisdiction (as a sort of property) for themselves and their heirs. The survival of government, both at the top and the provincial level, may have been too precarious in India and the Islamic Middle East.

5. Political fragmentation will not favour innovation and growth if it leads to prolonged and highly destructive wars rather than limited warfare or peaceful competition for manpower and capital. Initially, empires may raise economic growth because they stop such destructive wars, establish law and order and liberalize trade and capital movements. After some time however they introduce excessive taxes and regulations which stifle innovation, efficiency and growth. Alternatively, incessant warfare can be prevented by geographic barriers, cultural unity or some balance of power.

6. The innovative spirit generated by interstate competition may persist in the early stages of a new empire, but sooner or later it dies away.

7. Political fragmentation stimulates innovation and growth not only by promoting political competition and freedom but also by increasing diversity and the scope for comparison.

8. Quite apart from political fragmentation, innovation and growth also benefit from institutional pluralism within the political units. It matters whether there are competing legal instruments, as in European history but not under Islam, and whether religious institutions are sufficiently separated from the state, as in European and Japanese history.

NOTES

1. 'Europe is now divided into twelve powerful, though unequal kingdoms, three respectable commonwealths, and a variety of smaller, though independent states ... The abuses of tyranny are restrained by the mutual influence of fear and shame, ... monarchies have imbibed the principles of freedom, or at least of moderation' (Gibbon 1787, Vol. VI, Chapter 38: 328).

2. 'The competitive struggle (among the European nation states) created the largest opportunities for modern western capitalism. The separate states had to compete for mobile capital, which dictated to them the conditions under which it would assist them to power' (Weber 1923: 249). Note that, to some extent this was anticipated by Hume's friend Adam Smith (1776): 'The proprietor of stock is properly a citizen of the world, and is not necessarily attached to any particular country. He would be apt to abandon the country in which he is exposed to vexatious inquisition, in order to be assessed a burdensome tax, and would remove his stock to some country where he could, either carry on his business, or enjoy his fortune at ease. A tax that tended to drive away stock from a particular country would so far tend to dry up every source of revenue, both to the sovereign and to the society' (Vol. 2: 375 ff.). And he adds: 'The abuses which sometimes creep into the local and provincial administration of a

local and provincial revenue, how enormous so ever they may appear, are in reality, however, almost always very trifling in comparison with those which commonly take place in the administration and expenditure of revenue of a great empire. They are, besides, much more easily corrected' (Vol. 2: 253).

3. It has been supported by Brennan and Buchanan (1980: 180–86), North (1981: 23ff.; 1998), McNeill (1982: 114), Berman (1983: 553; 1998), Hall (1985: 102; 1988), Chirot (1986: 296), Rosenberg and Birdzell (1996: 136ff.), Kennedy (1987: 16–30), Engerman (1988: 14ff.), Weede (1988, 2000), Pipes (1999) and Mokyr (1990: 302). See also Baechler (1988).

    However, the hypothesis has been criticized by Goldstone (1987) and Pommeranz (2000).

4. In Simonton's correlation analysis of Western civilization (1975), political fragmentation has its strongest effect on creativity with a lag of 20 years.

REFERENCES

Armajani, Yahya (1970), *Middle East: Past and Present*, Englewood Cliffs, NJ: Prentice-Hall.

Baechler, Jean (1975), *The Origins of Capitalism*, originally published in French in 1971, Oxford: Basil Blackwell.

Baechler, Jean (1988), 'The origins of modernity, caste and feudality (India, Europe and Japan)', in Jean Baechler, John A. Hall and Michael Mann (eds), *Europe and the Rise of Capitalism*, Oxford: Basil Blackwell, pp. 39–65.

Berman, Harold J. (1983), *Law and Revolution: The Formation of the Western Legal Tradition*, Cambridge, MA: Harvard University Press.

Berman, Harold J. (1998), 'The Western legal tradition: the interaction of revolutionary innovation and evolutionary growth', in Peter Bernholz, Manfred E. Streit and Roland Vaubel (eds), *Political Competition, Innovation and Growth. A Historical Analysis*, Berlin: Springer, pp. 35–47.

Brennan, Geoffrey B., and James M. Buchanan (1980), *The Power to Tax*, Cambridge: Cambridge University Press.

Chirot, Daniel (1986), *Social Change in the Modern Era*, San Diego, CA: Harcourt Brace Jovanovich.

Engerman, Stanley L. (1988), 'Reflections on how (and when and why) the West grew rich', Interlaken Seminar on Analysis and Ideology.

Gibbon, Edward (1787), *The History of the Decline and Fall of the Roman Empire*, Basle: Tourneissen.

Goldstone, Jack A. (1987), 'Cultural orthodoxy, risk, and innovation: the divergence of East and West in the early modern world', *Sociological Theory*, **5**, 119–35.

Hall, John A. (1985), *Powers and Liberties, The Causes and Consequences of the Rise of the West*, Oxford: Basil Blackwell.

Hall, John A. (1988), 'States and societies: the miracle in a comparative perspective', in Jean Baechler, John A. Hall and Michael Mann (eds), *Europe and the Rise of Capitalism*, Oxford: Basil Blackwell, pp. 20–38.

Hume, David (1742), 'Of the rise and progress of the arts and sciences', reprinted in Knud Haakonssen (ed.) (1994), *Political Essays*, Cambridge: Cambridge University Press, pp. 58–77.

Jones, Eric L. (1981), *The European Miracle*, Cambridge: Cambridge University Press.

Kant, Immanuel (1784), 'Idea of a universal history from a cosmopolitan point of view', in Patrick Gardiner (ed.) (1959), *Theories of History*, New York: Free Press, pp. 22–34.

Kennedy, Paul (1987), *The Rise and Fall of the Great Powers*, New York: Random House.

Maddison, Angus (2002), *The World Economy: A Millennial Perspective*, Development Centre Studies, Paris: OECD.

Mokyr, Joel (1990), *The Lever of Riches. Technological Creation and Economic Progress*, New York: Oxford University Press.

Naroll, Raoul, et al. (1971), 'Creativity: a cross-historical pilot survey', *Journal of Cross-Cultural Psychology*, **2**, 181–8.

McNeill, William H. (1982), *The Pursuit of Power*, Chicago IL: University of Chicago Press.

North, Douglass C. (1981), *Structure and Change in Economic History*, New York: Norton.

North, Douglass C. (1998), 'The rise of the Western world', in Peter Bernholz, Manfred E. Streit and Roland Vaubel (eds), *Political Competition, Innovation and Growth: A Historical Analysis*, Berlin: Springer, pp. 13–28.

Pipes, Richard (1999), *Property and Freedom*, New York: A.A. Knopf.

Pomeranz, Kenneth (2000), *The Great Divergence. Europe, China and the Making of the Modern World Economy*, Princeton, NJ: Princeton University Press.

Rosenberg, Nathan, and L.E. Birdzell (1986), *How the West Grew Rich*, New York: Basic Books.

Schaefer, James M., Chitti M. Babu and N. Sudhakar Rao (1977), 'Sociopolitical causes of creativity in India 500 BC–1800 AD: a regional time-lagged study', paper presented at the meeting of the International Studies Association, St Louis, MO.

Simonton, Dean Keith (1975), 'Sociocultural context of individual creativity: a trans-historical time-series analysis', *Journal of Personality and Social Psychology*, **32** (6), 1119–33.

Smith, Adam (1776), *The Wealth of Nations*, reprinted 1976, Chicago, IL: University of Chicago Press.

Ting, S.S. (1986), 'The social psychology of Chinese literary creativity: an archival data anlaysis', unpublished doctoral dissertation, University of California at Davis.

Weber, Max (1923), *General Economic Theory*, reprinted 1961, New York: Collier.

Weede, Erich (1988), 'Der Sonderweg des Westens', *Zeitschrift für Soziologie,* **17**, 172–86.

Weede, Erich (2000), *Asien und der Westen*, Baden-Baden: Nomos.

2. The political pattern of historical creativity: a theoretical case

Jean Baechler

Even at the level of regional and local history, the historian cannot but notice that human creativity in all matters, not only economic ones, has a broad pattern of flashes of light extending into more or less sustained illumination, separated by long periods of somnolence. If the historian takes a world historical point of view and applies it to the last five millennia, the pattern becomes even more striking. Without entering into the details of the evidence, the historian sees that China experienced two major periods of cultural creativity, between the sixth and third centuries BC and the third and sixth AD; that India defined itself between the eighth and sixth centuries BC and between the third century BC and the third century AD; that Western Asia went through a series of peaks of achievement over many millennia; that Europe can boast of at least three major cultural upsurges, between the sixth and third centuries BC, the eleventh and fourteenth centuries AD, and since the seventeenth century.

Of course, the above dates can be contested and replaced by quite different ones, but nobody could argue that the flux of cultural and historical creativity is smooth and straightforward. The historian records the facts. The sociologist tries to explain them by comparing at least two and preferably many occurrences of analogous cases, and by imagining a theoretical framework. Such broad historical objects as those outlined here cannot possibly be explained by a crude line of argument of the kind: 'If X, then Y'. We can only hope to produce some theoretical cases which could be convincing enough as arguments and to find enough evidence in the facts for them to appear to be real factors in the production of these facts.

In order to introduce a useful discussion, I shall lean towards the theoretical side of the argument in trying to deduce the hypothesis that one of the main factors involved, and in fact in my view the most important factor, is a political pattern of fragmentation, in which a unified cultural area is divided among a plurality of competing polities. I could express my point of view in another way as follows. I would answer the question of the *Ortsbestimmung der Gegenwart* by arguing that modernity is defined both by the emergence of an entirely new stage of human history and by the convergence of all previous

18

human histories into one common history. For the social scientist, that historical occurrence raises the question of building new perspectives in world history. The task can only be based on comparative history of the kind tried by Max Weber. Successful comparisons need efficient tools. One tool is the political pattern. One tool, not *the* tool.

EXPLORATION AS HYPOTHESIS

Having chosen to prove our case not by induction out of historical records of analogous examples, but by deduction, we have to define the point of departure of the deduction, a point which has to be at least plausible. That point could be human fallibility, the fact that all human activities, taken as isolated and discrete attempts, almost inevitably result in failure. It is almost impossible to imagine a human being succeeding in his first attempt to find the answer to a cognitive question. He will almost certainly fail in his first efforts and reach a satisfying answer only after a series of attempts. This proposition is true not only for scientific knowledge, where it is obvious that no one truth has ever been found at once, but also for empirical knowledge, where general conclusions are drawn by induction and inference from a succession of cases and experiences. Apprenticeship in everyday life is a kind of empirical knowledge in this sense, which means that everybody, simply in order to become able to live reasonably successfully in a given social environment, has to master the necessary knowledge by a succession of failures. The same is true in all matters pertaining to what the Greeks called *poièsis*, the impression of a shape into a material or the materializing of a shape. It is difficult to imagine a potter succeeding in producing the best piece possible first time. He will need a succession of failed or imperfect attempts to succeed eventually.

The root of the problem is quite obvious. Knowing and making are complex enterprises, made up of a lot of interwoven elements, each of which must be grasped properly and put in the right place, and so more than one attempt is needed to find the answer to a question or to give a shape to a material. This is true not only of the individual actor, but also of the collective actor, an actor made up of at least two people acting together as a team. The solution to the problem is quite obvious too. Whenever one fails, one has to try again, till one eventually succeeds. The solution applies both to individuals and to teams. It can be approached in two ways. Either the same individual or team tries again and again to solve the problem, or different people try, individually or collectively, to solve it. When this second way is possible and taken, the solution to a problem tends to become independent of time and place. One can argue that some questions are answered by mankind as a whole and found eventually through all of human history.

One last detail is needed to complete the picture. One has to distinguish between two kinds of problems and solutions. In one kind, the problems and the solutions are known already because somebody has previously succeeded in surmounting his failures to find them. In that case, an individual or a team will also fail at the beginning of the training which leads to the mastering of the problems and the solutions, but since these are already known and mastered, the apprenticeship will succeed more quickly, unless a structural defect makes it impossible. Education and instruction, that is the acculturation of successive generations in a given cultural circle, work in this way. In the other kind, the problems are unknown, let alone the solutions. Something more or less new is emerging: a philosophical point of view, a way to produce resources better and cheaper, a literary genre, a style of architecture in places of worship, and so on. In this context, both the problems and the solutions are to be explored, giving opportunities to err and fail and succeed on a much larger scale, since nobody can know in advance what the eventual result will be. Greek philosophy or Elizabethan theatre can be understood and explained as explorations of fields of possibilities only in retrospect, once their histories are closed. All cultural achievements by human civilizations are of this second kind. They can always be interpreted as the exploration of fields of possibilities, an exploration by successive generations of individuals and teams, who may be scattered in time and space on the grandest scale till they encompass mankind and the whole earth.

Let us assume that human cultural products are achieved through exploration. Exploration itself can be thought of as being based on a sequence of different operations. The first is an attempt to raise the problem, the second to give a solution. Usually, just one try will not suffice. Thence, the second operation is failure. The two operations can be conceived as a trial in which a problem and its solution try to proceed from the virtual to the real through the efforts of people. The trial is useful and rational only if it enables tries aiming at the right target, albeit barely perceptibly, to be sorted from the plain failures. This selection operation is crucial because without it human fallibility could never be corrected. The selection can be made by the triers themselves or by other players. The latter is the rule when the time and the space involved exceed the reach of the individual and his counterpart. To be effective, selection has to be conceived as a social space, where triers offer the products of their tries and other people are demanders of the products, able to give an educated opinion on their quality and free to reject them if judged badly shaped. The demanders can be either offerers themselves, who control and criticize what the others offer, or consumers of the products. These three operations – try, fail, select – have to be sustained if the whole process of exploration is to lead somewhere positive. A fourth operation is needed, which we can call cumulation of the relative successes selected by the third one.

Somebody somewhere has to keep track of all the things selected by the previous operations. This cannot be done by the final consumers because they are interested primarily in the actual product presented to them, and do not care much about what came previously or what will come in the future. The cumulators have to be involved in the same exploration of the same set of problems. The remembrance of the successive stages of the exploration belongs to people who are competent, if not always as individuals then as a community, in selecting what is objectively right from the point of view of the problem raised. In other words, the fourth operation needs communities of peers. These communities are also in charge of the fifth and final operation, which could be called consolidation. Consolidation is not the same as cumulation. Cumulation means the ordering of succeeding selections, so that the whole pattern of the exploration can emerge, gradually or in jumps. Consolidation means that what has been achieved can be stored, guarded, managed and transmitted. At this stage, exploration joins education and instruction, in the sense that what has been achieved and consolidated can be circulated as a cultural product, either in a finite social circle or among mankind in general, if the product – for example, a scientific truth – has universal validity.

The concept of innovation and development as exploration divided into five linked operations raises two questions which are of the utmost importance to the historian and the sociologist. The first question can be put this way: what organizational pattern is best fitted to maximize and optimize exploration of the cultural realm accessible to human beings? This question leads straight to a second one: what are the best conditions offered by history for that organizational pattern to be implemented?

THE FRACTAL PATTERN IN HUMAN HISTORY

By 'fractal pattern' I mean an organizational structure consisting of multiple levels, each allowed and able to deal with all the problems raised at that level without interference from above or below, and all integrated from level to level so that a problem which cannot be solved at a lower level, can be at a higher level. The pattern could also be described as a structure bringing all the resources available in a given set to bear on a problem, as well as adapting the sizes of the sets involved and, consequently, of the resources mobilized to the problems raised: a local problem can be solved at the local level with local resources; a global problem could be solved at the global level with global resources; in between, intermediate problems can be solved at intermediate levels with corresponding resources. In order to work properly, the structure has to be built in such a way that each level can act on its own to solve the problem pertaining to it, without having to wait for a delegation of authority from the level beneath it. The whole pattern is simultaneously and without contradiction loose and focused, decentralized and hierarchical, adapted and adaptable.

The fractal pattern is the property of no particular segment of reality. It is actually the way reality works with complexity, and the more complex, the more so. Life itself is based on modular systems integrated into ever wider modular systems. Post-neolithic human societies, being more complex than Palaeolithic ones, adopt the fractal pattern spontaneously, usually with four levels: local, regional, political (the level at which war becomes a common outcome) and cultural (the level comprising everyone brought up under the same civilizational features). The most important fact for our purpose arises at that fourth level. Either it is politically integrated in one polity tending to encompass the whole civilizational area, or the area is divided into multiple polities. In the first case, we have a principality, a kingdom or an empire, depending on the size of the cultural area. In the second case, this area remains divided politically but not culturally, which means that exchanges of all kinds flow among all parts, except in time of war, when they may be temporarily interrupted.

One last point is needed. The fourth level of social integration can be politically divided in two different circumstances. Either an empire has collapsed and its collapse has allowed the underlying levels to become politically independent, but that independence can be only temporary and will last a few centuries at the most; or the political dispersion can be permanent and durable, that is the drive to building an empire has been definitively blocked. Why should that happen, when the drive towards ever larger polities has seemed irresistible since war was invented ten millennia ago? The answer is probably that a limited number of polities, five or ten perhaps, have been shaped by chance and history in such a way that none is strong enough to crush a coalition of all the others. When this situation occurs, imperialization can be postponed indefinitely by shifting coalitions and fluctuating balances.

If one looks at world history from this particular point of view, some striking broad features appear. Although the Palaeolithic age does not fall outside the theoretical framework, we can put it aside because there is no move toward political coalescence; on the contrary, the main movement is one of swarming and progressive expansion, without maintaining links between the hives. In fact, the best example of a true fractal pattern can be observed in the tribal world. The social structure is made up of a succession of four or five levels of social integration, beginning with the enlarged family and ending with the confederation of tribes. The problems which inevitably arise among human beings are treated by corresponding organs at each level, except at the top, where a tribal confederation has no permanent political organs: it is a mere defensive or offensive alliance, temporarily led by a temporary military chief.

This tribal stage has lasted for five to seven millennia everywhere, which means that the drive to political integration has been successfully blocked. The explanation fits our hypothesis: at each level of the tribal federation, a system of checks and balances, built on a few opposing and collaborating social units, prevents the rise of a political power strong enough to impose by war and force the formation of a polity uniting the whole social and cultural structure in one kingdom.

Eventually, kingdoms have arisen everywhere because there is always some hidden factor which gives some advantage to some part of the whole. The prevailing pattern for the last five millennia has not been the fractal but the monopolistic pattern, where one political centre tries to bring a whole cultural area into one unified, controlled structure. The widest monopoly is an empire controlling a whole civilization: China, India, and Western Asia in fact, Meso-America in the making, and Europe the great exception. If we accept the proposition that for the last few millennia the imperial pattern has been prevalent, we have to accept as a corollary that the fractal pattern could only be an exception induced, as we have seen, by two possible circumstances: either the break-up of an empire or a balance of power preventing an empire. The first occurred in China, India and Western Asia, the second in Europe, where there has never been a lasting empire – the longest having been Napoleon's for about ten years and Hitler's for about four years. If we look closer at the different occurrences, the picture becomes more complicated and somewhat blurred. China appears to have been the perfect model of an empire, beginning in 221 BC. It has lived through two long episodes of the fractal pattern: in the three centuries leading up to the empire and during the great interdynastic period, between the third and sixth centuries AD. At the other extreme, Europe is the perfect model of the fractal pattern, which has appeared three times in its history, in the city-states of Greece between the sixth and fourth centuries BC, in Western and Central Europe in the Middle Ages between the eleventh and thirteenth centuries AD, and in the whole of Europe between the sixteenth and nineteenth centuries AD. India and Asia – which stretch from the Mediterranean to the Indus and from Central Asia to the Indian Ocean – are intermediate cases, India leaning more towards the Chinese model and Asia towards the European one. But for our problem this picture is somehow misleading. The imperial pattern, even when as perfect as in China, is only tentatively monopolistic, in the sense that a political centre of supreme importance is effectively in place but its ability to control everything in the empire is very limited. The consequence is that in China the local, regional and provincial levels each enjoy great autonomy and develop marked peculiarities, but with the capital still setting the tone. The evolution in India, having followed the Chinese path till the third century and the building of the Mauryan empire, took an entirely new course after its collapse, marked by a complete disjunction of the political and the social pattern. The former became wholly amorphous and the latter took the unique shape of the caste system, which is as purely fractal in pattern as the tribal world. In Asia, the interdynastic periods are long enough to make the empires – the Achaemenides, the Abbasids and the Ottomans – the exception. In the absence of empires, the whole area becomes divided into mutually exclusive entities, each developing the monopolistic pattern, so that the result is entirely different from what can be observed in Europe.

In this tentative picture, a place has to be reserved for Japan. Culturally it belongs entirely to the Chinese model, but politically and socially it rather resembles Europe. Having tried, during the Nara period, to follow the Chinese path to a monopolistic kingdom, it failed entirely and began a long journey through the fractal pattern, culminating between the thirteenth and sixteenth centuries AD in a feudal pattern strangely reminiscent of feudalism in Europe between the tenth and thirteenth centuries. Both feudal periods are perfect examples of the fractal pattern and of the highest achievements in innovation and development.

THE FRACTAL PATTERN AND THE OPTIMIZATION OF EXPLORATION

Why should the fractal pattern, allowed and maintained by a balanced plurality of polities on one cultural area, contribute to political freedom, innovation and development? The answer, or one answer at least, can be found in the obvious fact that what we have called exploration is optimized by the fractal pattern, and in the less obvious facts that in order for that optimization to be implemented, political freedom is needed in each polity, and that the plurality of polities is a precondition of political freedom. Thus we have to explain two relationships and stages between plurality of polities and cultural optimization: the first between plurality and freedom, the second between plurality and freedom on the one hand and optimization on the other.

The relationship between plurality of polities and political pluralism – which means political power checked and balanced by a plurality of autonomous centres of decision-making within each polity – can be established both negatively and positively. Negatively, without a plurality political power becomes necessarily monopolistic and autocratic. This trend is unavoidable, since when political power in a given cultural area becomes concentrated enough to unify the whole area in one polity, it is also strong enough to eliminate all internal obstacles to its rule. All histories of political unification, be it from tribes to kingdom or from kingdoms to empire, are stories of the enlargement of both the polities and political power. That is the ultimate reason why during the last ten millennia the balance of political regimes available to humanity has shifted heavily from moderate ones to the autocratic kind, with some remarkable exceptions which are all correlated to the lack of political unification and, conversely, the coexistence of a plurality of polities. The best examples are ancient Greece and modern Europe. The negative argument could be put this way: a plurality of polities is conducive to political pluralism because imperialization goes hand in hand with autocratization.

The positive argument would need a more detailed account of the different regional histories. It would show how, on the one hand, each ruler is permanently embroiled in conflicts and wars with the others; needs, in order not to be vanquished, the support of the social elites; and has to buy their support by concessions of power, wealth and prestige. On the other hand, the elites obtain from these concessions strong local positions and the opportunity to build strong coalitions among themselves against the central power. The elites however have no interest in weakening the central power to the point where it could break down, because that would put their own polity at a disadvantage against the other polities and endanger their own survival. In other words, the rules of the game between rulers and elites are for each to check the power of the other without going so far as to ruin it. But the game is played only as long as there remains a plurality of polities. As soon as the possibility arises for one ruler and polity to conquer the others successfully and durably, it becomes necessary and advantageous for them to concentrate all the power available. The elites have an interest in the spoils of the conquest – those parts of the elites, at least, who will be lucky or clever enough to survive the conquest as part of the apparatus of the imperial power. This logic of the game can explain why, in the post-neolithic and pre-modern world, a balance among a plurality of polities has always been accompanied by regimes of the aristocratic–oligarchic variety, be they monarchical or not, and why the rupture of the balance led to more or less autocratic regimes.

The easiest way to show the relationship between political pluralism and plurality and the optimization of exploration is to argue in terms of demand and supply. The demanders are the rulers and the elites, who demand all kinds of resources, either necessary or superfluous, and who have the means both in wealth and in knowledge and taste of demanding the best available. The suppliers are the producers of all cultural items, craftsmen, poets, musicians, philosophers, architects, painters, thinkers, physicians, astrologers, theologians, experts in all fields of human endeavour. The most important point to understand and to keep in mind is that all products of human ingenuity come in the guise of themes and variations. The 'sacred place' theme can be developed either as a closed building or as an open space. If a closed building, it can take different shapes. If the shape is the Roman basilica, it varies to become the Maxentian or the Constantinian basilica. If a Constantinian basilica, it looks like the basilicas of Rome, Bethlehem or Jerusalem, and so on. The dialectic of theme and variation works at all levels, each theme being a variation on a previous theme and each variation becoming a new theme to vary on. From time to time, some variations are so strikingly new that the following variations seem to lead an entirely new path. The history of painting in Europe, let us say from Giotto to Cézanne, gives illuminating examples of this process. An even more dramatic illustration could be the emergence of the Gothic theme out of a variation on the Romanesque one. The histories of the sciences since the beginning of the seventeenth century can all be written in this language of theme and variation, the themes being the main theories and the variations their applications to narrower fields.

If one keeps all these features in mind at the same time, it becomes easy to grasp the positive and the negative reasons for the successes of the fractal pattern. Let us start with the supply side of the argument. Talents appear randomly in society at large, that is anywhere in the cultural area concerned, including the margins influenced by the culture. It would be wasteful and counterproductive to leave a single talent ignored and muted. On the other hand, talents differ in range and power. It would be wasteful and counterproductive to bury a great talent in a village or a cluster of villages making artefacts for the local people, or to propel a narrow talent to the highest level and allow him to define the themes or the variations for the whole area. In order to avoid these shortcomings, the obvious solution lies in a grid encompassing the whole area and making all levels of society communicate, so that a bright boy born in the remotest corner has a fair chance to reach the capital and that, by myriad movements of hiring and firing, of selection and exclusion, of consecration and condemnation, the grid becomes roughly peopled by the right persons in the right places – the best at the top, the worst at the bottom, the average in between. The fractal pattern maximizes the solution with one very precise advantage. There is no place in it for anybody, individual or coalition, to block new entrants indefinitely, in particular those endowed with a disruptive talent, disruptive in that it could disqualify all previous achievements. Established artists or scientists do not much like people proposing entirely new ways of creating or thinking. In a monopolistic pattern, they can control the new entrants if they can convince the people in power to stick to their cultural habits. In a fractal pattern, there is no centre of power able to do that. A ruler in one polity can decide to suppress the innovations, but he can succeed only in his own polity, not in the other ones. What he can try to achieve is to become prestigious enough to induce the other rulers to imitate him, but imitation is not subservience and does not lead automatically to duplication.

The producers are in competition among themselves to attain the highest positions and rewards accessible by their respective talents. As suppliers, they have to please the demand. There are two ways to achieve this. Either the producer follows the taste of the demander and sticks as closely as possible to the themes and variations accepted as traditional and well received in the area; or he can follow a more risky strategy and dare to shock tastes and habits by proposing a new variation or even a new theme. The latter strategy has little chance of success in a narrow social range because people are, in the main, conservative and afraid of being looked on as lunatics. In the tribal world, contrary to legend, there is complete freedom of opinion and expression, but opinions that people deem new are discarded as lunacies. In more stratified societies, the higher an individual climbs the social ladder, the more inclined he is to take bolder cultural steps. He is emboldened positively by emulation of his peers and by the ambition to distinguish himself, and negatively by the fact that he risks little in terms of reputation: a king has to be eccentric in the extreme to be perceived as a lunatic. At the top of the ladder are the rulers and their courts who have to convince everybody inside the polity that they are at the top and to show their counterparts outside that they are different. What is more, the rulers cannot decide to quit the game because the cost might be high. This constraint stems from the very containment imposed on the political power. Power is checked and balanced both from inside by the elites and from outside by the other polities and rulers. In this situation it is almost impossible for a ruler to show his strength and valour by resorting to force. He has to turn to prestige and to invest his wealth in prestigious products. Nobody can last by indulging in cultural dullness. Everybody wanting to be above his peers or different from them tries to distinguish himself by aspiring to a new variation or a new theme.

CONCLUSION

Both supply and demand are subject to endless competition and emulation, are unable to control or suppress freedom, innovation and development, and have strong incentives to pursue these. It is no mystery how the fractal pattern always and everywhere optimizes exploration of the fields of possibilities. At this point, before moving on to the application of the model to actual histories, it is necessary to remember that there is no place for a vision in terms of exclusive polarities, one being the fractal pole, entirely free of monopolistic tendencies, and the other the monopolistic pole, entirely devoid of fractal developments. It is much more useful and akin to the truth to postulate a continuum between the two poles and to define for each case study the point occupied along the continuum. It would appear, for example, that Europe in the eighteenth century was nearer the fractal pole than China under the Qing;

that the world today is much nearer still to it; that Ming China was less monop-olistic at the dawn than at the sunset of the dynasty; that the pre-dynastic and inter-dynastic periods in China have been the most creative and innovative; and so on. The model is not a yardstick to be applied rigidly and mechanically to the course of history, but a hypothesis and a method of inquiry. It is in this context that one could approach the issues of the rise of capitalism and even of the modern age. There is little doubt that one condition for their occurrence was the simple, troubling fact that Europe had never been an empire. But there is even less doubt that this was just one condition among others, since other-wise it could have happened earlier and many times in the tribal world. In fact this tribal world benefited hugely, contrary to received wisdom, from plurality and the fractal pattern, in producing almost the entire bulk of themes exploited by kingdoms and empires, till modernity introduced some real innovations such as science and the sciences.

COMMENT

Michael Cook

Baechler presents the insight that a unified cultural area divided among a plurality of competing polities is good for cultural creativity. When I call the idea in this form an insight, I am endorsing it in my capacity as a historian, but suspending judgement on behalf of social scientists. Hereafter I refer to it as 'the idea'.

Historians are opportunistic people. They clutch at anything that seems to work in their attempts to explain the past, and hang on to it. They are aware that the human behaviour they are trying to understand is very complicated, and that much of their own understanding of it is intuitive rather than scientific. They have little faith in attempts to develop rigorously defined, unambiguously testable hypotheses over the domain of history as a whole. They tend to suspect that such attempts will come to grief in one of two ways: either the hypothesis will be simple enough to be testable, and will then turn out to be wrong; or it will be wrapped up in so many qualifications that it will be compatible with any state of the world, and so prove unverifiable.

Social scientists, by contrast, hope that there is a middle ground between the simple-and-false and the complex-and-unverifiable, and if they can safely reach that ground, all power to them. On their behalf, let me set out some of the respects in which the idea as presented by Baechler at the start of his chapter would need to be sharpened to be fully testable. These points are not intended as criticisms of his chapter, nor am I trying to identify where he himself stands on these questions:

1. Is the federal pattern (to use Baechler's phrase as a convenient short-hand) a sufficient condition for cultural creativity? If the answer is 'yes', then the idea is being maintained in a strong form (strong in the sense that it claims a lot, and is thus easily testable): in Baechler's words, the federal pattern 'always and everywhere' delivers cultural creativity. If the answer is 'no', then the idea is being maintained in a weak form (weak in the sense that it claims less, and is thus less easily testable): other things being equal, the federal pattern will tend to deliver cultural creativity. It might well be that the strong claim would come to grief on the history of pre-modern South-East Asia, while the weak claim probably would not.
2. Is the federal pattern a necessary condition for cultural creativity? Again, we have strong and weak forms of the idea: the strong form is refuted if we find an instance of cultural creativity in a non-federal context, whereas the weak form is compatible with such instances. I tend to think that the

strong claim comes to grief on the early centuries of Islamic history, a period I will come back to in my comment on Kuran's chapter.

3. What is to count as a case of cultural creativity? Obviously this is a broad and vague conception. The title of this volume is more specific: innovation and growth (especially if we take 'economic' to qualify both nouns). But even here, how exactly would we decide whether or not there was enough (or too much) innovation, or growth in a given historical context to confirm or refute the hypothesis? Some of the chapters I think take the goods to be delivered by the federal pattern to be something like: 'those features of European economic life that enabled Europe to come out on top of world history'. This may not be very precise, but it is in some ways much more restrictive; for example the cultural innovations of the early Islamic period would not be relevant in such a perspective. In any case, the more precise the formulation, the more testable the idea.

4. What is to count as a case of the federal pattern? How many states does it take, and how unified must the culture be? Baechler himself is thinking of a spectrum rather than of two polar opposites. Again, the more precise the formulation, the more testable the idea.

5. Over what time scale must the goods be delivered? If the idea is that the effects of interstate competition should register within a few decades, we have a fairly strong claim; if within a few millennia, we have a much weaker one. There is likely to be a significant difference here between states where entrepreneurs have power, as in Italian mercantile republics, and states in which the incentive to treat the economy well is indirect.

What all this adds up to is that turning the idea into a testable hypothesis requires quite a lot of specification. In the absence of an agreed specification, a lot will depends on what each of us has in mind. But let me say again that I raise these difficulties on behalf of social scientists; as a historian I am quite happy to muddle through and be grateful for whatever fragmentary insights come my way.

COMMENT

Mark Elvin

All those who are interested in the history of political institutions are permanently in the debt of Jean Baechler, most notably for his *Démocraties* (1985). His later *Nature et histoire* (2000) is also of relevance to his present theme because of its treatment of general cognitive history. I am therefore conscious that in raising a few questions about Professor Baechler's approach in his chapter to the general historical relationships between political structures and creativity I am dealing with a summary of what is a monumental body of underlying work that I am far from having mastered to my satisfaction, particularly in the case of the second volume. I hope that both he and those reading this will therefore forgive the relative superficiality of what I have to say. I hope that it will nonetheless prompt some interesting responses.

Let us turn first of all to the central concept of 'creativity'. It is a flexible and evasive term. At its broadest it encompasses any previously locally unknown form of human behaviour, whether in politics, warfare, economics, technology, the plastic, musical, or verbal arts, recreations such as sports and gardening, or religion and philosophy. It is usually assumed that there is a critical cognitive component, but this does not necessarily have to be verbal (consider cooking). In this basic sense creativity is close to what economic historians term 'invention', but there are other historically crucial aspects. Economic historians also attach importance to what they call 'innovation', which is given in this context the rather special sense of the socio-economic consolidation of one or more inventions into regular profitableness and acceptance. Without this, inventions are short-lived and of little actual importance. But it is essential to distinguish the two processes. Inventors can be but are not necessarily effective innovators as well (think of Turing and the computer). A third aspect is what is called 'diffusion', the spread of an invention, plus the associated innovations based on it, into societies and cultures where it did not originate. Often this process requires an element of adaptation, which is a secondary but important form of creativity. Each of these three related phenomena needs relating in a distinctive way to the capacity of a society for creative behaviour or its lack of it. Thus the term is complex and needs unpacking.

We have also at all times to remember that creativity applies to much more than what goes into a museum of the arts and sciences. Devising the institutions to run a great empire – such as the Chinese imperial civil service examinations – also requires creativity. Nor is creativity always linked to what we would normally consider to be morally good or aesthetically admirable. The concentration camp, initially contrived by the British during the Boer War, but developed into something far more sinister by Lenin two decades later, was also – in its way – a creation. This comprehensive understanding of the full range of human creativity makes the assignation of periods of generally higher and lower creativity a more difficult undertaking than perhaps Professor Baechler acknowledges. We can manage it more easily with restricted subsets of the phenomenon: in economic technology for example, or in poetry, or military organization, training and tactics. But it is quite hard to be confident about general judgements, and evaluation almost inevitably enters into the issue. How for example does one rate the elaboration of much of the huge corpus of traditional Chinese medical theory? In my personal view a great deal of it – in contrast to a non-trivial percentage both of actual practice and of pharmacopoeia-based empirical knowledge – was nonsensical, but it is hard to see grounds for not seeing it as creative within the bounds of the definition I gave at the outset. It was certainly not without substantial historical impact either. So we likewise have to consider what we regard as useful to define as 'creativity' and why.

When we turn to the genesis of creativity, we need to make a rough and ready distinction between stimulus on the one hand and facilitation or inhibition on the other. I would suggest that somewhat different logics regarding political and other institutions apply to these two facets. Stimuli are challenges. They are extraordinarily various. They can emerge from changes in the environment, in the form of alterations in climate, or depletions of needed resources, or new diseases. They can appear from military threats to security – new enemies, new weapons. They can arise from the pressures of economic competition – new products, new rivals. I think they can also arise from the impact of psychological and even spiritual shocks – maybe the opening of the Americas and the world overseas to the European consciousness had something of this sort of effect. The impacts arising from the physical movements of people – explorers, invaders, migrants with ideas and skills that differ from those of the host populations, missionaries and the like – often play a major role in creating combinations of such stimuli. Within the realm of the mind, stimuli can even be internally generated through the fuller articulation of the logic of existing ideas: in mathematics for example, once you think through the solutions of equations that require square roots, the issue of the square roots of negative numbers in the end becomes unavoidable – and mathematicians, not without initial misgivings, create so-called 'imaginary' numbers. There is a law: no stimulus, no creativity. I would also hazard the guess that there is no clear and simple relationship between the frequency and intensity of such stimuli and different types of political structure, but that there are indirect but often powerful relationships between types of political structures and the types of stimuli that tend to occur. To take a crude example to save time, large cities and large armies, as well as large public works like the Chinese

Great Wall and the Grand Canal, have serious public health problems that do not arise with their counterparts on a sufficiently small scale. Sometimes, though, what we in retrospect see as a challenge is just treated at the time as a cost, and does not provoke efforts at a creative solution. There is no inverse law, since stimuli do not necessarily lead to creativity.

But stimulus is only half the story. Creative response to a stimulus requires, in general, both appropriate conceptual and physical tools, and both appropriate physical and organizational resources. In the last analysis specificity rules here, and satisfactory generalization is close to impossible. If I had nonetheless to indicate what seems to me the most important factor, I would suggest that it is the frequency or intensity in time in a given space of interactions between human beings. Consider for a moment an oversimplified but instructive model.

In an interacting group of N people there are approximately $I \approx N^2/2$ potential interactions. We divide N^2 by 2 because the interaction of person a with person b is the same as that of person b with person a. We say 'approximately' and write '$\approx$' because we omit the interactions of people with themselves, a with a, b with b and so on. If we label the potential interactions I, then the rate of change of I as N increases, or dI/dN, is N.

It is this non-linear effect that underlies the familiar change in the social character of large aggregations of people, especially in cities. Of course not everyone actually interacts with everyone else, or anything like it. The model formulation is merely a way of indicating an underlying tendency that is far from being fully realized. It is my suggestion that the most important single facilitation mechanism for creativity is the intensity per unit of space of interactions between people, since this tends to determine how efficiently and effectively commodities, techniques, ideas and beliefs, fashions and the various forms of power are exchanged and influence each other. Note that in this ultra-simple model the absolute size of the surrounding population in which a city-type aggregation is embedded has no formal effect: what counts is the intensity of the spatial localized effects. Of course when we turn to actual cases this is not adequate. We need also to consider the size and diversity of the hinterland from which people, commodities, ideas and so on are being drawn in; but so much is obvious. Note that we have in passing defined the essence of a city in pre-modern times.

This brings us back to political structures. Size is ambivalent. Its effects balance on a knife-edge. In some respects empires can be extremely good for creativity. They create a large zone of peace and, at times, free trade within which the easy and cheap circulation of people, goods and ideas is facilitated. In China the middle of the T'ang dynasty – the eighth century – saw the invention of one of the seminal inventions of the modern world, printing, perhaps initially due to competition between religions, since it seems to have first been used for multiplying religious texts. The Early Sung dynasty – late tenth and early eleventh centuries – saw the creation of mass production, in the state armaments industry, churning out millions of identical arrowheads each year. The Yuan or Mongol dynasty, in the thirteenth and fourteenth centuries, saw the invention of water-powered mechanized spinning of hemp and twisting of silk. In other respects, the problems of control created by vast political size can lead to the use of techniques that tend to suppress creativity, or creativity of certain types. The Neo-Confucian orthodoxy spread through most of the educated classes by the late-imperial state examination system in Ming and Qing China is a familiar example. The trouble, analytically, is that this sort of effect is not limited to overtly political structures. Try to imagine what might have happened to Western European creativity if the Counter-Reformation had been totally successful. The Catholic Church has had a long record of more-than-millennial institutional continuity, eventually on a worldwide scale, that makes even Chinese imperial institutions look a trifle transitory and localized. If a triumphant Counter-Reformation had for example everywhere led to a society in the grip of the kind of bodies described by Châtellier in his book *The Europe of the Devout,* a religious version of what we would now recognize as Communist-style 'cells' and 'fractions', European modernity might have been a long time coming. Not that the Counter-Reformation was without its own, but different, creativity. Think, just to begin with, of Palestrina.

This brings me to my final theoretical point. Ideas and techniques cross political boundaries. The most spectacular example in history is that of 'hell-purgatory'. I use this hyphenated form because Buddhist 'hells' are all, *stricto sensu,* 'purgatories' in being for a limited duration – and, for that matter, like everything else of a composite nature, in the last analysis illusions. This concept, of appropriate post-mortem punishment of an individual for offences committed during his or her lifetime, seems to have originated in Persia or North India very roughly 3000 years ago, or maybe somewhat less, and then made its way both west to the Mediterranean world (recall the efforts of Lucretius to persuade his readers not attach credence to 'Acheron') and east to central Asia, China, Korea and Japan by a variety of vectors, and in a variety of forms that acquired different cultural imprints. Although it became inter-twined with politics in the West in various ways – being a useful tool for social control – it seems to have had a history to a very great extent independent of it. As one of humanity's most macabre and influential inventions it can serve as a warning of linking creativity too tightly with political structures, even if such links undoubtedly may and do exist.

Last of all, a pendant. The withering of an earlier creativity under condi-tions when changes in political structures were not apparently that great (though sometimes small alterations may prove crucial) remains an analytical challenge. Why did major technological creativity fade away in late-imperial

China (though skilled fine-tuning and small inventions did not vanish)? Why did the great creativity in medieval Islam, exemplified by Ibn al-Haytham (Alhazen) in optical science and Ibn Khaldun, apparently die away in later centuries? I leave these issues with you for reflection.

References

Baechler, Jean (1985), *Démocraties*, Paris: Calmann-Lévy.
Baechler, Jean (2000), *Nature et histoire*, Paris: Presses Universitaires de France.
Châtellier, Louis (1989), *The Europe of the Devout: The Catholic Reformation and the Formation of a New Society*, translated by Jean Birrell, Cambridge: Cambridge University Press.

COMMENT

Erich Weede

Baechler distinguishes two patterns of rule or authority, imperial or autocratic on the one hand and federal or pluralistic on the other hand. I agree with the fruitfulness of the distinction, but I am slightly irritated by the choice of the word 'federal'. It carries connotations of a common legal superstructure which I would prefer to avoid. Although nineteenth century Europe was a case of Baechler's 'federal pattern', I perceive little legal superstructure encompassing Britain and Austria, France and Prussia. That is why I prefer the term 'political fragmentation'.

The substance of theories, however, is more important than definitional issues. Here I fully agree with Baechler, in particular with the following two statements: (1) 'the plurality of polities is a precondition of political freedom', and (2) 'when political power in a given cultural area becomes concentrated enough to unify the whole area in one polity, it is also strong enough to eliminate all internal obstacles to its rule' (1988, p. 24). Like Baechler, I perceive beneficial consequences of political pluralism and negative consequences of empire.

Whereas Baechler is interested in creativity and cultural achievements, including architecture, music and poetry, I am personally inclined towards a narrower definition of the explanandum than Baechler is, at least partially for methodological reasons. In my view, progress in architecture, music or poetry is hard to evaluate. It is comparatively easier if one focuses on scientific, technological or economic development. Narrowing Baechler's focus and using my terms, one arrives at the testable proposition that political fragmentation or pluralism within a unified cultural area – and I hasten to add: within a fairly integrated economic area – contributes to scientific, technological and economic development. The rise of capitalism in the West (Baechler 1988, p. 28) is one illustration of this relationship. Another one might be China under the Southern Sung dynasty where the term 'Southern Sung' already provides a cue to some political fragmentation of China. At the beginning of the second millennium Southern Sung China achieved a per capita iron production unequalled elsewhere before the industrial revolution in Britain.

Baechler advances a second insight with which I fully agree. Although he does not develop a full model of man, or action, or human behaviour, he insists on the fact of human fallibility. Unfortunately Baechler does not analyse the relationship between human fallibility on the one hand and political fragmentation, political pluralism (or checks and balances) and individual freedom on the other hand. Not knowing Baechler's analysis of this relationship, I shall try to offer my own understanding of it. If human error is likely and pervasive, then a good social order is characterized by minimizing the risk of big errors affecting entire societies rather than of small errors affecting erring individuals themselves, and by maximizing the likelihood of quickly detecting and correcting errors. You get many small errors by decentralized decision-making. If individuals are made responsible for the consequences of their errors and actions, then there exist strong incentives to overcome errors. By contrast, centralized or political instead of decentralized and private decision-making carries the risk of big errors. Moreover it is practically impossible to make central authorities or autocrats suffer the negative consequences of their errors and actions. Therefore it is much harder to overcome a few big errors by the mighty than many small errors by the many. Moreover, many small errors by decentralized and independent decision-makers may neutralize each other. For example if one producer of a good overestimates demand for this product, and another one underestimates demand for the same product, these errors need not affect the consumer. Under centralized decision-making mutual neutralization of erroneous judgements is hardly conceivable. If Baechler's image of man is essentially correct, then it follows that individual freedom and decentralized decision-making are desirable.

If one substitutes a narrower focus on economic development for Baechler's broader concerns with human creativity, then one detects a gap in Baechler's short analysis submitted here. Property rights are largely neglected. Since Baechler (1988) looked at property rights elsewhere in his writings, the neglection of property rights in this analysis does probably imply no denial of their importance. Still, I regard it as unfortunate for a number of reasons. First, the ideas of liberty and property are intrinsically linked. Without general acknowledgement of the idea of self-ownership, there is extremely little liberty. Second, as Smith (1776 [1976]) recognized, only the prospect of acquiring property makes people work rather than shirk. Third, Mises (1920) added that private property in the means of production is a prerequisite for a rational allocation of resources. Although some Western economists tried to prove Mises wrong, central planners in Soviet-type economies proved him right. Fourth, Hayek (1945, 1960) demonstrated that only decentralized decision-making, which is ultimately dependent on decentralized property ownership, permits the mobilization of knowledge scattered across millions of heads. Fifth, Friedman (1962), Bhagwati (1993) and others pointed out that private property underwrites political liberty and pluralism by enabling critics of rulers and authorities to speak up and still to survive. Since man has become sedentary, private property and political liberty have become part of a single package.

Once the pivotal role of property rights in economic and political development is recognized, one may return to Baechler's basic macrosociological proposition linking political fragmentation or pluralism to creativity and, at least, implicitly, to economic development and prosperity. Under political fragmentation, that is given the existence of many small principalities and/or independent cities, at least some people possessing and controlling resources enjoy the exit option. If rule becomes too oppressive or confiscatory, then some resource owners move out of a ruler's territory, thereby weakening its economy and tax base. By providing an exit option for at least some resource owners, political fragmentation or pluralism forces rulers to recognize private property rights, thereby permitting economic development, the overcoming of mass poverty and ultimately even modern democracy. Of course these ideas are not new. You find them in preliminary form in Max Weber's (1923 [1981]) work, you find them expressed with perfect clarity in Eric Jones's (1981) *European Miracle*, you find a most interesting refinement of them in Richard Pipes's (1999) *Property and Freedom*, and you find an application of them in my own comparisons of Asian and Western civilizations (Weede 2000).

In essence, there is no disagreement with Baechler (1988: 60) who elsewhere wrote something extremely similar to what I observed here, namely:

> Europe was made up of a market of markets in which rivalry and competition between polities whipped up energy and placed them beyond political seizure: an authority that was unreasonable in economic matters did not stifle them; it merely forwarded the prosperity of its rivals.

References

Baechler, Jean (1988), 'The origins of modernity: caste and feudality (Europe, India and Japan)', in J. Baechler, J.A. Hall and M. Mann (eds), *Europe and the Rise of Capitalism*, Oxford: Blackwell, pp. 39–65.

Bhagwati, Jagdish (1993), 'Democracy and development', in L. Diamond and M.F. Plattner (eds), *Capitalism, Socialism, and Democracy Revisited*, Baltimore, MD: Johns Hopkins University Press, pp. 31–8.

Friedman, Milton (1962), *Capitalism and Freedom*, Chicago, IL: University of Chicago Press.

Hayek, Friedrich August von (1945), 'The use of knowledge in society', *American Economic Review*, **35** (4), 519–30.

Hayek, Friedrich August von (1960), *The Constitution of Liberty*, Chicago, IL: University of Chicago Press.

Jones, Eric L. (1981), *The European Miracle*, Cambridge: Cambridge University Press.

Mises, Ludwig von (1920), 'Die Wirtschaftsrechnung im sozialistischen Gemeinwesen', *Archiv für Sozialwissenschaft und Sozialpolitik*, **47** (1), 86–121.

Pipes, Richard (1999), *Property and Freedom*, New York: A.A. Knopf.

Smith, Adam (1776), *An Inquiry into the Nature and Causes of the Wealth of Nations*, reprinted 1976, Oxford: Oxford University Press.

Weber, Max (1923), *Wirtschaftsgeschichte*, reprinted 1981, Berlin: Duncker & Humblot.

Weede, Erich (2000), *Asien und der Westen, Politische und kulturelle Determinanten der wirtschaftlichen Entwicklung*, Baden-Baden: Nomos.

3. Creative clusters, political fragmentation and cultural heterogeneity: an investigative journey through civilizations East and West

Dean Keith Simonton

Although historians often question the existence of any 'laws of history' (Norling 1970), it is certain that at least some historical generalizations have withstood considerable empirical scrutiny (Simonton 1990, 1994). Among these well-established regularities is the fact that creative genius is not randomly distributed over the history of any given civilization. On the contrary, illustrious creators tend to fall into temporal clusters separated by periods of relative sterility – Golden Ages and perhaps lesser Silver Ages punctuated by Dark Ages. For instance, Velleius Paterculus, a Roman historian, made the following observation over two millennia ago:

> For who can marvel sufficiently that the most distinguished minds in each branch of human achievement have happened to adopt the same form of effort, and to have fallen within the same narrow space of time . . . A single epoch, and that only of a few years' duration, gave lustre to tragedy through the three men of divine inspiration, Aeschylus, Sophocles, and Euripedes . . . The great philosophers, too, received their inspiration from the lips of Socrates . . . how long did they flourish after the death of Plato and Aristotle? What distinction was there in oratory before Isocrates, or after the time of his disciples and in turn of their pupils? So crowded were they into a brief epoch that there were no two worthy of mention who could not have seen each other. (Kroeber 1944: 17)

Several investigators have tried to document this phenomenon in specific creative domains or world civilizations. For instance, Schneider (1937) demonstrated the clustering of genius in the history of biology in the British Isles, and Sorokin and Merton (1935) established the clustering of creative genius in early Islamic civilization. Nonetheless the most extensive empirical demonstration of this phenomenon is to be found in *Configurations of Culture Growth* by Alfred Kroeber (1944), the distinguished cultural anthropologist. His demonstration began by compiling extensive lists of creative geniuses for most of the world's civilizations, especially the Western, Islamic, Indian, Chinese and Japanese. These geniuses made contributions to most of the major domains of creative achievement, namely science, philosophy, literature, music, painting, sculpture and architecture. After arranging the creators for a particular domain and civilization in chronological order, Kroeber showed how they tended to form 'cultural configurations'. Creative activity would first increase until the civilization reached a cultural climax, after which creativity would slowly decline, even mediocre creators becoming fewer and farther between.

Although Kroeber's methods were qualitative rather than quantitative, the clustering of creative genius has been amply established using rigorous statistical techniques, especially generational time-series analysis (Simonton 1984a). These tests have been conducted not just for Western civilization (Simonton 1975, 1976b) but also for the civilizations of China (Simonton, 1988b) and Japan (Simonton 1992, 1997). In the specific case of Chinese civilization for example, non-random trans-historical distributions have been identified for inventors, mathematicians, physical scientists, biological scientists, miscellaneous scientists, religious figures both native (Taoists) and alien (Buddhists), philosophers, non-fiction authors, poets, calligraphers, painters, sculptors, architects, artisans and musicians (Simonton 1988b). Stated forthrightly, no domain of creative activity failed to display some degree of genius clustering. Although these tests have not yet been carried out for all of the world's civilizations, such as the Islamic or Indian, Kroeber's (1944) qualitative results suggest that quantitative analyses would yield the same outcome for all civilizations. Every graph shows the same peaks and valleys in the appearance of creative genius.

Given the universality of this phenomenon, it should not be surprising that some social scientists have attempted to discern the factors responsible for creative florescence or stagnation with a civilization (for example Gray 1958, 1961, 1966; Kavolis 1963, 1964, 1966; Kuo 1986, 1988; Rainoff 1929). These factors include both internal forces such as role-model availability, and external forces such as war, political freedom and economic prosperity (Simonton 1981, 1984b, 1994). However in this chapter I wish to focus on just one possible cause, namely political fragmentation. This is defined as the number of independent or sovereign states into which a given civilization is divided at a particular time. After reviewing some empirical research on this subject, I will turn to a second factor that may be closely related to political fragmentation, namely cultural heterogeneity. The research on the latter variable may help clarify the research findings on the former.

POLITICAL FRAGMENTATION

From the Golden Age of Greece to the Italian Renaissance, creative vitality has often been concomitant with political fragmentation. A number of philosophers, historians and scientists have argued that this association constitutes a general rule. For example Candolle (1873) held that great scientists are most likely to appear in small independent countries, or at least in confederations of small sovereign states. Likewise, Toynbee (1946), in his book *A Study of History*, claimed that the emergence of a 'universal state' was negatively correlated with the creative activity of a civilization. Nonetheless, the first empirical test of this conjecture did not appear until 1971 in a pilot study conducted by Naroll and his students.[1] Naroll based the analysis on Kroeber's (1944) raw data. Drawing the creative geniuses from Chinese, Indian, Middle Eastern and European civilizations, he then tabulated them into century-long periods. The number of sovereign states was then calculated for each civilization area over the same historical intervals. The correlation between these two measures was 0.29. Interestingly, Naroll also investigated the effects of wealth, geographical expansion, democratic government and external challenge, but the tests were not confirmatory. Hence, according to this pioneer empirical inquiry, political fragmentation was the only factor associated with the appearance of creative geniuses in these four civilization areas.

I came across this journal article about the time that I was searching for a topic for my doctoral dissertation in social psychology. I therefore decided to investigate this question using more powerful analytical methods, especially the dynamic time-series models used in econometrics (Simonton 1974, 1975). These techniques enabled me to examine a wider range of variables and to control for possible methodological artifacts. Although my original plan was to study the same civilizations as covered in Naroll et al. (1971), my dissertation committee dissuaded me from doing so. As a consequence, I decided to focus on Western civilization owing to the greater availability of data. The study began along the lines of Kroeber's study, compiling a long chronology of approximately 5000 eminent creators. Then, adapting a strategy used in Sorokin's (1937–41) classic work on *Social and Cultural Dynamics*, these figures were assigned to 127 consecutive 20-year periods or 'generations', where the assignment was based on Kroeber's (1944) floruit of the fortieth year (Simonton 1988a). The next step was to tabulate several predictors into the same generational time series. Besides political fragmentation, these included imperial instability, political instability, war and persecution. These data were used to test a dynamic multiple regression model in which the number of creators at generation g was regressed on the number of creators at generations $g - 1$ and $g - 2$, the amount of political fragmentation, imperial instability, and political instability at generation $g - 1$ (lagged effects), the amount of war and cultural persecution at generation g (synchronous effects), plus several control variables (for example to correct for exponential trends in the dependent variable; see Lehman 1947, Price 1963, Taagepera and Colby 1979). In line with the hypothesis, the number of creators at generation g was indeed a positive function of the amount of political fragmentation at generation $g - 1$, that is 20 years earlier. This lagged effect was interpreted in terms of political fragmentation acting as a developmental influence (Simonton 1984a). That is, creators who are around 40 years old in generation g will be around 20 years old in generation $g - 1$, making them susceptible to various influences in the socio-cultural milieu. Political fragmentation was then supposed to nurture the creative potential of talented youth.

I followed up this investigation by conducting several others that examined the relation between political fragmentation and creative activity, but with the focus on philosophical creativity. Thus one study examined the differential eminence of 2012 Western thinkers active between 580 BC and AD 1900 and found that the greatest philosophers were more likely to emerge during periods of high political fragmentation (Simonton 1976b). In another I examined how various political conditions, including fragmentation, effected the emergence of the various philosophical belief systems investigated by Sorokin (1937–41). In this case the degree of political fragmentation at generation $g - 1$ had a positive impact on the number of thinkers in generation g who advocate empiricism, scepticism, criticism, fideism, materialism, temporalism, nominalism, singularism and the ethics of happiness (Simonton 1976c). Because most of these philosophical positions are associated with the scientific worldview, these relationships imply that political fragmentation may have been a factor in the emergence of modern science, just as Candolle (1873) had suggested (Simonton 2002).

In one respect these findings were most provocative. Not only was political fragmentation correlated with various aspects of creativity, but it had also proved itself to be the most consistent and potent predictor among the several political factors studied. On the other hand it was somewhat frustrating not to be able to pin down the specific form of the causal relationship. Sometimes political fragmentation operated as a synchronous influence, and at other times it functioned as a lagged or developmental influence. It was difficult to tease out the optimal causal formulation because political fragmentation exhibits an exceptional degree of autocorrelation. That is the number of independent states at generation g correlates 0.97 with the number of sovereign nations in generation $g - 1$ (Simonton 1976a). Naturally, this degree of historical inertia makes perfect sense. Rome was not built in a day, nor was the Roman empire. Neither did the empire disintegrate over night. It usually takes decades for nations to come and go. Even so, this temporal consistency makes it virtually impossible to discriminate between synchronous and lagged effects.

In any case, my plan was to attempt to replicate my dissertation research on other civilizations. Yet this plan was pre-empted by others who had similar designs.

INDIAN CIVILIZATION

James Schaefer was one of the students who had collaborated with Naroll in the 1970 investigation. Having seen the results of my dissertation research (Simonton 1975), he decided to replicate and extend the 1971 results using the time-lagged methods first introduced in my inquiry. To do so, he collaborated with two anthropologists at Sri Venkateswara University in India. The index of creativity was based on Kroeber's (1944) work and spanned from 500 BC to AD 1800. The indicator included great philosophers, scientists, philologists, sculptors, painters, dramatists and other writers. In addition they tabulated a measure of political fragmentation based on both English and non-English histories.[2] The correlation between the two indicators was 0.73, an impressive figure. The correlation remained statistically significant after partialing out the number of political decision-makers during the same periods.

Unfortunately, two aspects of this study undermine its effectiveness as an empirical test. First, because the chronologies in early (pre-Muslim) Indian history are very approximate, the investigators used centuries rather than generations as the unit of analysis. Given that there are five generations per century, this appreciably reduces the sensitivity of the analysis, particularly with respect to the search for cross-lagged correlations. Second, to avoid the problem of autocorrelation, which biases the statistical tests, the investigators decided to examine only every other century, which reduced the sample size by half. A more powerful test would have retained all centuries and then employed the kinds of analytical remedies so common in econometrics (Simonton 1975). Nevertheless, the general conclusion I drew back in 1975 was confirmed. For India as well as the West, political fragmentation is positively correlated with the number of creative geniuses over the course of a civilization's history. Hence some of the clustering of genius may again be attributed to this political factor.

Schaefer never published this analysis, but did read his results at a meeting of the International Studies Association. And he kindly sent me a copy. After reading the paper I was inspired to redouble my data collection efforts with respect to Chinese civilization. Within a few years I had gathered a data base of over 10 000 eminent Chinese creators and leaders, and was on the verge of collecting the necessary political measures, when my work was again pre-empted.

CHINESE CIVILIZATION

Shing-Shiang Ting, a native of Taiwan, had applied for admission to our graduate programme, seeking me as his sponsor. His explicit aim was to conduct a study for China similar to that which I had carried out for Western civilization. He followed my procedures very closely, with but one major exception: he decided to confine the sample to just literary creators. Even so, because he had access to sources available only in Chinese, he managed to accumulate a collection of approximately 7000 writers. To his and my surprise, the degree of political fragmentation was negatively correlated with the number of literary geniuses (Ting 1986). Moreover, this negative association could not be easily dismissed. Besides controlling for several potential artifacts in a multivariate time-series analysis, he tested the effect using three distinct operational definitions of literary creativity, and always obtained the same result, with consistently high effect sizes in all three equations. This disconfirmation raised the obvious issue of why the results for China departed so drastically from those for India and the West.

One answer may be that my graduate student may have discovered an idiosyncrasy of Chinese literature. Perhaps more consistent results would have been obtained had he examined other domains of creative activity. For instance, the relation between political fragmentation and creative genius might have been different had Ting examined generational fluctuations in the appearance of major Chinese philosophers. The Golden Age of Chinese philosophy took place during the Zhou dynasty, after it had disintegrated into numerous independent states. It was then that all of the indigenous schools of thought emerged, including Taoism, Confucianism, Mohism and Legalism. Furthermore, Chinese imperial systems displayed a distinct inclination toward imposing ideological conformity. When Shi Huangdi, the founder of the Qin dynasty, finally unified China, he immediately ordered the burning of all books that were not to his liking, thereby incurring the eternal enmity of all subsequent Confucian scholars.

Yet rather than separate out Chinese literary creativity from other forms of creativity, it might be better to rethink the implications of political fragmentation. It may very well be that the latter variable serves merely as an approximate indicator of a more fundamental factor that provides the actual proximate cause of creative activity in a civilization. To be specific, the crucial reality may be that political fragmentation is strongly but not perfectly associated with cultural diversity or heterogeneity. It is the latter socio-cultural condition, then, that supports creative development. Large empire states, in contrast, tend to impose cultural homogeneity and thereby precipitate a decline in the appearance of creative genius (Hume 1741–42/1875). This connection was suggested by Kroeber (1944) when he surmised that 'it is certainly true that high achievements by suppressed nationalities are rather rare' (p. 794). Given this interpretation, the results for China may not be that discrepant after all. In particular, it is necessary to consider the following two circumstances that would undermine the expected linkages among political fragmentation, cultural heterogeneity and the appearance of creative clusters (Simonton 2002).

First, Chinese history is probably distinctive in that it represents almost exclusively the record of a homogeneous nation, culture and civilization. Most cultural minorities in the territorial core of China – as distinguished from those in peripheral areas like Tibet – all but vanished early in the emergence of the Chinese nation. As a consequence, an increase in the number of independent states is not strongly associated with nationalistic movements. On the contrary, often the emergence of new states would represent the conquest of Chinese peoples by invading non-Chinese 'barbarians'. This situation contrasts greatly with what tended to happen in the civilizations of India, Europe and Islam. In the latter cultures, imperial expansion often meant the oppression of cultures sometimes quite different from those of the conquerors. The Moghul conquest of India in the sixteenth and seventeenth centuries, for example, entailed the submission of indigenous Hindu peoples to alien Islamic invaders descended from Mongolians of Central Asia.

Second, Chinese literature is highly distinctive in its use of a writing system that transcends the spoken language. Chinese is actually a collection of mutually unintelligible languages (sometimes incorrectly called dialects). Although the differences among these languages are comparable to those that separate the Romance languages of Europe, the Chinese languages are all written in the same way. As a result, any tendencies toward nationalism could not take voice in a corresponding literary movement, unlike what happens in other civilization areas. When the Roman empire began to fall apart, various vernaculars began to rival the Latin language. As nationalism increased, these vernaculars could become the independent languages of new nations. With this emergence would invariably come a new national literature, beginning with epics like *The Cid* and the *Song of Roland* and eventually culminating in the masterpieces of Dante, Rabelais, Camoens and Cervantes.

In light of these arguments, it behoves us to scrutinize cultural heterogeneity and its connection to both political fragmentation and creative genius.

CULTURAL HETEROGENEITY

Many scholars have indicated the significant link between cultural diversity and creativity (Koestler 1964). Thus one creativity researcher identified 'exposure to different and even contrasting cultural stimuli' as a significant 'creativogenic factor' (Arieti 1976: 320, emphasis removed). Likewise, Sorokin (1947/1969) claimed that the creativity of individuals or groups is enhanced when they live

> at the point of intersection of cross-currents of various appropriate or relevant systems of meanings and values. Since any new system of meanings is a blend of two or more existing systems, such a union occurs more naturally amidst several crosscurrents of different ideas, beliefs, and patterns. Such a milieu contains richer material for a new synthesis or creative combination than a cultural milieu of monotonous stereotypes. The point of junction of various cultural streams supplies a larger number of the elements necessary for a new creation. (p. 542)

One possible manner of attaining this exposure is to become an immigrant. Galton (1892/1972) long ago observed: 'it is very remarkable how large a portion of the eminent men of all countries bear foreign names' (p. 413). According to Park (1928), 'one of the consequences of migration is to create a situation in which the same individual . . . finds himself striving to live in two diverse cultural groups'. Consequently, 'the "cake of custom" is broken and the individual is freed for new enterprises and new associations' (p. 881). A classic example is the pre-eminence of Jews among the Christian nations in which they reside (Arieti 1976, Hayes 1989, Veblen 1919).

Moreover, empirical studies have documented the auspicious fortune of immigrants to a new land (Bowerman 1947). For example a study of twentieth-century eminent personalities revealed that nearly one-fifth were either first- or second-generation immigrants (Goertzel et al. 1978). This pattern even holds in the sciences, where cultural diversity tends to be somewhat less than in the arts (Simonton 1988c, 1999). In one sample of highly eminent scientists, 25 per cent were second-generation immigrants (Eiduson 1962). Among distinguished mathematicians, 32 per cent were foreign-born (Visher 1947) and 52 per cent were either foreign-born or second-generation Americans (Helson and Crutchfield 1970). One recent investigation scrutinized the origins of the most influential figures in the physical and life sciences of the United States (Levin and Stephan 1999). Judging from citation impact and membership in the National Academy of Sciences, 'individuals making exceptional contributions . . . are disproportionately drawn from the foreign born' and 'are also disproportionately foreign educated, both at the undergraduate and graduate level' (p. 1213).

These findings are in accord with two other sets of findings. First, bilingualism is positively associated with creative capacity, at least once controls are introduced for any initial socio-economic disadvantages (Carringer 1974, Lambert et al. 1973, Landry 1972, Lopez et al. 1993). Second, members of the native-born population can attain some of the same advantages enjoyed by immigrants if they immerse themselves in an alien culture. For instance Ellis (1926) observed that a very high proportion of the British geniuses he studied had spent their early years living abroad for a considerable time. If one does not reside in another country early in life, at least there remains the option of studying abroad. Nobel laureates, for instance, illustrate this alternative, a very high percentage having gone to foreign universities to complete their education (Moulin 1955; also see Poffenberger 1930). Of course the latter option often presupposes some degree of proficiency in a second language.

These empirical findings all come from studies of individuals rather than whole cultures or civilizations. Yet there is already some research indicating that cultural heterogeneity is linked with the creativity of socio-cultural systems and at the same time heterogeneity has some non-trivial connection with political fragmentation. The evidence comes from two civilizations: the Western and Japan.

WESTERN CIVILIZATION

Nikolay Danilevsky, the Russian historical philosopher, proposed a 'second law of the dynamics of great cultures' which claimed that 'in order for the civilization of a potentially creative group to be conceived and developed, the group and its subgroups must be politically independent' (Sorokin 1947/1969: 543). As a consequence, the main means for subjugated peoples to resuscitate their creativity is to revolt against the oppressive empire under which they are submerged. Hence, creative clusters should emerge in response to nationalistic revolts and rebellions against imperial states. There is evidence for such an effect operating over and above the impact of political fragmentation. This was found in the study I conducted for my doctoral dissertation (Simonton 1974, 1975). Among the variables I measured was 'imperial instability', a count of civil disturbances directed against an imperial state. The data analysis indicated that the number of creative geniuses in generation g tends to be a positive function of the intensity and frequency of such popular revolts, revolutions and rebellions in generation $g - 1$. Furthermore, the evidence was more secure that imperial stability acted as a developmental influence. Presumably these events increase the exposure of young talents to a diversity of cultural beliefs, ideas, practices, customs and mores.

Admittedly this investigation did not include a direct measure of cultural heterogeneity. Thus the above conclusion is only inferential. Still, a later study provided a more immediate connection between the hypothesized variables (Simonton 1976a). Added to the generational measures of political fragmentation, imperial instability and cultural creativity was an indicator of ideological diversity. The latter measure was based on Sorokin's (1937–41) assessments of philosophical beliefs. In essence, ideological diversity was a count of the number of distinct positions advocated by thinkers in a given generation. The time-series analysis then divulged two main findings. First, political fragmentation, imperial instability and ideological diversity are all correlated positively with the number of creators. Second, political fragmentation and imperial instability are both positively associated with ideological diversity. The only complication was that political fragmentation affected ideological diversity after a generation lag, whereas the impact of imperial instability on ideological diversity operated contemporaneously.

Although the latter result fits with the general argument, it suffers from the disadvantage that ideological diversity does not provide the best possible indicator of cultural heterogeneity. In the first place, the former measure is confined to intellectual history, ignoring heterogeneity in other domains of creativity. Even worse, the measure does not necessarily incorporate the influx of foreign ideas. Even if some of the intellectual movements during the course of Western civilization were external imports (for example Manichaeism and Christianity), many others were indigenous creations (for example Cynicism, Stoicism and Epicurianism). Consequently, it is really essential that cultural heterogeneity be assessed more adequately.

JAPANESE CIVILIZATION

After completing a study of genius in Chinese civilization (Simonton, 1988b), I decided to turn my attention to another Far Eastern culture: Japan. One investigation examined the determinants of female genius, such as the negative role played by Confucian philosophy and political militarism (Simonton 1992). Another looked at whether the eminence of a Japanese genius was influenced by his or her temporal placement within the cultural configuration (Simonton 1996). Yet another study applied generational time-series analysis to detect whether cultural cross-fertilization had a beneficial effect on achievement over the course of Japanese history (Simonton 1997). Japanese civilization was ideal for this purpose because its history has shown exceptional variation in the degree to which its culture has been open to foreign influences. At one extreme, Japan has sometimes opened the floodgates to the onrush of alien ideas, such as Chinese culture, Buddhism and, most recently, modern Western civilization. At the other extreme, Japan has sometimes totally shut its doors to the outside world, occasionally imposing the death penalty on those who violated its policy of deliberate cultural isolation.

The study began with a sample of 1803 eminent Japanese in 14 achievement domains: politics, war, business, religion, medicine, philosophy, non-fiction literature, fiction literature, poetry, drama, painting, sculpture, ceramics and sword making. The figures were assigned to 68 consecutive 20-year intervals from AD 580 to 1939.

I then defined three alternative measures of Japanese openness to foreign influences:

1. The number of foreign immigrants who left a mark on Japanese history. Examples include Chinese Buddhist monks, Korean artists and Christian missionaries.
2. The number of eminent Japanese who travelled abroad, that is who left the main islands of Japan to visit civilized regions like China, Korea, Europe or the United States.
3. Outside influences in which native Japanese studied under foreigners, went abroad to study, or admired, developed or imitated the style or ideas of foreigners – the most inclusive of the three measures.

I then computed the cross-correlations between the time series assessing fluctuations in national achievement and those gauging fluctuations in cultural openness to the non-Japanese world. Several significant cross-lagged correlations emerged. For instance, the number of eminent medical figures in generation g was a positive function of the frequency of foreign travel in generation $g - 2$. Other creative domains that exhibited similar cross-lagged effects were poetry, fiction, non-fiction, painting and sculpture. The two-generation lag was typical. Apparently the influx of outside ideas must be first assimilated by one generation before it can exert a developmental impact on the next generation.

CONCLUSION

Over three decades have transpired since Naroll et al. (1971) first investigated the relation between a civilization's level of political fragmentation and the amount of creative genius. Although the Naroll inquiry encompassed four civilizations, subsequent work has examined just one civilization at a time. My first replication of the relationship concentrated just on Western civilization (Simonton 1974, 1975). However, that replication was conducted using a more extensive sample of creators and a more rigorous methodology (generational time-series analysis). In addition, political fragmentation was shown to be positively associated with the differential eminence of Western philosophers (Simonton 1976b) and with the emergence of philosophical positions linked to scientific activity (Simonton 1976c). A subsequent study by Schaefer et al. (1977) partially extended the first set of results to Indian civilization. Even though the methodology was not as strong as that applied to Western civilization, it at least confirmed a positive relation between the two variables.

Then came a big surprise: Ting (1986) showed that the appearance of literary genius in Chinese civilization was negatively correlated with political fragmentation. This disconfirmation was then explained in terms of the hypothesis that it is cultural heterogeneity that provides the crucial factor, political fragmentation only proving relevant insofar as it is associated with such heterogeneity. This explanation had the advantage of incorporating some earlier findings with respect to Western civilization: the connections among political fragmentation, imperial instability, ideological diversity and cultural creativity (Simonton 1976a). Here imperial instability is a measure of nationalistic revolts and rebellions against empire states, while ideological diversity is an indicator of the variety of philosophical positions advocated by a given generation of thinkers. Because ideological diversity is not equivalent to a gauge of cultural heterogeneity, the decision was made to examine the impact of the latter variable more directly. In this case, the target civilization was Japan. After assessing fluctuations in Japan's openness to foreign influences, the generational time-series analysis showed that the influx of alien ideas was positively linked to creative activity, usually after a two-generation lag (Simonton 1997).

As often happens in many research programmes, what was originally hypothesized to be a relatively simple causal function turned out to be far more complicated after empirical examination. The primary problem is probably political fragmentation as a phenomenon. Unlike many other factors that underlie the appearance of creative clusters, it is extremely autocorrelated in generational time series. After all, most national entities endure for a century or more (Sorokin 1927). This contrasts greatly with factors such as peace and prosperity that change rapidly even on a year-to-year basis (Rainoff 1929, Schmookler 1966). The political fragmentation's inertia makes it difficult to pin down precisely how it affects creativity. Does it operate simultaneously or only after a generational delay?

Another problem with the construct is that it is associated with many other factors that may exhibit positive, negative or zero associations with cultural creativity, with or without a lagged effect. For example, political fragmentation is associated with balance-of-power wars, whereas political unification is associated with imperialistic wars. Yet only the former class of war has a negative correlation with creative activity (Simonton 1980; see also Fernberger 1946, Price 1978). On the other side of the picture, political fragmentation is no doubt associated with greater opportunities for creativity in such domains as painting, sculpture and literature. Numerous small states, at least when wealthy, signify a plentiful supply of patrons trying to attract the brightest and the best to their courts. Political unification, in contrast, by centralizing all patronage to one imperial court, can prove a detriment to creativity except in those domains where concentrated funds are necessary to finance the achievements. The most obvious instance is monumental architecture, such as the Egyptian pyramids, the Athenian Parthenon, or the Roman Coliseum.

All these problems notwithstanding, two conclusions remain. First, if we ever wish to understand why creative genius clusters over the course of a civilization's history, political fragmentation must certainly be considered among the potential factors. Even in the case of China it appeared as a predictor, albeit in a negative direction. Second, although the impact of political fragmentation may differ across civilizations, the differences likely have some rationale. In particular, the impact of political fragmentation may partly depend on whether it is indicative of cultural heterogeneity. In relatively homogeneous cultural systems like China, the two factors are decoupled, whereas in highly heterogeneous systems like India and the West, the two factors are intimately connected.

It would be fascinating to examine how this principle applies to the case of Islamic civilization. Islam began as a highly homogeneous culture based on a single language (Arabic) and religion (based on the Koran), and began its political life as a universal state (the Caliphate). Yet it eventually differentiated into a heterogeneous civilization with multiple languages (Arabic, Persian, Turkish and Urdu among the most prominent), religious sects (Sunni and diverse forms of Shiism), and political systems (a veritable confusion of empires, sultanates, slave states and principalities). Because at least one historian of Islamic civilization has suggested that the high point of creativity did not appear until after the disintegration of the Caliphate (Armajani 1970), it is most probable that this culture follows the same pattern as already observed for India and the West. By the same token, as a civilization that spread precipitously by the military or economic conquest of prior civilizations, Islam is put in a unique situation *vis-à-vis* other civilizations, East or West. To some yet to be determined extent Islam recurrently resuscitated its creative potential by having to assimilate a conquered culture. The prototypical case is the Moghul civilization that emerged as a distinctive hybrid of Islamic (Persian and Central Asian) and Hindu civilizations. Cases like this need to be systematically scrutinized in future research.

APPENDIX

Table 3.1   Creativity and political fragmentation

Civilization, century	Number of eminent creators	Number of independent states
China		
500–401 BC	7	7
200–101 BC	18	1
AD 100–199	23	1
AD 400–499	12	4
AD 700–799	20	?
AD 1000–1099	38	40
AD 1300–1399	18.6	3
AD 1600–1699	38.6	4
India		
500–401 BC	6	23
200–101 BC	1	21
AD 100–199	4	17
AD 400–499	18	23
AD 700–799	6	14
AD 1000–1099	6	11
AD 1300–1399	2	12
AD 1600–1699	8	7
Middle East		
AD 900–999	94	11
AD 1200–1299	29	4
AD 1500–1599	0	8
AD 1800–1899	0	7

Note: The data cover only every third century.

Source: Naroll et al. (1971).

Table 3.2 Creativity by domain and number of states in the history of India

Century	Number of Indians of reputation						Number of independent states
	Philosophy	Science	Philology	Drama	Literature	Total	
500–401 BC	–	–	–	–	–	–	8
300–201 BC	–	–	–	–	–	–	19
100–1 BC	–	–	–	–	–	–	12
AD 100–199	4	1	–	(1)	2(1)	7	18
AD 300–399	4	–	1	3	3(2)	11	26
AD 500–599	–	2	1	–	1(1)	4	34
AD 700–799	4	–	–	1	1(1)	6	42
AD 900–999	4	–	–	1	(1)	5	43
AD 1100–1199	–	1	–	1	6	8	56
AD 1300–1399	–	–	–	–	2	2	29
AD 1500–1599	–	–	–	1	6	7	26
AD 1700–1799	–	–	–	–	1	1	8
Total	16	4	2	7(1)	23(6)	52	–

Note: Numbers in parentheses indicate persons repeated from other fields.

Source: Schaefer et al. (1977), Table 4 and Table 5, column 4.

NOTES

1. Table 3.1 in the Appendix to this chapter reproduces the raw data of Naroll et al. (1971).
2. Their data on creativity and political fragmentation are reproduced in Table 3.2 attached to this chapter.

REFERENCES

Arieti, S. (1976), *Creativity: The Magic Synthesis*, New York: Basic Books.
Armajani, Y. (1970), *Middle East Past and Present*, Englewood Cliffs, NJ: Prentice-Hall.
Bowerman, W.G. (1947), *Studies in Genius*, New York: Philosophical Library.
Candolle, A. de (1873), *Histoire des sciences et des savants depuis deux siècles*, Geneve: Georg.
Carringer, D.C. (1974), 'Creative thinking abilities in Mexican youth', *Journal of Cross-Cultural Psychology*, **5**, 492–504.
Eiduson, B.T. (1962), *Scientists: Their Psychological World*, New York: Basic Books.
Ellis, H. (1926), *A Study of British Genius*, revised edn, Boston, MA: Houghton Mifflin.
Fernberger, S.W. (1946), 'Scientific publication as affected by war and politics,' *Science*, **104**, August, 175–7.
Galton, F. (1892), *Hereditary Genius: An Inquiry into its Laws and Consequences*, 2nd edn 1972, Gloucester, MA: Smith.
Goertzel, M.G., V. Goertzel and T.G. Goertzel (1978), *300 Eminent Personalities: A Psychosocial Analysis of the Famous*, San Francisco, CA: Jossey-Bass.
Gray, C.E. (1958), 'An analysis of Graeco–Roman development: the epicyclical evolution of Graeco–Roman civilization', *American Anthropologist*, **60**, 13–31.
Gray, C.E. (1961), 'An epicyclical model for Western civilization', *American Anthropologist*, **63**, 1014–37.
Gray, C.E. (1966), 'A measurement of creativity in Western civilization', *American Anthropologist*, **68**, 1384–1417.
Hayes, J.R. (1989), *The Complete Problem Solver*, 2nd edn, Hillsdale, NJ: Erlbaum.
Helson, R., and R.S. Crutchfield, (1970), 'Mathematicians: the creative researcher and the average PhD', *Journal of Consulting and Clinical Psychology*, **34**, 250–57.
Hume, D. (1741–42), 'Of the rise and progress of the arts and sciences', in T. H. Green and T.H. Grose (eds) (1875), *Essays Moral, Political, and Literary*, London: Longmans, Green, pp. 174–97.
Kavolis, V. (1963), 'Political dynamics and artistic creativity', *Sociology and Social Research*, **49**, 412–24.
Kavolis, V. (1964), 'Economic correlates of artistic creativity', *American Journal of Sociology*, **70**, 332–41.
Kavolis, V. (1966), 'Community dynamics and artistic creativity', *American Sociological Review*, **31**, 208–17.
Koestler, A. (1964), *The Act of Creation*, New York: Macmillan.
Kroeber, A.L. (1944), *Configurations of Culture Growth*, Berkeley, CA: University of California Press.
Kuo, Y. (1986), 'The growth and decline of Chinese philosophical genius', *Chinese Journal of Psychology*, **28**, 81–91.

Kuo, Y. (1988), 'The social psychology of Chinese philosophical creativity: a critical synthesis', *Social Epistemology*, **2**, 283–95.

Lambert, W.E., G.R. Tucker and A. d'Anglejan (1973), 'Cognitive and attitudinal consequences of bilingual schooling: the St Lambert project through grade five', *Journal of Educational Psychology*, **65**, 141–59.

Landry, R.G. (1972), 'The enhancement of figural creativity through second language learning at the elementary school level', *Foreign Language Annals*, **4**, 111–15.

Lehman, H.C. (1947), 'The exponential increase of man's cultural output', *Social Forces*, **25**, 281–90.

Levin, S.G., and P.E. Stephan (1999), 'Are the foreign born a source of strength for US science?' *Science*, **285**, August, 1213–14.

Lopez, E.C., G.B. Esquivel and J.C. Houtz (1993), 'The creative skills of culturally and linguistically diverse gifted students', *Creativity Research Journal*, **6**, 401–12.

Moulin, L. (1955), 'The Nobel Prizes for the sciences from 1901–1950: an essay in sociological analysis', *British Journal of Sociology*, **6**, 246–63.

Naroll, R., E.C. Benjamin, F.K. Fohl, M.J. Fried, R.E. Hildreth and J.M. Schaefer (1971), 'Creativity: a cross-historical pilot survey', *Journal of Cross-Cultural Psychology*, **2**, 181–8.

Norling, B. (1970), *Timeless Problems in History*, Notre Dame: Notre Dame Press.

Park, R.E. (1928), 'Human migration and the marginal man', *American Journal of Sociology*, **33**, 881–93.

Poffenberger, A.T. (1930), 'The development of men of science', *Journal of Social Psychology*, **1**, 31–47.

Price, D. (1963), *Little Science, Big Science*, New York: Columbia University Press.

Price, D. (1978), 'Ups and downs in the pulse of science and technology', in J. Gaston (ed.), *The Sociology of Science*, San Francisco, CA: Jossey-Bass, pp. 162–71.

Rainoff, T.J. (1929), 'Wave-like fluctuations of creative productivity in the development of West-European physics in the eighteenth and nineteenth centuries', *Isis*, **12**, 287–319.

Schaefer, J.M., M.C. Babu and N.S. Rao (1977), 'Sociopolitical causes of creativity in India 500 BC–1800 AD: a regional time-lagged study', paper presented at the meeting of the International Studies Association, St Louis, MO.

Schmookler, J. (1966), *Invention and Economic Growth*, Cambridge, MA: Harvard University Press.

Schneider, J. (1937), 'The cultural situation as a condition for the achievement of fame', *American Sociological Review*, **2**, 480–91.

Simonton, D.K. (1974), '*The social psychology of creativity: an archival data analysis*', unpublished doctoral dissertation, Harvard University.

Simonton, D.K. (1975), 'Sociocultural context of individual creativity: a transhistorical time-series analysis', *Journal of Personality and Social Psychology*, **32**, 1119–33.

Simonton, D.K. (1976a), 'Ideological diversity and creativity: a re-evaluation of a hypothesis', *Social Behavior and Personality*, **4**, 203–207.

Simonton, D.K. (1976b), 'Philosophical eminence, beliefs, and zeitgeist: an individual-generational analysis', *Journal of Personality and Social Psychology*, **34**, 630–40.

Simonton, D.K. (1976c), 'The sociopolitical context of philosophical beliefs: a transhistorical causal analysis', *Social Forces*, **54**, 513–23.

Simonton, D.K. (1980), 'Techno-scientific activity and war: a yearly time-series analysis, 1500–1903 AD', *Scientometrics*, **2**, 251–5.

Simonton, D.K. (1981), 'Creativity in Western civilization: extrinsic and intrinsic causes', *American Anthropologist*, **83**, 628–30.

Simonton, D.K. (1984a), 'Generational time-series analysis: a paradigm for studying sociocultural influences', in K. Gergen and M. Gergen (eds), *Historical Social Psychology*, Hillsdale, NJ: Lawrence Erlbaum, pp. 141–55.

Simonton, D.K. (1984b), *Genius, Creativity, and Leadership: Historiometric Inquiries*, Cambridge, MA: Harvard University Press.

Simonton, D.K. (1988a), 'Age and outstanding achievement: what do we know after a century of research?', *Psychological Bulletin*, **104**, 251–67.

Simonton, D.K. (1988b), 'Galtonian genius, Kroeberian configurations, and emulation: a generational time-series analysis of Chinese civilization', *Journal of Personality and Social Psychology*, **55**, 230–38.

Simonton, D.K. (1988c), *Scientific Genius: A Psychology of Science,* Cambridge: Cambridge University Press.

Simonton, D.K. (1990), *Psychology, Science, and History: An Introduction to Historiometry*, New Haven, CT: Yale University Press.

Simonton, D.K. (1992), 'Gender and genius in Japan: feminine eminence in masculine culture', *Sex Roles*, **27**, 101–19.

Simonton, D.K. (1994), *Greatness: Who Makes History and Why*, New York: Guilford Press.

Simonton, D.K. (1996), 'Individual genius and cultural configurations: the case of Japanese civilization', *Journal of Cross-Cultural Psychology*, **27**, 354–75.

Simonton, D.K. (1997), 'Foreign influence and national achievement: the impact of open milieus on Japanese civilization', *Journal of Personality and Social Psychology*, **72**, 86–94.

Simonton, D.K. (1999), *Origins of Genius: Darwinian Perspectives on Creativity*, New York: Oxford University Press.

Simonton, D.K. (2002), *Great Psychologists and their Times: Scientific Insights into Psychology's History*, Washington, DC: APA Books.

Sorokin, P.A. (1927), 'A survey of the cyclical conceptions of social and historical process', *Social Forces*, **6**, 28–40.

Sorokin, P.A. (1937–41), *Social and Cultural Dynamics*, (vols 1–4), New York: American Book.

Sorokin, P A. (1947), *Society, Culture, and Personality*, reprinted 1969, New York: Cooper Square.

Sorokin, P.A. and R.K. Merton (1935), 'The course of Arabian intellectual development, 700–1300 AD', *Isis*, **22**, 516–24.

Taagepera, R., and B.N. Colby, (1979), 'Growth of Western civilization: epicyclical or exponential?' *American Anthropologist*, **81**, 907–12.

Ting, S.-S. (1986), 'The social psychology of Chinese literary creativity: an archival data analysis', unpublished doctoral dissertation, University of California, Davis.

Toynbee, A.J. (1946), *A Study of History*, (abridged by D. C. Somervell, vols 1–2), New York: Oxford University Press.

Veblen, T. (1919), 'The intellectual pre-eminence of Jews in modern Europe', *Political Science Quarterly*, **34**, 33–42.

Visher, S.S. (1947), 'Scientists starred, 1903–1943', in *American Men of Science: A Study of Collegiate and Doctoral Training, Birthplace, Distribution, Backgrounds, and Developmental Influences*, Baltimore, MD: Johns Hopkins Press.

4. Lessons from the history of Imperial China

Pak Hung Mo

INTRODUCTION

There are several mysteries commonly expressed by students of Chinese civilization. They include the following.

Why has there been a persistent under-utilization of technology for improving the welfare of the society? An example is the impressive achievements in the mediaeval economic revolution during the Sung dynasty (AD 960–1275). During the period, economic growth had been accompanied by the invention of new production techniques. However, in the Ming (AD 1368–1644) and Ch'ing (AD 1645–1911) dynasties, the Sung inventions were underutilized and new inventions were almost entirely absent. Why and how did the dynamism of the 'Medieval Renaissance' disappear?

What forces support the formation of the world's largest enduring state? Why have larger states normally broken up into fragments after a certain period of time while China, though it often suffers from invasion, rejuvenates itself because of 'the extraordinary integrative and absorptive power of Chinese civilization, a power which no invader before modern times was able to withstand'? (Needham 1954: 119). In most of its history, China proper has seldom been under more than two administrations since the unification of the Ch'in dynasty in 221 BC

The relatively detailed and long historical record of Chinese civilization and its unusual evolution can provide some important lessons that can enlighten our future development. In this chapter, we attempt to explain the above-mentioned mysteries. Based on the understanding, we discuss briefly the arrangements of domestic and international governance that can facilitate our future development. Our reasoning follows the work of Mo (1995). It suggests that the stagnation of Chinese civilization is due to maximization of self-interest by the autocrats in an environment lacking effective international competition. In order to curb the development of domestic non-governmental forces, the autocrats destroyed non-governmental organizations directly and designed intricate institutions that could destroy the factors essential for economic development. We also suggest that a major reason for the lack of effective international competition is the vastness and diversity of the land in and around China proper.

The chapter is organized as follows. In the next section, we explain the behaviour and effects of the imperial autocrats in different international environments, exemplified by the observations in the Sung and Ming dynasties. The third section discusses the role of pictographs in the evolution of imperial China and the fourth section is the concluding remarks.

THE THEORY AND OBSERVATIONS

The take-off of a civilization starts with having a production surplus that makes investment and the provision of essential public goods possible. However, when surplus exists, rent-seeking groups will appear. They are defined as groups that intend to capture the surplus without contribution. If the rent-seeking groups are also the groups that monopolize the use of violence and set the rules of the community, they will use their power to extend their position of exploiting the surplus of the society. We call these rent-seeking groups the 'exploitative government', in contrast to the 'functional government' that exists to provide public goods to the economy.

Unfortunately, the major functions of government are defining and enforcing property rights, and organizing military force to protect the state against invasion. Naturally, the controllers of the government machinery who monopolize the use of violence become the strongest rent-seeking group to exploit the social surplus. Their behaviour and evolution are exemplified by the history of China, which has endured for more than 2000 years.[1]

A well-established feudal system was founded by the Chou dynasty in 1122 BC. The customs, political system and technology of the Chou people were spread throughout China proper. After defeating the Shang dynasty, it was reported that more than 1000 states were established by the Chou dynasty. From their establishment to the unification by Ch'in in 221 BC, the whole period was taken up by competition, synthesis and imitation among the states with similar technological levels. The survival possibilities of the states, and hence of the autocrats, were therefore dependent on the states' relative economic and military strengths. The fierce competition among the despotic rulers forced them to design and adopt institutions favourable to economic development and hence the military strength of the countries. This resulted in the most important and exceptional period in the formation of China and her culture. On the other hand, after the unification of Ch'in in 221 BC, with China's superior technology, labour force, and cultural and natural endowment, the unified empire became the dominant political power in the region.

Apart from some relatively short periods of disintegration between dynasties, the autocrats seldom experienced long-lasting and fierce competition as they had done in the Ch'un Ch'iu and Warring States period (722 to 221 BC). Without effective competition, instead of enriching the states and strengthening the army, the autocrats indulged in conspicuous consumption and chose policies to extend their privileges and to raise their chances of maintaining power. The production surplus was allocated to further the interests of the autocrats rather than promoting the welfare of the country. Their behaviour and its effects were exemplified by the policies of Han Wu Di (reigned 140 to 87 BC) as discussed in Mo (1995), which resulted in long-lasting stagnation in imperial China.

Although competition did resume during the periods of disintegration between dynasties, such as in the periods of Three Kingdoms (AD 221–264) and the Northern and Southern dynasties (AD 311–580), it was accompanied by constant destruction due to anarchy, barbarian invasion and political instability.[2]

Without a stable provision of basic public goods and a sufficient production surplus under these conditions, technological and economic development became difficult even though the environment was competitive.[3]

Taoism and Buddhism, which entered from India, became the dominant intellectual and religious forces in this turbulent period. The renewal of the unified empires of Sui and T'ang in AD 589 was followed by a period of political stability and military and geographical expansion. The empires were the result of the sinification of the barbarians during the period of disunity. Although T'ang was one of the most celebrated and powerful dynasties of imperial China, the underutilization of technology and counterproductive policies intended to restrict the development of domestic non-governmental forces were still commonly observed. The T'ang dynasty adopted the equal distribution of land with laws confiscating the property of the rich. The dynasty was therefore supported by small tenant farmers. The livelihood of the majority of people was thus totally dependent on their small piece of land, which was in turn totally under the control of government. They also developed an examination system that recruited bureaucrats according to their poetic ability.[4] However it is the sharp contrast between the government policies in the Sung (AD 960–1275) and Ming (AD 1368–1644) dynasties that reveals the deleterious role of the autocrats in the development of China since the unification of Ch'in in 221 BC.

From the tenth to the thirteenth century, China under the Sung dynasty advanced to the threshold of a systematic experimental investigation of nature, and created the world's earliest mechanized industry (Elvin 1973). The Chinese world experienced a significant transformation, the range of which was no less than that of the changes in the Warring States period. The term 'renaissance' was adopted by Gernet (1972), among others, to describe the period. The period was characterized by a return to the classical tradition, the diffusion of knowledge, the upsurge in science and technology, a new philosophy, and a new view of the world. However this period was both the climax and the end of scientific and technical progress. From around the early Ming dynasty, scientific and technical progress declined until the full encounter with the Western civilization.

From its beginning to its end, the Sung dynasty faced severe international competition and was finally replaced by the Mongol Yuan dynasty (AD 1276–1367). Sung was the first Chinese dynasty that was forced to pay regular tribute to neighbouring 'barbarians' for most of its reign. The Ming dynasty, however, after the expulsion of the remnants of the Mongol forces from the north and the north-east, enjoyed two and a half centuries without serious external threats. The difference in the level of international competition in the two dynasties led to a significant difference in government policies and hence a divergence in economic development. We will discuss the major differences that determined the economic development of the dynasties. They include the attitude towards tradition and reforms, the structure of governance, and the attitude and policies towards innovation and trade.

THE ATTITUDE TOWARDS TRADITION

An outstanding characteristic of the Sung period was dissatisfaction with past ideas. Substantial revenues were required for military expenditures due to the strong competing nations, Liao and Hsia.[5]

The situation resulted in attempts to remedy the deficiencies of the defence system and to solve the financing problem. However, since the problems could not be separated from their economic, social and political institutions, they finally affected most institutions in the dynasty. The attempts were exemplified by the reform of the minister called Wang An Shih (AD 1021–86), which was strongly supported by the emperors. The reform had several features.

Since the adoption of Confucianism as the only official teaching by Han Wu Di (reigned 140–87 BC), Wang was the first prominent Confucian bureaucrat to advocate ignoring all traditional practices and to propose drastic reforms to strengthen the economic and military strength of the nation.

His major objective was to improve administration so that it could increase national wealth and provide additional sources of tax revenue without increasing the tax burden on the populace. For that purpose, the government introduced policies intended to help small merchants and peasants. For example, government trade bureaus offered loans at a rate of 2 per cent, purchased surplus stocks at fixed prices and arranged for the exchange of goods. They also abolished compulsory labour service and introduced agricultural loans to prevent the rich from exacting heavy interest from the poor.

Since the adoption of Confucianism as the only official teaching, Chinese government had seldom intended to serve as a functional government focused on providing essential public goods. However Wang's policies were intended to serve the country's needs rather than to accomplish the ideals of Confucianism. He raised the importance of practical subjects in the recruitment competition for government posts. Candidates for the bureaucracy were urged to study methods of practical administration rather than exhausting themselves in the strenuous cultivation of the art of essay writing.[6]

Public schools were established in prefectures and sub-prefectures in order to raise the supply and quality of the candidates.

He proposed entrusting good-quality people delegated with important responsibilities to select their own subordinates according to their qualifications. Traditionally, all bureaucrats were allocated by central government for the sake of imperial control.

To summarize, Wang and his supportive autocrats intended to introduce more efficient institutions in order to deal with the intense international competition in the period.

THE STRUCTURE OF GOVERNANCE

Sung government was the only dynasty that had minimal records of intervention by eunuchs and imperial relatives. The political system of the Sung dynasty allowed free discussions in which contradictory opinions could be expressed. The elite bureaucrats had never played such an important role in the government since the Ch'in dynasty (221–206 BC). The emperors themselves played only a secondary role. In contrast, the Ming government was characterized by the complete centralization of all power in the hands of the emperor, and by the development of secret police forces entrusted with the task of supervising the various levels of administration. Another peculiarity of the Ming dynasty was the great influence acquired by the eunuchs as a result of the excessive centralization and secretiveness of the autocrats. Even the nature of power in the countryside was changed. While manorialism was prevailing in the Sung dynasty, there was a shift from landlord power localized in the country to managerial gentry in the Ming dynasty. Formal administrative power was put into the hands of the biggest landowners for the collection of tribute grain, and they were given extensive privileges. The local non-government force in the Sung dynasty was therefore converted to be a sub-bureaucratic organization. Another remarkable institution set up by Ming Tai-tsu (reigned AD 1368–98) was a functional division of the population. People whose fathers were peasants, soldiers or craftsmen by birth were destined to remain unchanged. This further consolidated the control of central government over the people at the expense of efficiency. These extreme autocratic tendencies, and the absence of non-governmental forces and private capital, were hardly favourable to economic development.

THE ATTITUDE AND POLICIES TOWARDS TRADE

Traditionally, an important motive for controlling trade was to extract revenue from it. However this was very different from the motive for suppressing it. As observed in Mo (1995), when the autocrats faced no effective international competition they tended to suppress non-government forces including big families, merchants and industrialists. This is observed again when comparing the policies in the Sung and Ming dynasties, as exemplified by their policies on overseas trade.

Because of the significant military threats on the northern borders, the Sung dynasty had to support not only an enormous army, but also a large increase in the number of bureaucrats to serve it. The government took substantial measures to stimulate foreign trade to meet the financial burden. A maritime trade commission to supervise and tax merchant ships was established. In AD 987, four separate trade delegations were sent to South-East Asian countries carrying goods such as silk and porcelain. The delegations offered special licenses to foreign merchants and Chinese merchants going abroad. During the T'ang dynasty (AD 618–906) there had been only one port – Guangzhou – that was allowed to trade with foreigners. Sung opened up seven more points along the Guangdong and Fujian coasts, as well as a dozen naval bases from which armed vessels patrolled the coast to protect merchant fleets from Japanese and other pirates. Moreover, supportive measures were employed to facilitate the domestic economy and trade in order to raise more revenue. They included substituting taxes on shops, products and trade for the control of prices, markets and the requisitioning of craftsmen and labour.

Without effective international competition, the Ming dynasty adopted policies of reducing contacts between Chinese and foreigners, and of stopping private ventures overseas by Chinese merchants. At one point the ban was extended to coastal shipping, so that 'not an inch of planking is allowed on the seas'. The underlying reason for the policy was that a large overseas or even a coastal trade would lead to centrifugal coastal centres of power and the need for naval forces if they were to be controlled, which was bound to be difficult, dangerous and expensive (Elvin 1973: 221). Without the need to deal with international competition, it was not worthwhile for the autocratic government to allow the development of maritime non-governmental forces that were potentially difficult to control.

THE ATTITUDE TOWARDS KNOWLEDGE AND TECHNOLOGY

Under the harsh international competition, the Sung dynasty was a period of remarkable progress in military techniques. The military pressure induced the spirit of research, invention and experimentation characteristic of the period. New kinds of weapons were invented and perfected. Inventions were encouraged by rewards. A treatise on the military art that appeared in the year 1044 evidenced the remarkable evolution in the period. Moreover the Sung retreat to the south led to the development of a substantial navy with bases on the rivers and coast. Some of the craft had 25 paddle wheels. However, this very fast type of boat had appeared as early as the eighth century and its history might go even further back than that (Gernet 1972: 310).[7]

Innovations also flourished in the private economy. Private printing was popular and water-powered machines for spinning hemp thread appeared. The main driving force behind the innovations was the supportive government policies. It adopted a policy of editing and printing the standard texts on mathematics, medicine, agriculture and warfare, as well as the Confucian scripts. Moreover, state-sponsored education in the prefecture appeared. Great efforts were made to improve irrigation, raise productivity and disseminate knowledge in the rural economy. These policies raised the national knowledge level to new heights.

The economic and technological revolution of the Sung dynasty stopped as abruptly as that of the Warring States period. The obvious decline appeared in the textile industry. After a detailed study of the technological evolution of the period, Elvin (1973) stated:

> We are compelled to conclude that, at least in the case of textiles, the basic obstacle in the way of further technological progress in China after this time was not a lack of better scientific knowledge. Rather it must have lain in a weakening of those economic and intellectual forces which make for invention and innovation. (p. 199)

In retrospect, the decline is only an effect generated by the change of government policies reflecting the change in the international environment. Another example is the decline of military technology.

The high level of military technology, particularly the use of gunpowder and maritime technology, fostered by the wars between the Sung, Liao and Hsia and the Mongols was bequeathed to the Ming dynasty. However with the disintegration of Mongol power the Ming dynasty faced no serious rivals in Eastern Asia. Throughout the period the Ming government did little to improve upon what it had inherited. Moreover, in order to limit plausible threats from its people, the autocrats intended that no one should use these weapons and the people were not allowed to know how they worked or to spread the knowledge. Similarly the early Ming naval fleet, which comprised 6450 ships, the largest of them being able to carry 500 men, was allowed to decline and virtually disappeared in the later part of the dynasty. The advanced maritime technology was not utilized, stopped growing and was gradually forgotten after the government prohibited the building of large vessels and overseas trade.

In summary, the above analysis allows us to understand a major mystery in the evolution of China. In order to eliminate the potential development of non-governmental forces, the Chinese autocrats in the Ming dynasty adopted anti-technology and anti-trade policies. In the early Ming period, the empire had a huge production surplus with the strongest sea power and the most advanced technology in the world. However without effective international competition, they did not adopt the expansive policies of their Western counterparts but chose to employ a closed-door policy in order to restrict the growth of non-governmental forces. As a result the dynamism of the Mediaeval Renaissance mysteriously disappeared.

RESPONSE TO AN INCREASE IN DOMESTIC NON-GOVERNMENTAL FORCES

People naturally seek to improve their living quality by innovation and invest-ment that will result in the accumulation of private capital and economic power. Therefore when the inclination is less obstructed during the competi-tive period, domestic non-governmental forces will naturally grow stronger over time. In order to protect their vested interests, autocrats in the non-competitive period will adopt drastic policies to curb the stronger non-govern-mental forces developed in the competitive period. The behaviour is exemplified by the policies adopted by the autocrats in the Ming dynasty.

The first appearance of sustainable confrontation between the domestic non-governmental force and the imperial power happened in the Ming dynasty in the form of pirate merchants in the coastal regions. The technological improvements, particularly the maritime expansion, of the competitive Sung period had substantially raised the non-governmental forces and overseas trad-ing activities. In response to the rebellious non-governmental forces, the Ming dynasty changed the traditional structure of governance, forbade international

trade, designed the deleterious examination content to curb the growth of intelligence and obstructed the development of innovation and knowledge among
the commoners. This resulted in one of the most oppressive governments in
Chinese history.

THE ROLE OF OTHER PLAYERS

With the monopoly of the use of violence, the exploitative government was
free to design institutions to contain the non-governmental forces and to
extract the surplus of the country. The other players in the country, which
included the literati, merchants and peasants, reacted submissively to the institutions in general. Without other alternatives, they had to choose either to live
according to the rules designed by the autocrats or to revolt. Massive revolt
would result in anarchy that would destroy social stability and production. As
long as the living standard was higher under dictatorship than under anarchy,
the commons as a whole would choose dictatorship that brought law and order.
They would revolt only when the output level under the rule of the autocrats
was lower than the subsistence level.

PICTOGRAPHS, SIZE OF THE EMPIRE AND COMPETITION

Note that it was the great size of the Chinese dynasties that brought them huge
and diverse surpluses, making the adoption of the exploitative policies of the
Chinese autocrats possible. When China proper was made up of smaller states,
no government could afford to close itself off. It would have faced effective
international competition and not been able to survive under exploitative policies. The sheer size of the Chinese empires removed the need for the autocrats
to manage them efficiently for their survival purpose. If the size of the empire
relies on its productivity, or state of technology, it is likely to be unstable. Any
changes in productivity and technology among the related political actors will
result in irreversible changes. However, China is probably the most successful
and largest enduring civilization in the world. Although it was broken up into
small states during the dynastic cycles and even totally occupied by non-
Chinese in the Mongol Yuan and Manchus Ch'ing dynasties, the capacity of
Chinese society to rejuvenate itself and prosper appeared limitless. Why have
large states usually broken up into fragments after a certain period of time
while China can survive? This can be attributed to its particular carrier of civilization – the pictorial Chinese character.

The Chinese character communicates information through 'pictures' that are independent of pronunciation and therefore can be easily utilized by races with diverse spoken languages. Chinese writing consists of isolated characters. Each character represents a single unchanging word that remains eternally the same regardless of how it is used. This is similar to our Arabic numerals 1,2,3 and so on, that carry the same meaning in all countries though pronounced differently. The writing was unaffected by the phonetic changes that occurred in the course of time, by dialectal variations, or even by differences in linguistic structure. Whenever people cannot communicate orally the written text permits mutual comprehension. Thus Chinese writing became a sort of universal means of expression in every part of Asia subject to Chinese civilization or influence (Gernet 1972). This characteristic has resulted in two effects of incalculable importance upon the development of Chinese civilization.[8]

It has given China an unparalleled literary and hence cultural continuity in time. Once possessing the knowledge of the written language, one can read ancient classics written thousands of years ago. This has allowed the early classics to exert a profound and uninterrupted ideological influence upon generations of Chinese scholars.

It also gives China an equally striking literary and cultural unity in space. People with diverse beliefs, culture and dialects employ the same characters for their own expression and communication without infringing their cultural dignity, spoken languages or modes of life.

It is a misconception that Chinese is a pure, coherent race. China is better defined from a cultural perspective. Historically, the sinification of neighbouring countries and tribes was a continuous process. The process started from the feudal system in the Early Chou period (1122–771 BC), and ended in the invasion and sinification of the Manchus (AD 1645–1911) in imperial China. In many cases, the sinification was adopted voluntarily, as by the Manchus or in Korea and Japan. China was a melting pot of different people and cultures, and the tool of cultural unification was the pictograph, which carried Chinese civilization through thousands of years and provided an effective communication medium among hundreds of dialects. From the viewpoint of Chinese character learners, learning Chinese allowed them to gain from participation in the economic activities of the largest economy in the region. It also gave them access to the thinking, knowledge and technology of the time and of the last 1000 years. The learners finally became culturally Chinese, sharing similar information, technology and beliefs, even though they were racially different and had a wide variety of mother tongues. This characteristic of the Chinese character has contributed to the cooperation and coexistence of peoples of different spoken languages, culture and modes of life. However it also resulted in the formation of the single dominant force in the region during the imperial period, which created the environment for the repeated appearance of exploitative governments.

APPENDIX 4.1

Table 4.1 The flow of Chinese history

Period	Dynasty	Duration	Number of years and characteristics
Feudalism and Warring States	Western Chou	1122–771 BC	351
	Eastern Chou	771–221 BC	550
			900 years of synthesis and competition
Early Empire	Ch'in	221–206 BC	15
	Former Han	206 BC–AD 8	214
	Later Han	AD 25–220	195
			the beginning of 'hydraulic despotism'
	Three Kingdoms	AD 221–264	43
	Western Chin	AD 265–311	46
			disintegration and general political instability
		AD 311–580	269
			invasion and sinification of barbarians; political instability and destruction
Middle Empire	Sui	AD 589–617	28
	T'ang	AD 618–906	288
			nation based on small farmers
	Five Dynasties and Ten Kingdoms	AD 907–959	52
			disintegration and political instability

Table 4.1 continued

Period	Dynasty	Duration	Number of years and characteristics
The Medieval Renaissance	Northern Sung	AD 960–1126	166
	Chin/Mongol rule in north, Southern Sung in south	AD 1127–1275	148 contestable competition from the north and west
	Mongols (Yuan)	AD 1276–1367	91 non-traditional governance of the alien administration
Later Empire	Ming	AD 1368–1644	276
	Manchus (Ch'ing)	AD 1645–1911	266 the confrontation between governmental and maritime non-governmental force
Modern Era		AD 1912–1948	36 disintegration and political instability
	The People's Republic of China	AD 1949–	the era of global competition

Source: Adapted from Elvin (1973: 13). Years and duration are approximations in some cases.

Table 4.2 Chronological table of the tenth to fourteenth centuries

Outer Mongolia	North-western borders	North-eastern borders	North China	South China
				(907–923) Kingdoms of Shu in Szechwan
			FIVE DYNASTIES (at Kai-feng) (907–923)	(907–951) Ch'u in Hunan
			Later Liang (923–936)	(907–963) Ching-nan in Hunan
			Later T'ang (936–946)	(911–971) Southern Han at Canton
		(895–923) Shansi Kingdom of China	Later Chin (947–950)	(907–978) Min in Fukien
			Later Han (951–960)	(907–978) Wu-Yüeh in Chekiang)
		(946–1125) Empire of the LIAO (Khitan)	Later Chou	(902–975) Wu and Southern T'ang Kiangsi
			(951–979) Kingdom of Northern Han	
	(1038–1227) Empire of the Western HSIA		(960–1126) Northern SUNG at Kaifeng	
		(1115–1234) Empire of the CHIN (Jurchen) annexes North China in 1126		(1127–1275) Southern SUNG at Hangchow

(1206) Empire of the Mongols, accession of Genghis Khan
(1227) Annexes Hsia empire
(1234) Annexes Chin empire. Adopts the dynastic name of YUAN in 1271
(1276–79) Annexes Southern Sung empire
The Mongols are pushed back into Mongolia after 1368

(1368) Foundation at Nanking of the Chinese Empire of the MING

Source: Adapted from Gernet (1972: 299).

69

APPENDIX 4.2   THE CHOICE OF AUTOCRATS UNDER DIFFERENT ENVIRONMENTS

The dictator of an exploitative government is driven by the self-interest that depends on his or her expected survival period. For simplicity we assume that the amount of surplus the dictator can capture is already large enough, so that the dictator does not care about the absolute size of the surplus.[9] Her problem is to maximize satisfaction (U_t) by maximizing the expected survival period at time t, S_t:[10]

$$U_t \, [S_t(E_t - Z_t, N_0 + N_t)],$$

$$\text{with } \frac{\partial U_t}{\partial S_t} > 0, \quad \frac{\partial^2 U_t}{\partial S_t^2} < 0, \quad \frac{\partial S_t}{\partial ED_t} > 0, \quad \frac{\partial^2 S_t}{\partial ED_t^2} < 0, \text{ and } \frac{\partial S_t}{\partial N_t} < 0 \quad (4.1)$$

where E_t is the wealth of the nation, Z_t is the wealth of the external competitor which is exogenously determined, $ED_t = E_t - Z_t$, and N is the strength of the domestic non-governmental forces which is partly predetermined (N_0) and partly determined by government policies at time t (N_t).[11]

Suppose the wealth of a nation (E_t) depends on the current government policy mix (P_t) as well as that in the previous periods (P_{t-i}). The policies determine the incentive structure, cultivated norms, beliefs and the possibility set of the economic agents that in turn affect the wealth of the nation, such that:

$$E_t \, (P_t, P_{t-1}, \ldots, P_{t-n}), \text{ with } \frac{\partial E_t}{\partial P_{t-i}} > 0 \text{ and } \frac{\partial^2 E_t}{\partial P_{t-i}} < 0 \text{ for all } i, \, i = 0, \ldots, n$$

$$(4.2)$$

where P_{t-i} is the policy mix index in different periods. The higher the index, the higher the growth-promoting effect of the policy mix. However growth-promoting policies also facilitate the development of non-governmental forces like the development of private capital and economic organizations:

$$N_t \, (P_t, P_{t-1}, \ldots, P_{t-n}), \text{ with } \frac{\partial N_t}{\partial P_{t-i}} > 0 \text{ and } \frac{\partial^2 N_t}{\partial P_{t-i}} < 0, \text{ for all } i, \, i = 0, \ldots, n.$$

$$(4.3)$$

Substituting (4.2) and (4.3) into (4.1), the optimization problem implies:

$$\frac{\partial S_t}{\partial ED_t} \frac{\partial E_t}{\partial P_t} + \frac{\partial S_t}{\partial N_t} \frac{\partial N_t}{\partial P_t} = 0, \text{ where } ED_t = E_t - Z_t \tag{4.4}$$

Assuming the sufficient second order condition (SSOC) of the problem is satisfied:[12]

$$\frac{\partial S}{\partial ED} \frac{\partial^2 E}{\partial P^2} + \frac{\partial E}{\partial P} \left(\frac{\partial^2 S}{\partial ED^2} \frac{\partial E}{\partial P} + \frac{\partial^2 S}{ED \partial N} \frac{\partial N}{\partial P} \right) +$$

$$\frac{\partial S}{\partial N} \frac{\partial^2 N}{\partial P^2} \frac{\partial N}{\partial P} + \frac{\partial N}{\partial P} \left(\frac{\partial^2 S}{\partial N^2} \frac{\partial N}{\partial P} + \frac{\partial^2 S}{\partial N \partial ED} \frac{\partial E}{\partial P} \right) < 0 \tag{4.5}$$

Now we investigate the effect of an increase in international competition (Z) on the choice of the autocrat's optimal policy. Substituting the optimal policy choice (P^*) into (4.4) and differentiating it with respect to Z, we have:

$$\frac{\partial S}{\partial ED} \frac{\partial^2 E}{\partial P^2} \frac{\partial P^*}{\partial Z} + \frac{\partial E}{\partial P} \left(\frac{\partial^2 S}{\partial ED^2} \frac{\partial E}{\partial P} \frac{\partial P^*}{\partial Z} + \frac{\partial^2 S}{\partial ED \partial N} \frac{\partial N}{\partial P} \frac{\partial P^*}{\partial Z} \right) +$$

$$\frac{\partial^2 S}{\partial ED^2} \frac{\partial ED}{\partial Z} \right) + \frac{\partial S}{\partial N} \frac{\partial^2 N}{\partial P^2} \frac{\partial P^*}{\partial Z} + \frac{\partial N}{\partial P} \left(\frac{\partial^2 S}{\partial N^2} \frac{\partial N}{\partial P} \frac{\partial P^*}{\partial Z} \right) +$$

$$\frac{\partial^2 S}{\partial N \partial ED} \frac{\partial E}{\partial P} \frac{\partial P^*}{\partial Z} \right) \equiv 0 \tag{4.6}$$

Rearranging the terms:

$$\frac{\partial P^*}{\partial Z} = - \left(\frac{\partial E}{\partial P} \right)^2 \frac{\partial^2 S}{\partial ED^2} \frac{\partial ED}{\partial Z} / SSOC, \text{ or}$$

$$\left(\frac{\partial E}{\partial P} \right)^2 \frac{\partial^2 S}{\partial ED^2} / SSOC > 0, \tag{4.7}$$

$$\text{if } \frac{\partial^2 S}{\partial ED^2} < 0$$

Equation (4.7) indicates that when Z increases, self-interest maximizing autocrats will adopt a government policy mix that will be more favourable to economic development and to the non-governmental forces if S_{ED} is subject to diminishing returns.[13]

People naturally seek to improve their living quality by innovation and investment that will result in the accumulation of private capital and economic strength. Therefore if left unobstructed, exogenous domestic non-governmental forces, N_0, will naturally grow overtime. It is interesting to see how the exploitative government reacts to this exogenous development of non-governmental forces.

Differentiate equation (4.4) with respect to N_0:

$$\frac{\partial S}{\partial ED}\frac{\partial^2 E}{\partial P^2}\frac{\partial P^*}{\partial N_0}+\frac{\partial E}{\partial P}\left(\frac{\partial^2 S}{\partial ED^2}\frac{\partial E}{\partial P}\frac{\partial P^*}{\partial N_0}+\frac{\partial^2 S}{\partial ED\partial N}\frac{\partial N}{\partial P}\frac{\partial P^*}{\partial N_0}+\right.$$

$$\left.\frac{\partial^2 S}{\partial ED\partial N_0}\right)+\frac{\partial S}{\partial N}\frac{\partial^2 N}{\partial P^2}\frac{\partial P^*}{\partial N_0}+\frac{\partial N}{\partial P}\left(\frac{\partial^2 S}{\partial N^2}\frac{\partial N}{\partial P}\frac{\partial P^*}{\partial N_0}+\right. \qquad (4.8)$$

$$\left.\frac{\partial^2 S}{\partial N\partial ED}\frac{\partial E}{\partial P}\frac{\partial P^*}{\partial N_0}+\frac{\partial^2 S}{\partial N\partial N_0}\right)\equiv 0.$$

Rearranging terms, we have:

$$\frac{\partial P^*}{\partial N}=\left(-\frac{\partial E}{\partial P}\frac{\partial^2 S}{\partial ED\partial N_0}-\frac{\partial N}{\partial P}\frac{\partial^2 S}{\partial N\partial N_0}\right)/SSOC \qquad (4.9)$$

since:

$$\frac{\partial E}{\partial P}\text{ and }\frac{\partial N}{\partial P}>0$$

$$\frac{\partial P^*}{\partial N_0}<0,\text{ if }\frac{\partial^2 S}{\partial ED\partial N_0}<0,\text{ and }\frac{\partial^2 S}{\partial N\partial N_0}\leq 0. \qquad (4.10)$$

The analysis reveals that if the advance of non-governmental forces reduces the effectiveness of *ED* for the autocrat's survival, which is very likely, and if the detrimental effect of N on S is not subject to diminishing returns,[14] then an increase in non-governmental forces will induce more oppressive policies.

NOTES

1. A simple mathematical analysis of the autocrats' behaviour in different environments is attached in Appendix 4.2.

2. For the course of Chinese history, see Table 4.1 in Appendix 4.1. For the conditions in the disintegration periods, see Gernet (1972).

3. Although general social and economic conditions were not remarkable in the period due to political instability, it seems that inventions and their applications were still quite active. The match was invented in AD 577 (Temple 1991: 98), the umbrella around the fourth century AD (Temple 1991: 96), the paddle-wheel boat around the fifth century AD (Temple 1991: 193), and land sailing in about AD 550 (Temple 1991: 195).

4. Under the political stability and huge production surplus in the dynasty, the incentives generated under the examination system resulted in remarkable literary accomplishments in poetry. However they contributed nothing to economic development and hence generated no threats to the autocrats. Please see note 7.

5. Table 4.2 in Appendix 4.1 describes the international environment facing the Sung dynasty.

6. In the Ming and Ch'ing (AD 1644–1911) dynasties, recruitment competitions degenerated and became an apparatus that retarded rather than assisted social advancement. In the Ming period, the *pa ku* or 'eight-legged essay' that was rigid in form and difficult to master became the dominant recruitment subject. Talented men were made to waste their time and energy in an elegant, but useless, literary accomplishment. Their independent thinking and innovative activity were thus suppressed. Apart from working as administrative assistants to the emperor, they became useless literate and indoctrinated Confucians. They were therefore totally dependent on the mercy and under the control of the autocrats. A similar intention was documented in the remark of one of the most celebrated emperors, Li Shih-min (AD 598–649) in the T'ang dynasty. When he was watching the candidates around the examination hall, he said: 'All the best talents under the sky were induced to enter my container.'

7. This reveals the underutilization of technology when competition was lacking in the previous dynasties. Recent excavations have found that as early as 119 BC, there were at least 46 state-run iron foundries throughout China. In Henan, the scale of cast-iron production was massive by any standard. The core or salamander left from one of the damaged crucibles used in smelting was found to weigh 20–25 tons, a capacity not reached in Europe until well into the eighteenth century (Merson 1990: 21). With a similar level of technology, in AD 806, T'ang China was producing 13 500 tons of iron a year, but by 1078, during the Sung dynasty, this had risen to 125 000 tons. Technology underutilization is further evidenced by the policies in the Ming dynasty.

8. They are suggested by the writers of the *Far Eastern Leaflets* (1942).

9. This simplification will not affect our major conclusions.

10. Since U_t is a monotonic transformation of S_t, we can get identical implications by assuming the autocrat is maximizing S_t in the following analysis.

11. The non-governmental forces include economic organizations like industrial and agricultural enterprises as well as political organizations. They may have effects on the wealth of nations. However for our purpose we assume that the non-governmental forces and the wealth of nations are driven by governmental policies. This has no substantial effect on our conclusions.

12. For simplicity, we drop the subscript t from the variables in the following equations.

13. The survival possibility of a nation is less likely to have diminishing marginal returns with respect to the economic power difference. However the survival possibility of autocrats is likely to be subject to the law of diminishing returns. This is because, besides economic power, the survival possibility of the autocrats depends on many other complementary factors such as domestic social stability, the size of the middle class and the popularity of the autocrats among the people.

14. Although finally the effect of N on S will be subject to diminishing returns, it is likely that at some levels it may enjoy increasing returns, particularly when the level of non-governmental forces is near its critical mass.

REFERENCES

American Council of Learned Societies (1942), 'The Chinese language as a factor in Chinese cultural continuity', *Far Eastern Leaflets* 1–6, Washington, DC, 28–29, reprinted in Derk Bodde (1981) (ed.), *Essays on Chinese Civilization*, Princeton, NJ: Princeton University Press.

Elvin, Mark (1973), *The Pattern of the Chinese Past*, Stanford, CA: Stanford University Press.

Gernet, Jacques (1972), *A History of Chinese Civilization*, translated by J.R. Foster, Cambridge: Cambridge University Press.

Merson, John (1990), *The Genius that was China: East and West in the Making of the Modern World*, Woodstock, NY: Overlook Press.

Mo, Pak Hung (1995), 'Effective competition and economic development of imperial China', *Kyklos*, **48** (1), 87–103.

Needham, J. (1954), *Science and Civilization in China*, vol. I, Cambridge: Cambridge University Press.

Temple, Robert (1991), *The Genius of China*, London: Prion, Multimedia Books.

COMMENT

Mark Elvin

No satisfactory analysis of China's economic and technological performance over the long run can be based solely on the ascription to it of relatively unchanging so-called 'Chinese' characteristics, even if these may well have played a part in more complex mixes of causes. At the time of Mediterranean antiquity, China was probably very slightly behind the West economically. During the Western Middle Ages she was well ahead. In the course of the seventeenth and eighteenth centuries, the West caught up with and then over-took her, leaving her far behind by the end of the nineteenth century. In the course of the twentieth century China struggled, with gradually increasing effectiveness, to recover some of the lost ground.

A dynamic analysis is thus needed in which each major epoch has an appropriate distinctive overall character. The basic strength of Professor Mo's approach is that he recognizes this. He frames both his formal model and his descriptions in terms of a varying balance of power between, on the one hand, external competitive pressures that stimulated the promotion, or at least the acceptance, of economic growth by the government because the survival of the regime depended on it; and on the other hand, the (assumed) tendency of an autocratic system of the Chinese type to seek to ensure its political survival against internal threats by repressing economic vitality in non-governmental sectors. Thus for example he attributes the post-medieval decline to early Ming repressive policies at a time when China's regional economic and strategic preponderance, though far from absolute, could only be challenged with difficulty. (A case in point is Vietnam, which broke away in the early fifteenth century.) Specifically, 'in order to eliminate the potential development of non-governmental forces, the Chinese autocrats in the Ming dynasty adopted anti-technology and anti-trade policies'.

The outcome is an original attempt to encapsulate the fluctuations of Chinese economic history in a set of interlocking mathematical formulae. This is a heroic aim, and one that is likely to have imitators and successors, but I think that in its present form it is still only partially successful. There seem to be several probable reasons for this. Government policy is treated as the decisive variable. It is assumed to respond to external forces that are, in the terms of the model, aleatoric. It is also assumed that state policy decisions, once taken, were more or less fully effective, whatever their nature. This last point seems far from justified for pre-modern times. After the Sung, the filters of the mandarinal bureaucracy, local sub-bureaucracies, the local notables who slowly turned into what scholars have called the 'managerial gentry', and the effect of substantial distances and an ever larger population size on communication, were rarely overcome at more than moments in space and time.

Again, no causes are assigned for endogenous non-governmental growth or innovation.[1] It seems to be assumed that these will spring up of their own accord unless repressed and that, other things being equal, they will be politically destabilizing. No explicit justification is offered for these two assumptions, nor is it made clear if the latter is a general phenomenon or found only in polities of a certain type to which imperial China belonged.

No attention is paid to forms of competition other than that between states. Thus, competition between religions seems to have been the motive force behind the invention and spread of woodblock printing in China more than 1000 years ago, with Buddhism in the lead role. Much later, in the eighteenth century, the Jesuits, who were almost unique among pre-modern observers in knowing both East and West, wrote of how in China the ever-growing population at this time 'puts merit ceaselessly in competition with merit, diligence with diligence, and work with work, in a manner that prevents large fortunes'. Late-imperial China, ruled by a bureaucracy selected through competitive examinations, with almost no hereditary power-holding aristocracy (the imperial family excepted), and partible inheritance among male heirs, was possibly the most socially mobile of all developed pre-modern non-immigration societies. Competition could thus also be internal. The model seems to suggest that it was politically destabilizing, but Manchu-Qing China, with a high level of competition, lasted in a stable form for at least 200 years (in round numbers, 1650 to 1850). Is there a contradiction here with the historical record?

Next, are we focusing on total or per capita 'development'? Manchu-Qing China was not without external military challenges in the eighteenth century, notably in the north-west from loose polities based on Mongols and other non-Chinese groups, but it was in the main an age of secure Chinese strategic security. It was also a period of spectacular quantitative growth, based mainly on extra inputs of land (though of increasingly poor quality) and of labour, through reclamation and demographic increase respectively, with a number of improvements in both the average level of practice and modestly in techniques. There was little if any growth in income per capita. Insofar as there was a cause for this quantitative efflorescence it would seem to have been prolonged internal peace as much as anything else. The theory thus may need to draw a sharp analytical line between the quantitative and qualitative types of growth.

The model does not make provision for a number of long-term trends in Chinese economic history that broadly seem to have cut across shorter-term fluctuations. The first of these is the increase in population, which rose from around 65 million in the eighteenth century AD to over 400 million in the middle of the nineteenth, albeit with two major periods of decline (centred approximately on the fourteenth and seventeenth centuries). The second was the rise of relatively free markets from about the ninth century on. This trend began under a weakened centralized empire, continued under the European style of fragmentation of the Five Dynasties and Ten Kingdoms, and then on again under the Sung dynasty, continuing with modest ups and downs to the end of the empire. Thus it cut across the pattern defined by the model. The third trend is the eventual crystallization, after many changes, of a personally free legal status for almost the entire population by the later seventeenth century. Free status had tended to flourish in periods of strong central power as smallholding peasants were favoured as an easily accessible source of taxes by the state. It tended to decline during eras of internal turmoil as peasants were forced into dependency, or even sought it for the sake of protection. Even under the Sung, the Golden Age of qualitative growth, one-fifth at least of the rural population was, so far as we can guess at the size of a group normally not entered in the administration's registers, in a status that was essentially a form of serfdom. To the extent that personal freedom is a valuable economic input, the Manchu-Qing period should have done somewhat better.

A fourth trend of major importance was the gradual depletion, region by region, of the natural resources that could be economically accessed with pre-modern Chinese technology. By the end of the later empire most potential farmland of reasonable quality had been opened up except in frontiers like Manchuria, most easily engineered irrigation systems had already been built, the 'buffers' once provided against bad years by hunting in the forests and the gathering of wild plants were much diminished, and in many places wood and/or water were in short supply. Maintaining existing hydraulic systems often consumed a large amount of labour, resources, money and scarce administrative skills just to stay in the same place. In terms of its relation with the natural environment, the rural economy was far from being a constant entity over the very long run. The patterns of ownership also changed. The long-term trend, though subject to frequent reversals, was towards the privatization of land-holding. The state slowly relinquished control over non-agricultural land (the so-called 'mountains and marshes'), economic development based on the military became restricted to certain frontier zones (such as parts of Guizhou in Ming and Qing times), and farms passed into the ownership of individuals and families, especially after the collapse of the so-called 'equitable fields system' in the eighth century. In contrast the water-control systems remained at all times either under state management or at least state supervision and community management. By late-imperial times control of the means of production in the Chinese rural economy manifested a fairly clear dualism: private land and collective water. (Though there were a few cases of the small-scale commercialization of water supply, and the buying and selling of water rights.)

None of these overall trends, and only some of their fluctuations, can be easily related to the model, at least so far as I can see.

Turning now to the issue of periodization, I am in broad agreement with Professor Mo's divisions, but there are some difficulties that need discussion as they are symptomatic of the obstacles in the way of any clear-cut analytical formulation. In the case of qualitative advances in technology, looking at spinning-machines suggests one pattern, looking at the construction of seawalls another. The appearance, and then the disappearance, of water-powered mechanized spinning during the thirteenth and the fourteenth centuries seems to mark a clear divide between an age of high technical creativity and one in which it was lower. Under the Sung, however, the quality of the seawalls that guarded the eastern coast was poor, and they frequently had to be rebuilt. Methods improved during the Ming, with a switch to interlocking stone construction, and the use of pine-tree trunks as foundations, and they reached a high degree of sophistication by the middle of the Qing with groynes, and glacis. The two diachronic patterns are quite different.

If we admit economic institutions as legitimate creations, then we are obliged to recognize as important the rise under the Qing of guilds of fellow-regional merchants (the *huiguan*). These associations facilitated the shift of the focus of interregional commerce from arbitrage to regular trading relationships in this period.

If we go farther still and consider creativity outside the economic sphere as relevant to our enquiry, we obtain the interesting result that the hypothesis of heightened creativity in times of political fragmentation does in some respects better than that limited to economics. There were three major periods of political fragmentation: (1) the pre-imperial ages of the Springs and Autumns and then of the Warring States; (2) the Three Kingdoms that followed the breakup of the Han empire, and then, after a short-lived reunification, the Northern and Southern Dynasties; and (3) the tenth to the thirteenth centuries, when the Northern Sung and then the geographically much reduced Southern Sung struggled with the Qidan in the north-east, the Xixia or Minyak state in the north-west, and the Jurchen in the north, before the entire Chinese world was overwhelmed by the Mongols. The first and third were economically highly creative, the second much less so, though it was very culturally creative (with nature poetry, the development of calligraphy as an art form, alchemical experimentation, the sinification of Buddhism, and so on). Conversely, periods of unification were often also culturally creative. Thus the late Ming and the first two-thirds of the Qing saw the rise of the Chinese novel, which reached a quality in the eighteenth century that compared favourably with its Western contemporaries.

Doubts can also be raised as to the extent to which the competing states in the second period, and again in the third period, can be legitimately described as being within a framework of overarching cultural unity. There would seem to have been considerable variety in this regard, though a significant measure of Chinese influence cannot be denied in most instances.

Let us conclude by looking at some aspects of the formal model. It is focused on the concept of the expected survival at a given time (S_t) of an individual ruler. I would prefer to recast this in terms of a regime, a system or even a dynasty. The best analysis to date of regime breakdown, Jack Goldstone's *Revolution and Rebellion in the Early Modern World* (1991), which includes the Ming in its case studies, demonstrates the systemic nature of such collapses. Key factors include the splitting of the ruling class, insufficient satisfactory employment for the elite, and a fiscal crisis arising from the lack of an acceptable way of raising revenues for expanding but necessary functions of the state. Popular grievances in general only become critical in combination with these factors. In what follows I have therefore taken the liberty of shifting to the systemic interpretation, and readers should be aware that Professor Mo's own interpretation of his formulae is slightly different.

Expected regime survival at t is defined as a function of two quantities. These are (1) the difference between the 'economic power' E_t of the focal polity and that of its competitors Z_t, summarized as the 'economic difference' ED_t; and (2) the '[economic ?] strength of domestic non-governmental forces' created by the sum of governmental and non-governmental actions, and symbolized as $N_0 + N_t$. The constraints imposed are (1) that a positive increase in the 'economic difference' increases expected survival, and (2) that an increase in domestic non-governmental 'strength' decreases expected survival. That is, economic growth can have two diametrically opposed political consequences. I have some difficulty in accepting this as a generally valid proposition, though it may well be correct under certain circumstances.

I am unable to follow the formalization of equations 8, 9 and 10 because I do not see in what independently measurable units 'policy' $(P_t$ and $P^*)$ can be quantified. (Definition in terms of a policy's estimated effects on income after implementation might be possible, but the lack of any independent parameters would then make it impossible to compare the constituent nature of one policy with that of another, as well as raising other problems.) The author's conclusion is clear enough, however: higher N_0 in general, like higher N_t, reduces the expected survival of a regime or ruler. One wonders however if the 'rent-seeking groups' in power in the state of whom the author speaks could not have appropriated increased rents under these circumstances. Would this not be classified as increasing the government's 'economic power' at the same time as reducing the 'force' of the non-government sector?

At all events, the model does seem to create something of a gulf between the governmental and non-governmental sectors that seems to leave little space for the 'functional government' of which Professor Mo rightly speaks elsewhere. The traditional Chinese state was in fact ideologically committed to the ideal of 'the people's livelihood' (*minsheng*) and at least in some respects took this obligation seriously, notably in the construction and maintenance of the larger hydraulic systems, building seawalls and river levees, and so on.

Overall, this chapter makes a valuable contribution to sharpening up and focusing the debate by suggesting a way in which the central arguments might be formalized, but it is, as I think the author would accept, only a first exploratory step along a long and difficult path.

Notes

1. For the sake of brevity, I lump together in this term the three rather distinct processes of initial creation (invention), practical and profitable use (innovation) and subsequent spread to new regions and states (diffusion).

References

Goldstone, Jack (1991), *Revolution and Rebellion in the Early Modern World*, Berkeley, CA: University of California Press.

COMMENT

Toby E. Huff

Hung Pak Mo's contribution to this volume raises many questions of perspective, analysis and interpretation. Mo rightly points to the Sung period of China's history as one of considerable creativity and innovation. Indeed most China specialists would agree that the Sung period was one of renaissance and in some respects revolution. Certainly there were major changes in land ownership, a state and educational reorganization and, above all, a great upsurge in commercial activity. Some have suggested that the levels of economic output (as measured by tons of iron produced) achieved an all-time high during this period, from which they dropped by 50 per cent during the next three centuries, with the result that by the 1930s they were not as high as they had been in the late eleventh century in the Northern Sung (Hartwell 1962, 1982). This is one of the great paradoxes of China and its delayed modernization.

As Mo's analysis unfolds, however, it seems to neglect the major institutional structures that were put in place by China's elites, and which lasted from the Sung, through their consolidation and amplification in the Ming, all the way to the end of the Ch'ing in 1911. At the same time his suggestion that the explanation of the failure of China to undergo economic and cultural development 'is due to the self-interest maximization of the autocrats' seems to imply that the elites who ruled China for centuries – indeed more than 1000 years – were usurpers who did not represent Chinese culture and its deeper values. Given the mode of selecting these elites, namely via the civil service examinations that focused exclusively on the classical Chinese heritage, that suggestion needs reformulation. From the point of view of economics, 'Institutions are the rules of the game in a society or, more formally, are the humanly devised constraints that shape human interaction.' Furthermore, as Douglass North continues, 'Institutional change shapes the way societies evolve through time and hence is the key to understanding historical change' (North 1990: 1).

Mo's analysis seems to have an underlying concern with the problematic raised by Mark Elvin a quarter-century ago; namely 'why did [China] not at some point break up permanently into separate states like those of Europe, but remain an empire with provinces the size of European states?' (Elvin 1973: 20). This question may not seem to be fruitful at first sight – though it was extremely useful for Elvin's analysis for he brought the need for scientific and technological prowess into the equation of empire-supporting necessities. On the other hand, looking at the European context, the collapse of the Roman empire and the lack of any other Europe-encompassing empire thereafter, was conjoined with the appearance of the scientific and industrial revolutions.

Those revolutions were conjoined with a democratic initiative that resulted in the rise of parliamentary representation (Strayer 1970). As I shall suggest, at a time when Europe was moving toward a formal recognition of community based organizations and professional associations, China was going in the other direction, that is towards an extraordinary centralizing of power and intellectual initiative.

China's success in saving its empire may thus be at the cost of a successful scientific and technological revolution, as well as democratic governance. In my comments I shall emphasize the institutional side of the equation that can give rise to economic and scientific development and which is under-emphasized in Mo's chapter.

Sung Reforms and the Civil Service Examinations

The institutional impediments that blocked intellectual as well as civil autonomy are probably mostly the same ones that impeded economic development in China. They are opposite sides of the same coin.

The historical record of China regarding the development and imposition of the civil service examinations is now fairly clear. Although vestiges of it go back to the T'ang dynasty and possibly earlier, it was the Sung officials who put the civil service examination firmly in place for the purpose of recruiting government officials (Franke 1963; Miyazaki 1976; Lee 1985, 1989; Elman 2000 among others). At the same time that the civil service examinations were put in place for the recruitment of all government officials, it was also decided to make the Confucian classics the main subject of study. Except for a brief period during the late Ming dynasty, there was never a time when there was an inclusion of scientific subjects in the civil service examinations (Needham 1954, 1969: 179; Elman 2000). A recent discovery, reported by Elman, is that during the late Ming, policy questions were introduced that required knowledge, some of it quite technical, of astronomy, calendrical calculations and mathematics as applied to musical harmonics. This was never a very large portion of the examinations, but it does indicate that for a period of time during the Ming dynasty some candidates were required to answer questions about the Chinese astronomical system, why there were errors in calendars, how they were rectified, and whether there was a method of explaining the celestial movements. Likewise questions were asked on Chinese musical harmonics and on the mathematically stated basis of the relationship between pitch and the length of an instrument.

In all of these 'policy' questions in the domain of natural studies, the main concern was preserving the present harmony and explaining why things were done as they were. As Elman points out, the minority of candidates who qualified on these naturalistic questions were not licensed to become 'scientists', but rather were trained in something approximating 'history of science' (Elman 2000: 482, 483, note 63). What is remarkable however, according to Elman, is not that the Ming examinations included such questions (dropped soon thereafter in the Ch'ing), but that the Ming literati successfully encapsulated natural studies within a system of political, social and cultural reproduction that guaranteed the long-term dominance of the dynasty, its literati and the Ch'eng-Chu orthodoxy. (Elman 2000: 468). Furthermore these examinations were based almost entirely on memorization. The implication of that decision – reaffirmed in every generation and ruling group until its abolition in 1905 – was that the government, the bureaucrats and so on did not encourage the study of the natural sciences but the memorization of classical subject matter. Mo focuses on the attempted reforms of Wang An Shih (d. 1086), who did indeed launch some heroic reform efforts, but which quickly failed to be taken up. Undoubtedly Wang An Shih was a progressive thinker and reformer who put in place a variety of reforms that helped ease peasants' tax burden, and made important reforms in the state bureaucracy, while expanding subjects for the examination system. It was during Wang's short-lived term that examinations were focused on law (the *ming-fa*), and also mathematics, but not the natural sciences (Lee 1985, Elman 2000). Both of these specialized examinations were soon abolished, which is one reason why Chinese law did not evolve very much, and why district magistrates, who served as police and prosecutors at the local level, often had to employ law clerks who knew actual legal practice through experience but had generally failed the state examinations (on non-legal matters) (see Watt 1972, MacCormach 1996).

Mo also speaks of a 'new philosophy' emerging in the Sung period. This appears to be a reference to Neo-Confucianism which was the project of the great philosopher Chu Hsi (d. 1200) and his fellow travellers referred to by Elman as the 'Ch'eng-Chu orthodoxy'. What he accomplished was a new and condensed version of the Confucian classics which became the primary subject matter of the civil service examinations. Consequently those books, along with Chu Hsi's commentaries on them, became the required subjects of memorization for the following 600 years. Benjamin Elman estimates that by 1787 'over 500 000 characters of textual material had to be memorized to master the examination curriculum of the Four Books and the Five Classics', and that was not all (Elman 2000: 373, Miyazaki 1976: 16–17). Surnames and other material had to be memorized.

This version of Confucianism became so deeply embedded in Chinese elite culture that no one dared to offer on the examinations any interpretation of them but that which was taken from the Neo-Confucian canon. Anyone who did was guaranteed never to get a job in the government. When this examination system was then buttressed with the requirement of writing essays in the stylized 'eight-legged' form to which Mo alludes, an extremely restricted intellectual system was put in place.

In a word, the institutional and intellectual trends put into motion in the Sung period, then elaborated in the Ming dynasty, led to an increasingly rigid ideological and cultural outcome. Still more damaging was its effect on the development of modern science, which as we know did not occur in China. Without going into the details of this complex system, it may be noted that all candidates for the civil service (who could not buy an office or degree) had to take the examinations at the village, province and finally 'metropolitan' level, offered once every three years. Later there were 'palace examinations' conducted by the emperor. It was through this process that 'degrees' were awarded in China for hundreds of years. Since there is no sense in which it can be said that students taking these examinations were taught natural science, it should not be surprising that the system did not produce a cadre of scientists or independent-minded philosophers. The system was run by bureaucrats who themselves had mastered the examinations, and hence ultimately received government positions. It was they who established the examinations and set the questions for each class of examinees. At the same time, no independent body or 'faculty' of professors could emerge, as the whole system was imbedded in the state bureaucracy. Although some students might attend independent academies, all students undertook studies under the guidance of a master scholar precisely for the purpose of passing the state examinations, not for intellectually independent study. There was no other alternative if a career in government was sought.

Of course it can be said that highly knowledgeable scholars did emerge who were expert in areas that we would call the natural sciences, that is in astronomy, optics, medicine and mathematics. Indeed the most remarkable thing about China in this regard is the extraordinary range of beginnings that occurred in many areas: these are found in such wide-ranging fields as hydraulics, clock works, pharmacology and pharmacological taxonomy, alchemy, immunology and medical inquiries, very detailed observations of astronomical events such comets, eclipses, nova and sunspots, and even rudiments of probabilistic thinking. But the scholars who carried out these inquiries and laid pioneering foundations did not form professional guilds, associations, corporations of physicians, much less autonomous universities. Yet in the end, institutions matter, as many economists have reminded us (North 1990, Paul 1994). Without appropriate institutional foundations, fertile seeds of intellectual brilliance fail to grow into hardly plants.

Consequently, due to this lack of institutional support (and I leave out issues having to do with the 'internal' content of Chinese scientific thought), Chinese scholars did not rise to the innovative level of Copernicus and Galileo, nor did Chinese astronomers incorporate the fundamentals of the geometric astronomy of the Arabs (based on Greek assumptions) that many think the Chinese had access to in the 'Eastern' bureau of astronomy (Needham 1954, vol. 3: 50). Likewise, in the highly important field of optics the medieval Chinese opticians fell far short of the level reached by Ibn al-Haytham (Needham 1954, vol. 4. Part 2: xxiii).

In a word, the Chinese were in a position very similar to the Middle Eastern natural philosophers in that they were forced to do all their studies privately and independently, outside any formal institutional structure comparable to Western universities. Consequently in many areas they did not equal the Arab-Muslim achievements (as noted above). Clearly the lack of institutional support – that the Europeans had – made independent and innovative intellectual thought exceedingly difficult to produce. In the realm of technology, the studies of Joseph Needham and many others have shown how creative Chinese individuals could be. But that picture is always clouded by the non-use and often aborted development of important innovations (as shown by Elvin 1973).

The Legal Infrastructure

If we consider the problem from the point of view of law and legal administration (the really fundamental institutional structure), we see many deficits and compounding relationships. The legal system in China was essentially a punitive system designed to punish wrongdoers while it emphasized the Confucian idealized relationships, especially filial piety and the five relationships (emperor–subject, husband–wife, father–son, older brother–younger brother, friend–friend). It was a top-down system with all authority originating in the emperor, down through his administrative offices to the local magistrate. There were no spheres of autonomy in any area. Cities, towns and villages were not legally autonomous entities but seats of the residence of imperial authority. There were no legally autonomous guilds or professional associations, nor any autonomous universities. Those entities that bore that label were more in the nature of state-sponsored academies, whose curricula had to be based on the official Neo-Confucian philosophy. The legal idea of a corporation with its bundle of rights was unheard of, as it was in Islamic law. Even the legal profession itself could not emerge under these circumstances, and those who attempted to assist others who had legal troubles, were punished as 'legal tricksters' (Watt 1972, MacCormach 1996).

The law was administered strictly by state officials who responded to complaints by individuals. One did not lodge a complaint against a person accused of some violation but rather petitioned the court (district magistrate) for relief from a situation that had gone bad. No intermediate bodies or individuals were allowed to intervene. Since the law was seen solely as a punitive instrument of government, no provisions were made for legal enablements (Bodde and Morris 1973, Schwartz 1968). Just as there was no conception of the need for monetary restitution, no provisions were available that would enhance merchants or economic transactions. Officials mainly wanted to know how to increase their powers of taxation, to maximize revenue. Merchants were in general placed at the bottom of the status hierarchy, and when merchants were able to gain wealth for their families, they wanted their sons to study for the civil service examinations so that they could gain a state position, the major source of wealth and power. Many if not all of the major commodities such as salt, grain, copper, iron, tea, transport and so on were run as state monopolies. When in the late nineteenth century the Ch'ing elite decided that industrial development was a good thing that ought to be encouraged, the refrain was that this was too important to leave to the merchants, that is the government should run and control it (Chan 1980: 421ff).

In short, the Chinese empire was an autocracy that did not allow for any zones of independent authority, administrative or intellectual. This stands in stark contrast to the European situation in which groups of all sorts were recognized as having legal rights of existence, autonomy and self-government. Starting in the twelfth and thirteenth centuries (corresponding roughly to the middle Sung period), all sorts of collective entities were granted legally autonomous status as 'whole bodies'. Cities and towns, merchant guilds, charitable entities, professional guilds such as physicians and surgeons, and of course universities (among many others see Michaud-Quantin 1970, Berman 1987). Each of these entities could make its own rules and regulations, and in some cases establish its own courts. But in general they enjoyed self-government and often had the right to be represented before the King's court. These developments made Europe highly polycentric and these trends led directly to parliamentary representation (Strayer 1970). Nothing like this occurred in China nor in the Muslim world.

Seen in this light the scientific revolution represents a vast overthrow of established religious and moral authority, unlike anything that could (or did) take place in China or the Muslim world. From an institutional point of view it was made possible by the existence of relatively neutral spaces, namely universities (but also autonomous cities and towns), that from their inception were considered legally autonomous. They were organized and run by academics, not state bureaucrats. This was something that could not be envisioned in the Chinese situation.

If one looks to the situation as it applied to commercial enterprise and democratic participation, the same blockages, rooted in Chinese law and administration, stood in the way. Freedom of action, of contract, of self-governance were all absent. Reducing centralized control might have allowed the provinces to fragment into semi-autonomous states, and perhaps put an end to the 'empire';

but one might have expected that interstate competition would have yielded greater creativity and new economic alternatives as well as a semblance of self-governance.

References

Berman, Harold (1987), *Law and Revolution*, Cambridge, MA: Harvard University Press.

Bodde, Derk, and Clarence Morris (1967), *Law in Imperial China*, reprinted 1973, Philadelphia, PA: University of Pennsylvania Press.

Chan, K.K. (1980), 'Government, merchants and industry to 1911', in John K. Fairbank and Kwang-Ching Liu (eds), *The Cambridge History of China*, vol 11, Cambridge: Cambridge University Press, pp. 416–62.

Elman, Benjamin (2000), *A Cultural History of Civil Service Examinations in Imperial China*, Los Angeles, CA: University of California Press.

Elvin, Mark (1973), *The Pattern of the Chinese Past*, Stanford, CA: Stanford University Press.

Franke, Wolfgang (1963), *The Reform and Abolition of the Traditional Chinese Examination System*, Cambridge, MA: Harvard University Press.

Hartwell, Robert (1962), 'A revolution in Chinese iron and coal industries in the Northern Sung, 960–1127', *Journal of Asian Studies*, **21** (2), 153–62.

Lee, Thomas H.C. (1985), *Government Education and Examinations*, Hong Kong: University of Hong Kong Press.

Lee, Thomas H.C. (1989), 'Sung schools and education before Chu His', in William de Bary and John Chaffee (eds), *Neo-Confucian Education: The Formative Period*, Berkeley, CA: University of California Press, pp. 105–36.

MacCormach, Geoffrey (1996), *The Spirit of Traditional Chinese Law*, Athens, GA: University of Georgia Press.

Miyazaki, Ichisada (1976), *China's Examination Hell. The Civil Service Examinations in Imperial China*, New York: Weather Hill.

Michaud-Quantin, Pierre (1970), *Universitas: Expressions du mouvement communautaire dans le moyen-age latin*, Paris: J. Vrin.

Needham, Joseph (1954), *Science and Civilization in China*, 7 vols, in progress, New York: Cambridge University Press.

Needham, Joseph (1969), *The Grand Titration. Science and Society in East and West*, London: George Allen & Unwin.

North, Douglass C. (1990), *Institutions, Institutional Change and Economic Development*, New York: Cambridge University Press.

Paul, David A. (1994), 'Why are institutions the "carriers of history"? Path dependence and the evolution of conventions, organizations and institutions', *Structural Change and Economic Dynamics*, **5** (2), 205–30.

Schwartz, Benjamin (1968), 'On attitudes toward the law in China', in Jerome A. Cohen (ed.), *The Criminal Process in the People's Republic of China*, Cambridge, MA: Harvard University Press, pp. 62–70.

Strayer, Joseph (1970), *The Medieval Origins of the Modern State*, Princeton, NJ: Princeton University Press.

Watt, John R. (1972), *The Magistrate in Late Imperial China*, New York: Columbia University Press.

COMMENT

Erich Weede

In essence, my own analysis of Chinese economic development (Weede 2000, Chapter 4) as well as the general approach outlined by Baechler fit with Mo's analysis. Interstate competition forced Sung rulers to serve their subjects better than Ming or Manchu rulers. What I miss in Mo's analysis is more detailed information about property rights in imperial China as well as an attempt to explain the rise of contemporary China under a leadership still nominally committed to Communism.

In Weberian terms (Weber 1922/1964), imperial China's political system was patrimonial rather than feudal. Under patrimonialism the staff of the ruler is dependent upon him for their livelihood. Under feudalism, by contrast, the staff of the ruler consists of vassals with resources of their own. They possess land. Moreover they command the loyalty of warriors. Therefore patrimonialism permits much more arbitrary rule than feudalism, as defined by Weber. In feudalism, but not in patrimonialism, we find the ideas of reciprocity and complimentary rights and obligations at the top and at the bottom of the ruling class. Since feudalism – because of the balance of power between king and self-equipped vassals commanding their own troops – enforces the recognition of rights, including property rights, below the level of the ruler, it provides a much better starting point for development towards a non-exploitative state than patrimonialism. Throughout the second millennium China never benefited from feudalism, as defined by Weber.

Weber's (1922/1964) general analysis – rather than his specific analysis of China (Weber 1920/1972) about which I am less enthusiastic – provides a second important insight. In his view, independent, self-equipped citizens and defensible cities contributed much to Western political and economic development. Like feudalism China lacked this second domestic check on arbitrary power for most of the second millennium. Feeble beginnings of independent cities in Southern China in the first part of the second millennium were strangled under the Ming dynasty together with international trade.

The property rights of merchants, peasants and gentry in China were more insecure than in the West because neither interstate competition nor feudalism nor independent cities were strong enough in China to challenge emperors and their patrimonial administrations. As Yang (1987: 49–53) points out, Chinese emperors could successfully claim to be the ultimate owners of all the land in China. Therefore all other property rights in land had to be attenuated, weak and insecure.

As Yang (1987: 21) or Tu (1990: 43) also point out, the ideas of law and equality under the law never grew roots in imperial China. The dominant anti-legalism among the Confucian staff of Chinese emperors may be a result of power relations within imperial China. But it must have made the protection of private property more difficult than in Western civilization where law and lawyers became successively more important since the rediscovery of Roman law at the beginning of the second millennium.

According to Yang (1987: 29, 64), no group suffered more from insecure property rights as well as arbitrary and frequently confiscatory discrimination than merchants. Their insecurity must have interfered with market exchange. By not recognizing and not respecting the property rights of merchants, Chinese emperors effectively reduced the size of the market. Already Adam Smith (1776/1976) taught us that the size of the market limits the division of labour, and that the division of labour permits productivity gains. Ultimately attacks on the property rights of merchants must reduce economic development and growth.

These observations on the imperial past of China directly prepare us for the question, how could nominally still Communist-ruled China grow as fast as it did since 1979, given the deplorable state of the rule of law in mainland China even today? In my view the Chinese must have applied a kind of substitute for the rule of law. Or there must have been incentives for rulers to respect the property rights of investors. These incentives are provided by interstate competition. Overseas Chinese, for example, may invest their capital in mainland China, in Taiwan, in South-East Asia or elsewhere. In order to protect its reputation, the Chinese government has to act as if it were committed to the recognition of private property rights. Acting 'as if one cared' is good enough for the real world. Market competition forces producers to act as if they cared for the welfare of consumers. It does no harm that they ultimately care for their profits only. Likewise, a government by nominal communists that acts 'as if' it recognized private property might be good enough for promoting growth.

As Weingast (1995) and Montinola et al. (1995) added, the devolution of economic decision-making from the central government to provincial, county, city and township governments further intensified the competition between local and regional governments for the favour of investors. In order to gain the favour of investors from inside and outside China, local and regional governments have to act 'as if' they respected private property rights, they have to try to be more effective and less corrupt than neighbouring regions and townships. Local and regional governments are forced by competition into a race to the top.

In my view the general spirit of these additional observations looks compatible with Mo's approach. Both of us seem to believe that government does more harm than good unless constrained by interstate competition. Therefore the economically very successful competition between the miniscule Republic of China on Taiwan and the People's Republic of China under Mao Zedong may have contributed to the monumental improvement of the mainland Chinese economy under Deng Xiaoping.

References

Montinola, Gabriella, Yingyi Qian and Barry R. Weingast (1995), 'Federalism, Chinese style: the political basis for economic success in China', *World Politics*, **48** (1), 50–81.
Smith, Adam (1776), *An Inquiry into the Nature and Causes of the Wealth of Nations*, reprinted 1976, Oxford: Oxford University Press.
Tu, Wei-Ming (1990), 'Der industrielle Aufstieg Ostasiens aus konfuzianischer Sicht. Po', in S. Krieger and R. Trauzettel (eds), *Konfuzianismus and die Modernisierung Chinas*, Mainz: von Hase und Koehler, pp. 41–56.
Weber, Max (1920), *Gesammelte Aufsätze zur Religionssoziologie*, vol 1, reprinted 1972, Tübingen: Mohr.
Weber, Max (1922), *Wirtschaft und Gesellschaft*, reprinted 1964, Köln: Kiepenheuer und Witsch.
Weede, Erich (2000), *Asien und der Westen: Politische und kulturelle Determinanten der wirtschaftlichen Entwicklung*, Baden-Baden: Nomos.
Weingast, Barry R. (1995), 'The economic role of political institutions: market-preserving federalism and economic development', *Journal of Law, Economics, and Organization*, **11** (1), 1–31.
Yang, Tai-Shuenn (1987), *Property Rights and Constitutional Order in Imperial China*, PhD dissertation, Bloomington, IN: Indiana University.

INNOVATIONS IN THE CHINESE HISTORY OF SCIENCE

Li Chen and Ugurlu Soylu

The following figures and tables have been compiled by Li Chen and Ugurlu Soylu from the 21 volumes of Joseph Needham's monumental work about the Chinese history of science.[1]

Following Needham, the 575 innovations have been assigned to a century or dynasty according to the date of their occurrence or, where this is not known, according to the date at which they were first reported. A few innovations could not be clearly assigned to a dynasty. They have been omitted in the division by dynasty. Of course the innovations could not be weighted by their importance. The disaggregated data are available from the editors upon request.

Notes

1. Joseph Needham, editor. Seven volumes, started in 1954. *Science and Civilization in China.* Cambridge: Cambridge University Press. Volumes 4–7 are each divided into several books.

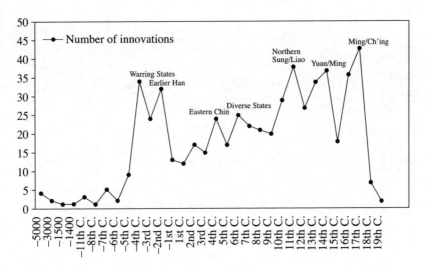

Figure 4.1   Innovations in the Chinese history of science (by century)

Note: *Liang, Chhen, later Wei, Northern Ch'i, Northern Chou, Early Sui

Table 4.3 *Innovations in the Chinese history of science (by century)*

Year/century	Agriculture	Astronomy	Botany	Bridge work	Chemistry	Hydraulics	Mathematics	Mechanical engineering	Medicine	Military	Navigation and discoveries	Physics	Shipping	Total
-5000	3		1											4
-3000	2													2
-1500	1													1
-1400							1							1
-11th C.	2						1							3
-8th C.						1								1
-7th C.			1		2	1	1							5
-6th C.												1	1	2
-5th C.				1		1						7		9
-4th C.	6		5		21		1					1		34
-3rd C.	9		3		3	7	2							24
-2nd C.	2		2		20		3		2		1	2		32
-1st C.	6		2		1	3			1					13
1st C.	1	4	1	1	10	2								12
2nd C.	2	1	2	1	1		2							17
3rd C.	2	4			14	1					1	2	4	15
4th C.	2	4	1		6	1	1				1			24
5th C.	3	2		1	1						2		2	17
6th C.	10	4	6	1	6	1	1		1		2		1	25
7th C.	1	8	4		3					1	2			22
8th C.		9			12	1			1		2	3	2	21
9th C.		3			20	1				1		1		20
10th C.		4	3		7	5				2	1		1	29
11th C.	2	7			3			2		2	3	5	4	38
12th C.		4	3		3	1		8	2	1	4	5	1	27
13th C.	3	11			1		3		1	4	1	2		34
14th C.	1	2			20		3	23		2	1			37
15th C.	3	1	2								7	1	2	18
16th C.	3		6		16	2	4			2		3		36
17th C.	3	2	2		1			18						43
18th C.		2						4						7
19th C.		1												2

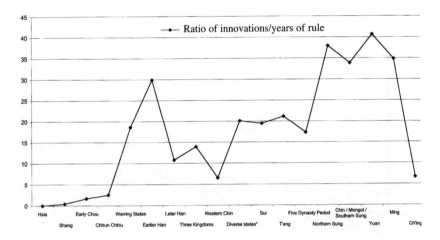

Figure 4.2   Innovations in the Chinese history of science (by dynasty)

Notes: *Eastern Chin, Liu Sung, Chhin, Northern Chou

Table 4.4 Innovations in the Chinese history of science (by dynasty)

Dynasty	Year	Duration	Agriculture	Astronomy	Botany	Bridge work	Chemistry	Hydraulics	Mathematics	Mechanical	Medicine	Military	Navigation and discoveries	Physics	Shipping	Total	Total* 100/duration
Hsia	-2000 to -1521	479														0	0,00
Shang	-1520 to 1031	489	1													2	0,41
Early Chou	-1030 to -723	307	2		1	1										5	1,63
Chhun Chhiu	-722 to -481	241	2		1		1	1						1		6	2,49
Warring States	-480 to -222	258	8		5		21	2	3					8	1	48	18,60
Ch'in	-221 to -207	14														0	0,00
Earlier Han	-206 to +8	214	15	2	7		21	8	4		3		1	2	1	64	29,91
Later Han	+25 to +220	195	2	1		2	11		1						4	21	10,77
Three Kingdoms (first partition)	+221 to +264	43		2				1					1	2		6	13,95
Western Chin	+265 to +311	46	1	1			1									3	6,52

	Dates														
Invasion and political instability (second partition)	+311 to +580	269	10	7		21	1	1			5			54	20,07
Sui	+581 to +617	36	4	1			1			1				7	19,44
T'ang	+618 to +906	288	1	17	4	22	3	1	1	2	5	4	2	61	21,18
Five Dynasty Period (third partition)	+907 to +959	52		1		6				2				9	17,31
Northern Sung	+960 to +1126	166	2	12	4	23	6		2	3	1	7	3	63	37,95
Chin/Mongol rule in north, Southern Sung in south	+1127 to +1275	148		13	3	4		4	8	3	7	4	2	50	33,78
Yuan	+1276 to +1367	91	3	2		3	1	1	23	2	1	1		37	40,66
Ming	+1368 to +1644	276	7	3	10	37	1	4	18	2	7	4	2	96	34,78
Ch'ing*	+1645 to +1911	150		3		2	1		4					10	6,67

Note: *The study ends at about 1800. The duration of the Ch'ing dynasty was adjusted respectively.

5. Advantages of centralized and decentralized rule in Japan

Günther Distelrath

PREFACE

Within the course of her history, Japan has experienced phases both of centralized order and those of orientation towards decentralized rule. In the process of transition between these phases, the influence of foreign powers and military attack from without, which might eventually have led to dynasty changes (as occurred several times in China), played only a minor role in Japan up until 1945. Nevertheless the country repeatedly followed foreign examples, especially when it came to legitimizing a central government; in part it was pressure from without that caused the centralization of the political order.

In this contribution I shall begin by giving a historical overview of the changes between the phases of more centralized and more decentralized constitution of the political, economic and social systems in Japan. I shall base my evaluation of the advantages and disadvantages of these orientations on the respective economic living standards of the population. Until the opening-up of Japan towards the modern international system in the mid-nineteenth century, it will be sufficient to rely entirely on internal factors, while thereafter the external influences became increasingly important. My discussion of Japan's modern developments will first focus on the country's departure from being a semi-colonized state[1] to its becoming an imperialist power and then give a brief picture of the switch from high-speed growth and 'catch-up' to the present stagnation.

Appraising the advantages and disadvantages of centralized versus decentralized rule from Japan's historical experience, I shall argue that the social and economic conditions tended to develop well in terms of the living standards of the population when there was a finely adjusted balance between factors of centralization and decentralization, for instance when legal security was established as a general framework, but – within it – enough space was provided for creative individual action. This is also true for international relations, which are determined by these two kinds of factors as well. The connection between my arguments concerning Japanese history and interstate

96

competition will become apparent in the case study of the Edo period (1603–1868) in section II, where I observe a 'proto-interstate' order. Since about 250 states or state-like units (*han*) coexisted and competed within the legal framework set up by a central government (*bakufu*) during that period, I come to the conclusion that that system might provide a good example for a working interstate order which is able to guarantee security and equal opportunity.

SECTION I. HISTORICAL OVERVIEW

Prehistory and Antiquity

Any scholar familiar with Japanese history will agree that all the great upheavals in the history of the country can be understood as fundamental changes of the political and economic set-up and that centralized and decentralized elements were arranged in a totally different manner from that prevailing during the preceding period. The division of Japanese history into periods, which after protracted debate became common in historiography, uses these great upheavals and system switches as benchmarks.[2] According to the terminology universally accepted by historians today, taking European history as a model, the period after prehistory (until 645) is called Japanese Antiquity (*kodai*, 645–1185), followed by the Japanese Middle Ages (*chusei*, 1185–1603), Japan's Early Modern period (*kinsei*, 1603–1868) and her Modern Age (*kindai*, since 1868). Sometimes contemporary history (*gendai*, since 1945) is also identified separately, which makes sense since, as will be shown later, the arrangement of the post-war system can be clearly distinguished from that of the pre-war period. Under the aspect of centralization versus decentralization, in this section I shall sketch out briefly each of the system switches to which this division of periods refers.

The change from prehistory to Antiquity can clearly be characterized as a movement towards centralization. Before the so-called Taiho reforms that took place after the year 645, we may call the system a totally decentralized one because Japan did not exist as a united state and local rulers (*uji*) divided up the territory amongst themselves. The centralization and founding of a state became possible after one of the kingdoms (*yamato*) had gradually gained supremacy and tried to institutionalize it. As a tool for this, the Chinese model of centralized state power was introduced by the post-645 reforms and thereby Japan came to know the rule of law for the first time. This first Japanese state based its existence on the legal institutionalization of all social and economic relations, defining them by their position within the new power structure. The court of the emperor which was now generally accepted as the centre of power

– the family of the Japanese *tenno* descends from these origins to this day – was able to establish a general legal code (*ritsuryo*) to obtain supremacy over the entire land, which of course meant that a large part of the agrarian tax revenue was captured and all former rivals eliminated or integrated into the new hierarchical order.

This movement towards centralization and the application of generally valid principles to the administration of the whole country brought about substantial economic advantages. Here I would like to draw attention to the exhaustive construction of wet paddy fields which requires irrigation systems only available in a well-functioning polity (*jori* system), the foundation of towns (mainly the capitals: the oldest Japanese cultural monuments and works of art date from this period)[3] as well as the establishment of the first Japanese currency system. The new system indeed brought forth highly important achievements and obvious advantages, because for the first time a framework for a comprehensive community was established throughout the land, and legal security replaced arbitrariness and patriarchal structures. In the context of the general discussion with respect to the advantages versus the disadvantages of centralized and decentralized orientations, it is worth noting here that the existence of some kind of a legal set-up appears to be a precondition for any development and is therefore presupposed.[4]

During the history of ancient Japan, tendencies indicating disintegration of the system occurred and increased in the course of the centuries. Local positions of power appeared, obtaining at first small but constantly expanding special rights and exceptions from the centralized order. Initially these local predominances occurred when positions within the centralized system became heritable. Some factions within the court nobility promoted local retainers, thereby establishing private landownership and tax sovereignties. In this connection, as in the early European Middle Ages, mention must also be made of the estates of the religious institutions – Buddhist temples and Shintoist shrines which were integrated into the centralized system but increasingly followed their own interests. Towards the end of the Japanese Age of Antiquity, the local power-holders (*bushi*, so-called military aristocracy) attacked the central imperial government as well as each other. From this point onwards, the *tenno* family was able to guarantee its status, which was merely nominal for most of the time, as supreme institution of the empire only by means of coalitions with the victorious combatants and by their integration into the categories of the governmental *ritsuryo* system.

Middle Ages and Early Modern Period

The definitive end of ancient Japan and the beginning of the Middle Ages became manifest when in 1185 the position of a *shogun* (which means supreme military commander) was introduced. The *shoguns* exercised the governmental power on behalf of the emperor. This new sovereignty displayed a number of institutions of the *ritsuryo* system, which, similar to Roman law in the European Middle Ages, legitimized the power structure through heritage. But the political system of the Japanese Middle Ages moved far away from the Chinese model which had been the blueprint for those institutions. Already the first *shogun* of the Kamakura period (1185–1333), Minamoto no Yoritomo (1147–99), was not entitled to exercise centralized power throughout Japan, but had to rely on a system of vassals and retainership. Because of the similarities of this system with the situation in the Holy Roman Empire – Japanese historiography and the division of periods was largely influenced by German historiography – this era was later called the Middle Ages (*chusei*). The similarities lay in the decentralization, if not fragmentation, of the feudal units.

The *shoen* (estates) became the basic units of social and economic life. According to time and region, the *shoen* showed a great variety of feudal relations, ranging from large agrarian manors including servants (comparatively few) to tax sovereignties over a number of independent households or only parts of their harvest incomes.[5] In Japanese feudalism of the Middle Ages, in a manner similar to that of Central Europe, the estates fragmented over centuries, and power could only be defined locally. The situation reached a state of almost complete decentralization. Towards the end of the Middle Ages there existed no generally accepted authority able to resolve conflicts peacefully according to superior principles. Instead military power became the decisive factor.

As in Europe, the Middle Ages in Japan is no longer exclusively viewed as a Dark Age because of a number of achievements that have been identified and acknowledged in recent research.[6] For example, as in the European Middle Ages, we find in Japan the establishment of private-law contracts, since commodity trading and the merchant class played an increasingly important role. Even in the realm of religion there are developments with parallels in the European Reformation movement: the 'sect of the pure land' (*jodoshu*) promoted a reform of the clerical system towards laicistic organizational structures. But the transition from the medieval system towards the Early Modern period in Japan saw even more violence than was prevalent in Europe.

In Japan, this transformation process was shaped by a century of civil wars (*sengoku-jidai*, 'age of battling countries' from 1467 to 1568). In this era the local lords (*samurai*) joined forces to create a system of vassalage, that is a system of mutual agreement on military assistance in the case of war. These agreements were increasingly concentrated around regional feudal lords (*daimyo*) and led to what in German is called *Landesherrschaft*, in contrast to the smaller *Grundherrschaft* of the Middle Ages.[7] The time of transition was marked by frequent conflicts between these feudal lords which devastated whole districts and decimated the population to a very considerable extent. At the final stage of this age, the Christian missionary activity that was just beginning also entered the power game. There were Christian *daimyo*, which with the assistance of the Spanish or Portuguese crown conquered large districts and positions of power. Within the Azuchi-Momoyama period (1568–1603), two of the military leaders, Oda Nobunaga (1534–82) and Toyotomi Hideyoshi (1536–98), gained control over large parts of Japan in succession, but the animosities continued until the decisive battle of Sekigahara in 1600.

Despite some future-orientated elements, the overall balance of the age of total decentralization in the Japanese Middle Ages, especially in its later phase, is highly negative, since it meant a predominance of military activity over all other fields of action. For the average citizen the conditions caused constant suffering, because military power overshadowed all other aspects of life. Warlords exercised unrestricted despotic rule over the people and the economy declined to a hitherto unprecedented degree. As an example I would like to mention the currency system: after Japan's Age of Antiquity there was no recoinage for 600 years. Towards the end of the Middle Ages the money in circulation consisted of the totally worn and torn coins minted centuries before, and of imported coins, mainly from China, with widely differing denominations. Every trade activity became very complicated since in each transaction the different qualities of the coins had to be evaluated with regard to their content of precious metal, and the coins had to be weighed.[8]

Legal certainty disappeared, arbitrary appropriations became normal, no reliable currency system existed. Within the context of our discussion, the diagnosis can only be that total decentralization is inevitably followed by disastrous consequences. If the law of the strongest prevails exclusively, the mechanisms which secure the welfare of the community as well as of the individual do not function: medium- and long-term mutual agreements and contracts; the reasonable expectation that the investments of today will reap profits in the future; the very belief that an upright conduct of life will provide advantages for oneself and one's descendants. Max Weber tried to incorporate and systemize observations of this nature when he differentiated between 'modern capitalism' and a capitalism of the 'adventurer type, or capitalism in trade, war, politics, or administration as sources of gain', motivated by compulsive greed, which is principally aimed at acquisition through force and the plundering of subordinates (Weber 1963: 320–21). I am critical of the Weberian view that individual motivation is constitutive for a 'modern' order, but I do concur with his general conclusion that positive and sustainable development of the community can only be achieved if the actions of individuals are integrated into a system of mutual obligations – be they constituted morally or institutionally.

Correspondingly, the system changes which were enforced after transition to the Early Modern period in Japan were greatly welcomed by contemporaries. After the installation of Tokugawa Ieyasu (1542–1616), the victorious general at the battle of Sekigahara, as *shogun* in the year 1603, the country experienced 250 years of lasting internal and external peace, of a well-adjusted social order and increasing economic prosperity. As will be shown in detail later (within the respective case study in section II), this system was based on national isolation (*sakoku*) from the international environment which became increasingly colonialist and imperialist, on a newly introduced class system with clearly outlined rights and duties for the individual, on a reliable framework for the economy (for example with regard to the currency and legal security) and on a mixture of centralized and decentralized elements which, with the benefit of hindsight, was quite appropriate. In section II I shall pay special attention to the establishment of a 'proto-interstate' order or a quasi-supranational system of regulating the coexistence and rivalries of the more than 250 *han* (domains) which appeared as state-like units at least since the mid-eighteenth century. Within Japan's Early Modern order, for internal reasons a number of tendencies leading towards the disintegration of the system developed around the middle of the nineteenth century. But the fact that these tendencies led to a revolutionary upheaval and to the establishment of a centralized state – the modern Japanese national state – was mainly due to external influences: the growing imperialist pressure to which the country was being subjected.

Modern Japan

The division of the world among the European and North American powers in the mid-nineteenth century reached East Asia as the last region of the world not yet being integrated into these powers' spheres of influence. After China had been partly colonized following the opium war of 1840–42, the imperialist powers concentrated their attention on the Japanese archipelago, where in 1854 a flotilla of the US navy under commodore Mathew Perry anchored in the bay of the shogunal capital Edo (today Tokyo). According to the 'policy of the open door', which represented the current approach towards East Asia and had as its goal the semi-colonization of the countries by forcing them to concede special rights, Japan too had to sign so-called 'unequal treaties',[9] which restricted to a great extent the trade sovereignty of the country. The opposition to this development within Japan, spearheaded by a number of domains in the south-west, finally succeeded in overthrowing the shogunal government by military force (the so called Meiji Restoration) in 1867/68. After a very short phase of reorientation, the new rulers who smashed all structures of the Edo period had to recognize that the state of semi-colonization and the danger of permanent subjection could not be changed suddenly, but could only be avoided by the rigorous establishment of a national state following the Western example.

The civil rights which were introduced in the following decades were, beyond European examples, mainly due to indigenous conceptions arising among the peasant population (for example within the *yonaoshi* and *ejanaika* rebellions of 1866–68)[10] and the merchant class with its increasing role in the Japanese common market of the late Early Modern period. But the centralized constitution of the young Japanese national state came about rather in response to international pressure. In part, the names of the new centralized institutions went back to the Age of Antiquity because such institutions had not been in existence in the meantime. The new institutions necessary in order to resist the pressure from outside were the national government, parliament, the national bank, a supreme court, the police, a permanent army and so on, and a central-ized education system. The latter had to serve a highly important function which, corresponding to Garibaldi's words on the young Italian national state, could be paraphrased as 'Now that we have Japan, we are in need of the Japanese'.

In the same way as in the other new national states of the late nineteenth century, the standardized educational system in Japan not only had to disci-pline the population for the rigidities of the industrial work process (resistance against them could be generally perceived in Japan at the end of the nineteenth century, too).[11] It also had the function of building a national identity. In order to achieve this, a uniform national tradition had to be invented consisting of loyalty to the emperor and the government and a predominance of Confucian social relations. A unique Japanese culture had to be developed. These were the goals of the imperial educational edicts of the year 1890.

With regard to military strength and the mobilization of the people, the success of this project can be dated at around the turn of the century when Japan appeared – in the Chinese–Japanese war (1894–95) and in the Russian–Japanese war (1904–05) – as an independent power within the impe-rialist competition, but total subordination of the population to national goals was never achieved, neither then nor later. It is of some considerable impor-tance that this last point is mentioned, since within the stereotyped perception which also penetrated large parts of the academic discussion, such a state of things is often claimed (for example concerning the motivation of the *kamikaze* pilots in the Second World War).

With respect to the question as to why Japan overcame the situation of semi-colonization far more successfully than most other countries affected, I would refer to the recent argument of Penelope Francks (2002) concerning 'growth linkages' between agricultural and non-agricultural activity. While other nations suffered long under the import of industrially manufactured goods from Europe and North America, which destroyed domestic manufacturing, according to this view the stage of development of the domestic industries in Japan with its high productivity, that is the good performance of the 'multiple rural households' within the Japanese common market for centuries, was chiefly responsible for a high degree of competitiveness, even under globalized conditions. It was also therefore the shortness of the phase of import pressure (especially in the textile industries) that enabled Japan to overcome the threat.

Harada and Kosai (1987) have tried to subsume the establishment of the first national system (1868–1945) and of the second (1945–) under the general concept of 'big game', which is based on the assumption that the modus of transactions and the path of development is constituted by the framework set up in the opening phase of each epoch. They claim that within the first phase of the Japanese national state, the system was on the one hand favourable to the *haute bourgeoisie* (known since the turn of the century as *zaibatsu*) by strengthening its influence on internal economic and political arrangements and on the other hand gave considerable voice to the military (*gunbatsu*).

In post-war Japan, Harada and Kosai again observe a big game phase of system building. This time, the general set-up for the socio-economic system of today's Japan was arranged by the occupying powers. In particular the American New Dealers within the administration of occupied Japan, whose policies had been without long-lasting effect in the US herself, found a new free field of operation there. They were responsible for the fact that the new framework for Japan's post-war society and economy would become directed largely towards equal opportunity, social balance and redistribution of wealth. What became well known after the appearance of Michel Albert's publication (1991) as 'Rhenish Capitalism' (*raingata shihonshugi*) – he explicitly included Japan in this category – is therefore not a system with long traditional origins, but is due to the lessons that both the Federal Republic of Germany and Japan, each under different conditions, drew from defeat in the Second World War and its causes.

After the Second World War, Japan, to a greater extent than the Federal Republic of Germany, returned to a centralized order which nevertheless was balanced by a number of decentralized elements. In Japan centralization has often been regarded as a problem up to today.[12] But there is certainly an increasing regional consciousness outside the metropolitan areas. Whereas in the era of high-speed growth everybody tried to study in the centres or find employment there in the big companies (a tendency existing since the 1880s, when *dekasegi* – going to the big towns and earning money – was the only way to increase wealth), today the relatively high standard of living in the peripheral areas is generally acknowledged. The cost of living there is low and accompanied by an infrastructure which has been based on subsidies for decades and is comparable to that of the centres. Today even an autonomization of the regional fiscal units has been under discussion, since the central government has had serious fiscal problems.

Furthermore, Japan's centralized post-war order has been balanced by equalization in the socio-political field. The power of the *haute bourgeoisie* (*zaibatsu*) was shattered by the occupying powers. In the meagre American social science literature on Japan dating from that time,[13] *zaibatsu* and the big landowners (*jinushi*) were identified as the main supporters of Japanese militarism (which did not prove to be true). In order to maintain democratization and demilitarization, which became the main goals of the occupying powers, they carried out a comprehensive land reform and the dissolution of the *zaibatsu* combines. Together with the highly progressive wage tax and other measures imposed by the New Dealers, this led to an egalitarian structure of the post-war Japanese society never previously experienced in history. In the countryside very small parcels remain predominant and responsible for the high subsidies in agriculture to this day, with all the problems that are so familiar from the European Union. In industry, the so-called intra-company socialism of the large Japanese enterprises gained ground.

In place of the combines which had been expropriated by the occupying powers, cross-share holdings and other horizontal links developed, which were eventually called *keiretsu*. For the structure within the companies this meant that management, in no way bound to any owner, took the lead. Furthermore the access to management positions was now left to competition within the companies, and top management had very few tools with which to enrich themselves. With these intra-company conditions, the mechanisms are already indicated that enabled the Japanese enterprises to succeed increasingly on the world market and that caused their 'aggressiveness': the influence of shareholder interests was minimal and the market position was crucial for decision-making.[14] Through the dissolution of the combines a situation emerged that was later called 'face-to-face competition': instead of the often oligopolistic structures in the pre-war period, there now existed between three and ten competitors of near-equal strength (in sales) within each industry. This led to keen competition amongst Japanese enterprises at first in Japan and later on the world market. Together with good economic policies, these are some of the domestic factors which allowed Japan to make effective use of the niche situation which opened up after the disaster of surrender in the Second World War and extend it over the course of several decades into a leading position worldwide.

From the international perspective, the rapid growth of world trade and the successful integration of Japan into the monetary system of Bretton Woods were the most important reasons for Japan's post-war success. The USA protected Japan for reasons of world politics in the first decades after the war, when for example they allowed Japan to retain the international exchange rates of 1949 until 1971, thereby providing very favourable trading terms. While Japan was one of the great beneficiaries of the regulations of those decades, she was probably the first victim of the era of deregulation that started in the 1980s. There is reasonable argument in Japan that besides domestic factors, it was mainly financial deregulation that contributed to the 'bubble economy' of the late 1980s and its burst in the early 1990s which caused the problems Japan continues to suffer today.[15]

Be that as it may, whether or not this argument proves to be true in detail, there is prevalent debate on the advantages and disadvantages of centralization or decentralization of the international economic order, to which some Japanese economists currently refer. I am attempting here to draw lessons from Japanese history. For a well-attuned balance between centralized and decentralized elements in a 'proto interstate order', the prime example might be the Japanese Early Modern age, the Edo period (1603–1868), when more than 250 state-like units coexisted and competed with each other on the Japanese common market.

SECTION II: CASE STUDY – THE EDO PERIOD

The Early Modern period in Japan is commonly identified with the time when Edo (today Tokyo) had the function of residence and capital of the Tokugawa shogunate from 1603 to 1867/68. It is hence also called the Edo period or sometimes Tokugawa period. Within the history of research, assessments of the Edo period have differed greatly. In earlier research both in Japanese and in European languages, the image of a Dark Age characterized by isolation, stagnation, suppression and excessive exploitation of the rural population predominates. Japan's industrialization in the second half of the nineteenth century has been viewed as a departure from its own traditions and the rigorous adoption of European and North American ways of thinking, judicial systems and production technologies. In more recent research some factors of stagnation are not denied, but they are seen as being easily compensated by a large number of dynamic developments in the economy and in society. Judging from the more recent research on social change, proto-industrialization and intellectual history, the Edo period should be referred to as an age of continued pre-industrial dynamics.

The constant developments which took place in Japan between the end of the Middle Ages and the eve of industrialization mark a considerable difference to the situation on the neighbouring Asian continent. Already the structure of society in the Japanese Middle Ages had been more similar to European feudalism than to the conditions in China and Korea. Slow but steady further changes in the Edo period contributed to the fact that the country entered the industrial age by no means unprepared. Fundamental to these developments was the establishment of a new legal set-up and a new social order. As mentioned in section I, the period of civil wars and political fragmentation ended with the victory of Tokugawa Ieyasu (1542–1616) at the battle of Sekigahara in 1600. In the ensuing decades great attempts were made to stabilize the country and to prevent it from falling back into chaos. The measures which balanced the powers were initiated first of all by the Tokugawa themselves in order to guarantee their supremacy, but soon they were welcomed by a large number of contemporaries, as we can learn from the sources.

I cannot deal here with all elements of the legal, political and socio-economic systems of Early Modern Japan such as the administrational order, the class division or the tax system, nor with the measures taken to secure peace and stability, such as the restrictions to the possession of arms. But it is worth mentioning that the voluntary isolation of Japan in that period is regarded by Immanuel Kant in his essay of 1795 on 'eternal peace' as a major advantage for the country in comparison to Europe with its frequent wars.[16] In this section I shall concentrate on the political superstructure, but I would like to indicate at the outset the social and economic developments of the age on which it was based. In the seventeenth century, agriculture, heavily damaged by the previous civil wars, had to be rebuilt (which is a great effort in the case of irrigation systems). Considerable advances were also made in infrastructure and communication systems. The late seventeenth century already saw a flourishing urban life in the shogunal capital Edo as well as in Kyoto, in the soaring commercial capital of Osaka and in more than 200 provincial towns. Worldwide, the tendency towards urbanization was probably most pronounced in Japan: at the beginning of the eighteenth century around 3.8 million people – 12 per cent of the population – lived in towns.[17] The population of Edo alone swelled to 1.1 million, making it the biggest town in the world (for comparison: London and Beijing had about 800 000 to 900 000 inhabitants in the eighteenth and early nineteenth centuries, while Paris had approximately 540 000).

The towns naturally developed a great demand for food and many other products which had to be delivered from the surrounding area or even from further afield. In the case of Edo for example, this caused a sharp rise in agricultural production in the surrounding Kanto plain. With the rise in production, the merchants became more and more important. They soon formed large enterprises, with their headquarters mainly in Osaka, concluding contracts and establishing networks throughout Japan and dealing with products such as paper, tea, sugar, cotton, timber, ceramics and so on. Miyamoto counted more than 200 products traded in Osaka in 1714; many of the trading volumes were surprisingly large.[18] The products came from putting-out systems (or cottage industries) all over the country, in some cases from manufacturers with paid labour. By means of this production and supply, a high standard of living was achieved and spread widely. It can be quantitatively assessed by Japanese economic historians today and is considered by Kito (1996: 445) as a 'highly developed ecological market economy' or 'high degree organic economy' (*kodo yuki keizai*).[19]

The superstructure and legal framework under which these social and economic developments took place and which has to be regarded as having been highly responsible for these achievements was the *bakuhan* system. This term refers to the dualistic structure of rule in Early Modern Japan, consisting of a centralized government by the *shogun* (called *bakufu*) and more than 250 domains (*han*). After the decisive battle of 1600, Tokugawa Ieyasu had not been able to bring the whole country under his direct control. Since then the direct rule of the *shogun* was limited mainly to the wider area surrounding Edo, several important towns including Osaka and Nagasaki as well as gold, silver and copper mines throughout the country to secure the resources for the metallic currencies issued by the central government. The rest of the country was divided into domains where the feudal lords (*daimyo*) – resident there since the Middle Ages or newly appointed by the *shogun* – had to set up castle towns as capitals of the fiefs and a sovereign administration including tax authorities and jurisdiction. The castle towns again were divided into quarters for *samurai*, merchants and artisans while in the countryside only the farmers remained in villages, with their own internal administrations.[20] Since the 1630s the families of the *daimyo* had been forced to reside permanently in Edo while the feudal lords themselves had to stay there every second year (*sankin kotai* system). This hostage system enabled the central government to control them and to guarantee countrywide peace, and at the same time to allow them to govern their fiefs. From time to time the central government was led by a strong *shogun* or administrator, but for the most part it was ruled by a council (*roju*) of four or five feudal lords.[21]

Thus in Early Modern Japan a political order was established which combined and balanced centralized and decentralized elements in such a way as to allow local and private initiatives (for example market forces), and simultaneously to contain institutions against chaotic developments. The system matured in the mid-eighteenth century to a 'proto-interstate' order. In previous decades the production and distribution of cash crops and manufactured goods had increased steadily while the importance of rice production, the basis of the revenues of both shogunate and domains, as well as the price of rice, showed a relative decline. At the same time the general tendency towards commercialization and consumption of traded goods raised public expenditure and caused problems for the budgets of both the central and the local governments.

In reaction to these developments, especially at the beginning of the so-called Tanuma era (1767–86) when Tanuma Okitsugu (1719–88) headed the shogunate's administration, the central government cut the subsidies for the domains drastically because of its own fiscal difficulties. From that point on, the *han* were forced to establish total fiscal independence and in order to guarantee and support it had to develop their own economic policies. They soon appeared as state-like units with sovereign budgets, trade policies, balances of payments and in a large number of cases their own (paper) currencies.[22] Furthermore the *han* became major players on the Japanese common markets, since they now 'exported' and 'imported' products, competed in price and quality, had exchange rates with the general coin currency and became stronger or weaker according to their market position. Because of this, since the second half of the eighteenth century a large landscape of economic scholarship had also been developing, involving the appearance of very different ideas. At least since the early nineteenth century, the scene had been dominated by system competition between *han*, pursuing what we would call today liberal, mercantilist or physiocratic directions.

What can be called the 'proto-interstate' order of Japan's Early Modern period lasted for around one century, from the mid-eighteenth to the mid-nineteenth century. Afterwards, as has been shown, the influence of imperialism forced Japan to open its microcosm and build up a centralized nation-state. Within the 'proto-interstate' order, the central government provided the framework to which the member states had to adjust their strategies and policies. This framework contained the following rules: (1) the absolute prohibition of military conflict among the states, (2) the obligation to maintain internal peace within the states (the central government would have intervened in the event of larger disorders), (3) a legal framework for economic competition among the states, and (4) supervision of the fairness of bilateral or multilateral relations. During this one century, the system was also perceived by contemporaries as an interstate order, since the term *koku* (meaning today 'country' or 'state') was used to refer to the *han* units. Under the rules of this system, it was quite possible that less-developed states at the periphery could catch up with the most-developed regions or even surpass them by offering good governance and adopting new economic strategies.[23] Thus Japan's experience in the Edo period could show us that interstate competition within a legal framework guaranteeing peace, fair competition and equal chances is not merely a utopian idea.

CONCLUSIONS

I would like to summarize the lessons that can be drawn from Japanese social and economic history concerning the advantages versus disadvantages of centralized and decentralized elements in the following four points:

1. The successive epochs are each characterized by a fundamental change in the importance and composition of centralized and decentralized factors. With the birth of the first Japanese state in her Age of Antiquity, a strongly centralized system was set up following a Chinese model. It was responsible for the fact that Japan became a civilization, whereas no written language had previously existed and the country was divided into tribal territories. But it could not withstand the emerging local and private interests for longer than five centuries. The dissolution of this centralized state and the rise of feudalism is – as also for Europe – commonly regarded as an essential step forward, enabling private ownership. But this system switch finally led to an era of all-pervasive internal military conflicts which strongly impaired the economic development of the country. The total decentralization of the late Middle Ages resulted in social and economic collapse, which led contemporaries to welcome any kind of re-regulation.

2. After this time Japan experienced a phase of isolation from the outside world, but within the country a microcosm including more than 250 smaller state-like units took shape. A well-adjusted composition of centralized and decentralized elements brought about legal security and the beneficial aspects of competition. I have acknowledged the advantages of this set-up and its possible function as an example of a functioning international system. Only as a result of pressure from without, Japan re-emerged as a centralized nation-state within the imperialist environment of the second half of the nineteenth century.

3. Japan's opening-up to the world market began under the conditions of semi-colonization, since the 'unequal treaties' limited her trade, political and juridical sovereignty. I have explained why the Japanese economy overcame that phase without falling into persistent dependence – namely, owing to the agricultural and non-agricultural linkages. The chaotic condition of the international system of the time induced the country to act as an imperialist power, a process ended by defeat in the Second World War.

4. Japan used her integration into the Bretton Woods system under special conditions (being supported by the USA for reasons of world politics) to become a fully-fledged industrialized nation, but has recently come up against serious problems since the so-called 'bubble economy' came to an end. The discussion as to whether these problems are mainly due to internal factors or caused by the deregulation of the international economic system, especially the financial markets, is still under way. In an attempt to learn from Japanese history within the scope of the case study on Japan's Early Modern period, I have presented an example of a 'proto-interstate order' which functioned for more than 250 years and which might give us a view of the nature of a just interstate arrangement.

Within her history, with respect to both the internal situation and international environment, Japan seems to have prospered when centralized and decentralized elements were in a well-adjusted balance, while she suffered decline in terms of the well-being of the population and the maintenance of peace when a disequilibrium occurred, and especially so when total decentralization caused chaotic conditions. In this sense, Japanese history also provides lessons for today's discussions on the constitution of the world economic order.

NOTES

1. The time from 1858 to 1899 is, in my view, Japan's age of semi-colonization. The country had been forced to sign so-called 'unequal treaties' with the Western powers, which implicated most-favoured-nation clauses, free trade rights for the companies of these nations within the opened ports, extraterritoriality (that is foreign jurisdiction for people from the signatory states) and a restriction of import taxes to 5 per cent and of export taxes to 20 per cent.
2. For the long-term development of Japanese historiography, see the book edited by Beasley and Pulleyblank dating from 1961, which remains instructive. For the discussion of the 1930s which shaped today's commonly shared division of periods, see Hoston (1986: 127–78).
3. If we exclude here the prehistoric archaeological findings.
4. For a comprehensive overview of the history of ancient Japan and the Middle Ages, see the two volumes of the *Cambridge History of Japan* (Shively and McCullough 1999, Yamamura 1990), respectively.
5. A good case study on *shoen* structures is Taranczewski (1988).
6. See for example Amino (1997).
7. German historiographical terminology seems to lend itself to the conditions in Japan much more readily than English, since the extent of decentralization of power in the Middle Ages was similar in Japan and Central Europe, while England (and also France) remained comparatively centralized.
8. For Japan's monetary history, see the 11 volumes edited by Tsuchiya and Yamaguchi (1972–76); for the currency situation in the Middle Age and the changes towards the Early Modern period, see especially Vol. 1, pp. 229–322.
9. Text of the treaties in English: the Center for East Asian Cultural Studies (1969).
10. For the latter see Zöllner (1997).
11. The German economist Karl Rathgen, who experienced the industrial revolution in Japan directly during his stay in the country in the late 1880s, wrote that the Japanese do not yet seem to be accustomed to continuous work (Rathgen 1891: 422).
12. See for example the problems of the overcrowded area of Tokyo and the many attempts to solve it, such as the plan of prime minister Tanaka Kakuei (1918–) in 1972 to establish a structure of medium-sized centres throughout Japan (*Nihon retto kaizoron*).
13. See Norman (1940).
14. See also Distelrath (1998).
15. For the arguments on this point, see for example Nakamura (1995: 172–224), Sawa (1993: 37–45) or Iwata (1995: 11–13).
16. Kant (1965: 121–2).
17. Figures from Nishikawa (1985: 38).
18. Miyamoto (1963: 83–8). Miyamoto's study is the first to state quantitative statistics on trade, prices and interest rates of the Edo period in a comprehensive manner.
19. For further details concerning the social and economic development of the Edo period, see for instance Distelrath (1996: 63–87), Nakane and Oishi (1990) as well as the study by Hanley and Yamaura (1977), which is already a near classic.

20. There were only very few exceptions to this division. At the beginning of the Edo period the local lords of the estates (*shoen*), which were being dissolved, could decide either to lay down their weapons and become peasants or move as *samurai* to the castle towns. Since there were both large domains and very small ones, the number of *samurai* and the size of the castle towns differed significantly.
21. These *daimyo* invariably came from one group called *fudai*, which was the term for those lords who had been allies of the Tokugawa before the battle of Sekigahara.
22. See Komuro (2001: 78–80).
23. There are only very few studies of these cases in the European-language literature (Roberts 1998 and my unpublished study: *Das Lehnsfürstentum Uwajima und seine Wirtschaftspolitik, 1615–1869*, 2003), but a large number in Japanese.

REFERENCES

Albert, Michel (1991), *Capitalisme contre Capitalisme*, Paris: Edition du Seuil.
Amino, Yoshihiko (1997), *Nihon shakai no rekishi* [History of Japanese Society], 3 vols, Tokyo: Iwanami Shoten.
Beasley, W.G., and E.G. Pulleyblank (eds) (1961), *Historians of China and Japan*, London: Oxford University Press.
Center for East Asian Cultural Studies (ed.) (1969), *The Meiji Japan Through Contemporary Sources*, Tokyo: The Center for East Asian Cultural Studies, vol. 1, pp. 16–65.
Distelrath, Günther (1996), *Die japanische Produktionsweise – Zur wissenschaftlichen Genese einer stereotypen Sicht der japanischen Wirtschaft*, Monographien aus dem Deutschen Institut für Japanstudien vol 18, Munich: Iudicium.
Distelrath, Günther (1998), 'Japans industrielle Organization – Industriepolitik, Arbeitsbeziehungen und Unternehmenskonstellationen', in Heinz Riesenhuber and Josef Kreiner (eds), *Japan ist offen – Chancen für deutsche Unternehmen*, Heidelberg: Springer, pp. 17–34.
Francks, Penelope (2002), 'Rural industry, growth linkages, and economic development in nineteenth-century Japan', *Journal of Asian Studies*, **61** (1), February, 33–55.
Hanley, Susan B., and Kozo Yamamura (1977), *Economic and Demographic Change in Preindustrial Japan, 1600–1868*, Princeton, NJ: Princeton University Press.
Harada, Yutaka, and Yutaka Kosai (1987), *Nihon Keizai Hatten no Biggu Gemu,* [The Big Game of Japan's Economic Development], Tokyo: Tôyô Keizai Shinposha.
Hoston, Germaine A. (1986), *Marxism and the Crisis of Development in Prewar Japan*, Princeton, NJ: Princeton University Press.
Iwata, Kikuo (1995), *Nihon-gata byodo shakai wa horobu noka* [Will the Japan-style Egalitarian Society perish?], Tokyo: Toyo Keizai Shinposha.
Kant, Immanuel (1965), *Politische Schriften*, Köln, Opladen: Westdeutscher Verlag.
Kitô, Hiroshi (1996), 'Seikatsu Suijun' [Standard of Living], in Odaka Kônosuke and Osamu Saitô (eds), *Nihon Keizai no 200 nen. Nishikawa Shunsaku kyoju kanreki kinen ronshû* [200 years of Japanese Economy. Festschrift for the 60th anniversary of Prof. Shunsaku Nishikawa], Tôkyô: Nihon Hyoronsha, pp. 425–46.
Komuro, Masamichi (2001), ' "Kagen" und die Entwicklung des ökonomischen Denkens in der Mitte der Edo-Periode', in Schefold Bertram (ed.), *Vademecum zu einem japanischen Klassiker des ökonomischen Denkens*, Düsseldorf: Verlag Wirtschaft und Finanzen, pp. 71–98.

Miyamoto, Mataji (1963), *Kinsei Osaka no Bukka to Rishi,* [Prices and Interest Rates in Early Modern Osaka], Tokyo: Sobunsha.

Nakamura, Takafusa (1995), *Gendai keizaishi* [Contemporary Economic History], Tokyo: Iwanami Shoten.

Nakane, Chie, and Shinzaburo Oishi (eds) (1990), *Tokugawa Japan. The Social and Economic Antecedents of Modern Japan*, Tokyo: University of Tokyo Press.

Nishikawa, Shunsaku (1985), *Nihon Keizai no Seichoshi* [History of Economic Growth in Japan], Tokyo: Toyo Keizai Sinposha.

Norman, E. Herbert (1940), *Japan's Emergence as a Modern State*, New York: Institute of Pacific Relations.

Rathgen, Karl (1891), 'Japans Volkswirtschaft und Staatshaushalt', *Staats- und sozialwissenschaftliche Forschungen*, **10** (4), Leipzig: Duncker & Humblot.

Roberts, Luke S. (1998), *Mercantilism in a Japanese Domain. The Merchant Origins of Economic Nationalism in Eighteenth-century Tosa*, Cambridge: Cambridge University Press.

Sawa, Takamitsu (1993), *Seijukuka Shakai no Keizai Rinri* [Economic Ethics for the Matured Society], Tokyo: Iwanami Shoten.

Shively, Donald H., and McCullough, William H. (eds) (1999), *The Cambridge History of Japan, volume 2: Heian Japan*, Cambridge: Cambridge University Press.

Taranczewski, Detlev (1988), 'Lokale Grundherrschaft und Ackerbau in der Kamakura-Zeit. Dargestellt anhand des Nitta no shô in der Provinz Kôzuke', *Bonner Zeitschrift für Japanologie*, 10. Bonn.

Tsuchiya, Takao, and Kazuo Yamaguchi (eds) (1972–76), *Nihon no kahei* [Currencies of Japan], 11 vols, Tokyo: Tokyo Keizai Shinposha.

Weber, Max (1963), 'The protestant ethic and the spirit of capitalism', in Mathilda W. Riley (ed.), *Sociological Research, volume 1: A Case Approach*, New York: Harcourt, Brace & World, pp. 320–7.

Yamamura, Kozo (ed.) (1990), *The Cambridge History of Japan. volume 3: Medieval Japan*, Cambridge: Cambridge University Press.

Zöllner, Reinhard (1997), 'Die Êêjanaika- Bewegung von 1867/68' in Antoni Klaus (ed.), *Rituale und ihre Urheber. Invented traditions in der japanischen Religionsgeschichte*, Hamburg: Lit, pp. 105–26.

COMMENT

Ken'ichi Tomobe*

'Advantages of centralized and decentralized rule in Japan' by Günther Distelrath covers a wide range of topics from the recent breakdown of the Japanese bubble economy to the long history of change between centralization and decentralization that lasted from the ancient era to the Edo period.

Though I am very interested in Distelrath's whole chapter, I especially agree with his argument concerning the balance of decentralization and centralization in Japanese history from the Sengoku to the Edo period. As some Japanologists and historians have pointed out, the political, economic and social systems of the Edo period constitute a large basis of modern Japanese capitalism since the late nineteenth century.

I think however the balance between decentralization and centralization changed especially after the Second World War due to post-war high-degree economic growth and the dominance of a single political party. Moreover the Japanese government official system, *kanryo*, also made a great contribution to the unbalanced situation of post-war Japan. Hereafter my comment is mainly concentrated on the socio-economic and political historical issues of Tokugawa Japan from the seventeenth to nineteenth century and is made up of three parts: (1) a new perspective of history broken up into 'events' and 'structures'; (2) Tokugawa feudal society; and (3) the development of a market economy in Tokugawa society.

A New Perspective of History: 'Event' and 'Structure'

From the viewpoint of macro socio-economic history, most of the present advanced capitalist nations such as Germany, France, Great Britain and Japan have undergone a stage of feudalism before capitalism. My idea is separate from Marx's stage theory of economic development, which entails strict rules due to historical materialism and is instead based on the historical experiences of these advanced countries. Though the definition of feudalism differs from country to country it holds as a general truth that some quality of feudalism did contribute to the development of capitalism.[1] Despite the fact that feudalism and capitalism oppose each other in many ways, continuity between the two also certainly exists. One of the macro-historical issues we should consider is the extent to which this continuity is true.

Social scientists and historians have a long history of debate on the transition from feudalism to capitalism.[2] One side has stressed the importance of commerce while the other has emphasized the change in mode of production at the time of transition from feudalism to capitalism. In recent times a new idea concerning the balance of population and land has developed. However I think it is more important to study the degree of freedom people had in producing and consuming, to what extent their expected production and consumption goals were met, and the process by which they accomplished their economic and social activities.

So far, thinkers of macro history have in general made light of individual facts compared to sets of macro data 'structures' and broad social theses. Now macro history needs to meet with a micro history constituted of individual events and individual units as done in anthropological research. For example, as we think about emerging crises such as the results of September 11 in New York, surely each crisis can be seen as an 'event' geographically moved within a very short time. These events can then be gathered into sets called 'structures'. Thus, by reconsidering the old-fashioned 'event–structure' relationship where seemingly random events can be linked to one another to form patterns, we can document the changes in society that are occurring today.[3]

As we translate such a new relationship between event and structure into the historical analysis of transition from feudalism to capitalism, we will be able to see how production and consumption statistics from peasant and feudal domains like *han* in Tokugawa Japan behaved when adhering to individual standards as opposed to national standards. We will be able to see how the competition between *han* induced by national standards in Tokugawa society led Japan to enter a historical period in which decentralization and centralization were well balanced.

Tokugawa 'Feudal' Society

The definition of 'feudal' society in this chapter is not a political governance by which the warrior class of the feudal domain (*han*) oppressed peasants under legal codes and extra-economic compulsion. Instead it means a centralized governance of Japan by the Tokugawa shogunate, especially in terms of military affairs and diplomatic relations.

In terms of centralized and decentralized aspects of the government, both military and diplomatic issues were centralized in Tokugawa Japan. Outside of military and diplomatic aspects, each feudal domain generally had economic, social and cultural freedom. Each Tokugawa domain was even allowed to issue their own local paper currency (*han-satsu*) and circulate it within their own areas. In some cases of strong feudal domains like Cho-shu, Satsuma and so on, the *han-satsu* circulated beyond their domains and were exchanged with Tokugawa specie such as gold coin (*koban*) and silver coins (*gin-ka*) certified by the Shogunate.[4]

Beginning in the middle of the Tokugawa period, around the eighteenth century, the decentralization of Tokugawa Japan increased in each feudal domain due to the development of local production (*tokusan-butsu*) as directed by the Tokugawa Shogunate.[5] In *tokusan-butsu*, each domain had dominant power not only over the production of local goods and foods, but also over their distribution and circulation by monopolizing their commerce. At the beginning, circulation was only confined to each domain's own area, but as the development of the market economy increased production, the covered area was enlarged to entire regions.

The freedom of economic activity in each feudal domain was basically undisturbed from the eighteenth century on. This decentralization of economic activity among other factors allowed the proto-industrialization of Tokugawa Japan.[6] By observing consumption trends during the age of proto-industrialization, which we must do in order to evaluate the development of the market economy, we can see that the Tokugawa shogunate did not interfere with the course of local culture, which each *han* had developed independently for a long time. This protection of local culture by the government facilitated the local people's acceptance of local diversity of production and consumption. It provided the energy for the development of the market economy in Tokugawa Japan.

In other words while the Tokugawa Shogunate society kept Japan united as a nation by centralizing governmental aspects such as diplomacy and military affairs, decentralization of economic, social and cultural affairs in local *han* allowed much progress to occur in society.

The Development of the Market Economy in Tokugawa Japan

In recent papers on proto-industrialization, it is pointed out that especially in Western European countries and Japan, family and family economy made great contributions to the development of market economy.[7] During the age of proto-industrialization in these countries, the family or household was the basic place of economic and social activity, and had its own life cycle due to aging and interaction of family members. It was through households that consumption and production commodities, labour, land and 'Z-goods' were exchanged within villages.

Especially when considering the development of market economy at the family or household level, introducing the concept of 'Z-goods' is very important.[8] Z-goods are basically goods, labour and services strictly produced and consumed within the household. As Tokugawa peasants encountered household goods and services similar to Z-goods on the market, they could directly calculate the price such commodities were worth. As a result a new phenomenon emerged in which peasants stopped producing their own Z-goods and instead spent their time earning higher wages to buy Z-goods from the market. As more and more peasants stopped producing their own Z-goods and took income jobs, the old-fashioned labour mentality began to wane, producing a backward-bending supply curve of labour.

Recently these arguments have become popular among socio-economic historians. What we need to know exactly, however, is how Tokugawa peasants organized Z-goods production within their family or household economy. Did they really depend on the backward-bending supply of labour? Is or was the mentality for labour supply really contrary to the market-oriented mentality both in theory and experience? To answer these questions, we have to adopt a different image of the market or market economy as a frame of reference to Tokugawa peasant economy.

Before the market economy, Tokugawa peasants organized various economic activities from agricultural production to wage labour and by-production during the slack season. Once labour and agricultural products began to be put on the market and given a price, peasants could estimate the price of other Z-goods, allowing Z-goods as a whole to become marketable.[9] If this is considered the starting point of market penetration into the family or household, most Tokugawa peasants were surely floating in a sea of market economy from the beginning of this period. Most likely, the stem family system evolved as a family or household formation by peasants to adapt to the penetration of such market economy into villages. Around the beginning of the seventeenth century, many peasants in Japan went out of their masters' houses to build their own residences in which the stem family formation was established and family members produced and consumed together.

What activities in the Japanese peasant family or household were house-keeping (like washing, cooking, nursing and breastfeeding)? When did the Japanese peasant woman eschew breastfeeding and nursing to earn more wages or income? Probably, during the great transformation of Japan as the rural world faced further development and penetration of the market economy.

NOTES

*   I would like to thank Andrew Lee who corrected my English. This research is financially supported by the Grant-in-Aid for Creative Scientific Research 2002–2006 of the Ministry of Education and Science in Japan.
1.   Concerning the idea, I partially depend on personal communication with Professor Akira Hayami.
2.   Hoppenbrouwers and van Zanden (2001) contains recent good papers on the issue.
3.   The old-fashioned concept of 'structure' is seen in Braudel (1977).
4.   Nishikawa (1978) is a good analysis of Choshu *han* budgets in the mid-nineteenth century.
5.   T.C. Smith (1988) called the decentralized Tokugawa pattern 'rural-centered growth'.
6.   Saito (1983) analyses the behaviour of Tokugawa peasants engaged in by-employment.
7.   See Oglivie and Cerman (1996) and Rudolph (1995).
8.   Hymer and Renick (1969) is the original paper on Z-goods. Recently, de Vries (1994) provides the argument of Z-goods related to the 'industrious revolution'.

9. Tomobe (2002) analyses peasant family or household production based on the village-collected data of Gifu prefecture in 1881.

REFERENCES

Anonymous (1994), 'The Industrious Revolution and the Industrial Revolution', *Journal of Economic History*, **54**, 249–70.

Braudel, F. (1977), *Afterthoughts on Material Civilization and Capitalism*, Baltimore, MD: Johns Hopkins University Press.

De Vries, J. (1994), 'The industrious revolutions and the Industrial Revolution', *Journal of Economic History*, **54**, 249–70.

Hoppenbrouwers, P., and J.L. von Zanden (eds) (2001), *From Peasants to Farmers? The Transformation of the Rural Economy and Society in the Low Countries (Middle Ages–19th Century) in the Light of the Brenner Debate*, Corn Publication series 2, Turnhout: Brepols.

Nishikawa, S. (1978), 'Productivity, subsistence, and by-employment in the mid-nineteenth century Choshu', *Explorations in Economic History*, **15**, 69–83.

Ogilvie, S.C., and M. Cerman (eds) (1996), *European Proto-Industrialization*, Cambridge: Cambridge University Press.

Rudolph, R.L. (ed.) (1995), *The European Peasant Family and Society*, Liverpool: Liverpool University Press.

Saito, O. (1983), 'Population and the peasant family economy in proto-industrial Japan', *Journal of Family History*, **8**, 30–45.

Smith, T.C. (1988), *Native Sources of Japanese Industrialization, 1750–1920*, Berkeley, CA: University of California Press.

Tomobe, K. (2002), 'Agricultural production function, labor productivity, and wage embedded in Meiji peasant productive behaviors: a quantitative analysis of Nohi Ryogoku Choson Ryakushi, ca. 1881', paper presented for the 13th Congress of the International Economic History Association, Buenos Aires, 22–26 July (KEIO-FCRONOS working paper series, no. 02–002).

DECENTRALIZATION IN THE HISTORY OF JAPAN

John Powelson

Relative to other countries, Japan has been decentralized from the beginning of history, but because of internal wars and other civil disturbances, that decentralization did not lead to significant economic development until approximately the thirteenth century. Thereafter, lower levels of society – farmers and merchants – formed village organizations that were the precursors of freedom, innovation and development. The most significant push towards these organizations and institutions occurred during the Tokugawa shogunate (1603–1868), with the development of modern farming, free merchants, new transportation, financial institutions, insurance companies and other instruments such as forward contracts, drafts and so on. All this occurred because the shogunate was too weak to stop it. This freedom reached its culmination in the 1920s but was stopped by high tariffs in the rest of the world and military adventurism by the Japanese army, which led to a war with China, economic sanctions, and finally to the Second World War. After the Second World War, the economic culture of the early twentieth century appeared to be restored, but the government – perhaps aping the military, perhaps feeling the sting of defeat – decided to exert central power once again and manage the economy: 'Japan Inc.'

In researching for my book, *Centuries of Economic Endeavor* (1992), I came upon a similarity in the economic development of North-Western Europe and Japan that (I believe) had been heretofore unnoticed. Decentralization and the diffusion of power had occurred in each area even before they had come into contact with each other early in the sixteenth century. Over and over again, in each area, the following sequence had occurred. Two major powers, call them king, church, emperor and nobility (for Europe) or shogun, emperor and nobility (for Japan) would be fighting each other (violently or non-violently) for some objective. A lower-ranking group, such as peasants, merchants or others, would ally itself with one or the other of the contending parties, demanding political concessions in exchange. If it won the struggle, the power of the lower group would be enhanced relative to the upper. If it lost, the lower-ranking group would bide its time until the next opportunity. Through numerous repetitions of this phenomenon, which are set forth in the book, power became diffuse in North-Western Europe and Japan, and the lower-ranking groups – taking advantage of their enhanced positions – obtained a freedom to innovate that existed nowhere else in the world.

Early in Japanese history, sovereign power was divided among two or more claimants. By 500, although in principle the emperor owned all land (still the primordial asset), in practice it was all privately held, with taxes paid to higher authorities, and ultimately to the emperor. Political pluralism consisted of various *uji* (clans) sitting in the court of the emperor.[1] These constantly quarrelled among themselves, and one family, the Soga, came to dominate the emperor, until it was defeated in 645 by a prince who later became emperor. Helping him was the Fujiwara family, which remained closely linked with the imperial house for the next four centuries. This dual power – royal emperor assisted by a commoner family – was a characteristic of medieval Japan.

Writing of the Taika ('Great Change') reform of 645, Jacobs reports: 'The Emperor, by agreeing to convert his personal political powers – then declining – into public powers, in order to maintain his titular authority, acknowledged a new balance of power'.[2] From that point on, the Fujiwara family gained increasing power over the emperor, marrying into his family, sometimes persuading the emperor to retire so that children of the Fujiwara might be brought up as new emperors. Two powerful families engaged in the Gempei War (1180–85) to gain control over the emperor. The winner, Minamoto Yoritomo, 'persuaded' the emperor to name him 'barbarian-suppressing general', or shogun. From that point on, until 1868, Japan was in principle ruled by the shogun, but during many periods the effective rule lay in landowners or the villagers upon their land.

Already in the ninth century, Japanese feudal estates were possessed by dual rulers, known as *honke* (noble patron) and *ryoke* (proprietor). Two centuries later, we find several more: *jishu* (owner), *ryoshu* (non-noble lord), *azukori dokoro* (middle-level manager) and *zuryo* (tax-collecting governor). Below them were tenants, free and half-free workers, and slaves. Except for the slaves all these had definable rights, known as *shiki,* which could be bought and sold.

Why did the Japanese, like the Europeans, allow both feudal officials and workers, first to have rights, but second, unlike the Europeans, to buy them and sell them? We can only suppose that some kind of balance of power had developed among them, both so that the emperor (and later the shogun) could not confiscate the rights, nor could each person impinge on the rights of others without buying them. Exactly how this balance of power emerged we have no way of knowing, but it is evidenced in many instances.

For example, Fairbank et al. write that the tax and law codes developed in 670 'were made piecemeal, with pragmatic compromises with existing institutions and the power of the various uji (clans)'.[3] Jacobs writes about the same period as one of 'constant coercion, coordination, and compromise ... a process repeated many times in Japanese history, first by the estates against the Taikwa imperialists in the court [seventh century], then by the markets, farmers, and the soldiers in the structure established by the estates (sho-en), and later by the merchants in the true, feudal structure'.[4]

Japanese historian Asakawa writes about the eighth century: 'The native

genius of the race for adaptability found its expression here in a free division
of the various interests and rights relative to land, in their investment in different lands, and in their almost infinite redivision and conveyance . . . the same
piece of land cultivated by one person soon giving titles and yielding profits
to many'.[5]

When Yoritomo, the first shogun, consolidated his victory by awarding the
lands of his enemies to his followers, he created two positions which later
became rivalries: *shugo* (provincial governor) and *jito* (estate steward):

> The jito, however, would not always pay the contractual amount of taxes. The
> resulting quarrels led to physical divisions of the property (*chubun*), sometimes
> worked out in compromise between the parties, sometimes imposed as punishments
> for non-payment of taxes, and sometimes decreed by [the emperor] in order to end
> an annoying dispute. The division might be made by separating out production units
> (*tsubowake chubun*) or by segmenting undifferentiated property (*shitaji chubun*).
> Sometimes the division was made in equal parts, sometimes not. A number of cases
> are cited in Mass.[6] The court did not always take the side of the *jito* as [the
> emperor's] representatives. In many cases it appeared most interested in enforcing
> contracts as they had originally been drawn.[7]

This quotation gives the impression of a multifaceted Japan, with no
concentration of power, either in the emperor, the shogun, the law courts or
other officials. Indeed this diffusion of power and compromise among contest-
ing groups has been a constant in Japanese history. 'A famous compromise
occurred in the fourteenth century, after the opposing military forces of the
shogun and one of the two rival emperors had occupied land to sustain themselves during the civil war. On conclusion of hostilities, the soldiers refused to
leave. Peace was established by permanent division of the yearly produce
between the absent proprietors and the soldiers'.[8]

Mass writes of *wayo* as a term often translated as compromise. 'Wayo was
not a mode of settlement adhering to any specific pattern but merely an expression of détente on any issue of long-standing dispute between jito and shugo'.[9]

Some have challenged the compromising nature of the Japanese. For example Najita argues that 'the characterization of Japan as a consensual society
proceeding along an evolutionary course or, at times, deviating from it, was
misleading'.[10] However these criticisms fail to compare Japan with the history
of other nations. While all nations reflect conflict and violence, the Japanese
have shown a greater ability than others to negotiate and compromise, to make
concessions by victors to vanquished, and to find ways for former adversaries
to trust each other. It is not possible for certain to state reasons for this but it
is logical to suppose – as I have – that the plural nature of Japanese society,
with no dominant power – political, military or economic – is the principal
cause of compromise-seeking.

During three centuries (1200–1500) a new cast of characters emerged, of which the most powerful were the *daimyo* who became feudal lords over estates known as *han,* which were similar to those of European feudalism. Village organizations and village militia also appeared. Two kinds of lower-level organizations evolved: *kuniikki,* made up of *bushidan* (warriors), and *tsuchi ikki,* composed of peasants.[11] Village governments evolved within the framework of the *han,* which sometimes held enough power to thwart the wishes of the *daimyo.* Sometimes they would appeal over the *daimyo*'s head to the shogun.

The *ikki* conducted rebellions:

Japan's history has been studded with peasant rebellions, caused by excessive taxes, forced loans, and demands for bribes; by daimyo and shogun monopolies and controls over prices and trade; by disputes over rights to land; and attempts by the lords to control peasant movements and behaviour. Both daimyo and shogun lived in fear of peasants, suspicious of their goings and comings, wondering what harm they would do next, or whether they would defect to other daimyo, or threaten the shogunate.[12]

The devolution of power to lower social levels is described by Davis:[13]

At about the time the first ikki organizations were being developed by minor bushi [warriors], the peasants of central Japan were creating similar political organizations for the purpose of waging their own struggles against shoen proprietors. This struggle was carried on in two ways. First, the new peasant political associations, forerunners of the characteristic village governments of the Edo period [1603–1868], aimed to assume all essential governmental functions relating to the daily life of the peasantry. These involved such matters as the management of projects requiring communal labor, but the most important, the transfer or adjudication of peasant disputes over land ownership and other vital matters from a shoen's headquarters in Kyoto to the village itself. This led to an enhancement of the average peasant's security of tenure. Second, the village government provided the unity and discipline necessary for direct confrontations with the shoen administration and its local agents. So long as the shoen proprietor was the principal opponent, such confrontations were normally limited to a single shoen, and wider peasant organizations or uprisings were quite rare during the fourteenth and early fifteenth centuries.

In 1428, however, a massive uprising swept Kyoto and the surrounding countryside, and as if this constituted a signal, more than a hundred similar rebellions followed before the end of the century. Nearly all these were larger than any of the ten or so recorded regional uprisings of the previous century.

During the period of the Warring States (sixteenth century), the *daimyo* warred against each other, virtually outside the control of the shogun. When Tokugawa Ieyasu conquered Hideyoshi and the other *daimyo* at the battle of Sekigahara in 1603, a new era in Japanese history emerged. But in the diffusion of power from higher to lower levels, it was simply a continuation of the past.

During the Tokugawa era (1603–1868) the power balance shifted in favour of merchants. In an edict of 1622, the shogun declared: 'Commercial transactions must be free, and no one shall act in the contrary or combine to raise prices'.[14] But this decree could not be enforced.

Peasants were frequently required by law of the domain to sell to monopoly merchants.[15] As new facets of trade and exchange opened, each was entrusted to some monopoly or semi-monopoly group: transport, principally between Osaka and Edo; foreign trade in port cities; exchange houses; and buying and selling of rice. For the most part these monopoly groups were registered and controlled by the city or the fief, although the shogun attempted from time to time to impose his own regulations. But the liberalism that could not be mandated grew by itself, not by control of monopolies but by their proliferation, not by enforcement of law but by its evasion, not by centralization of control but by its fragmentation. Liberalism was hindered primarily by guild restrictions: price controls and 'proper' procedures. But these might be offset by outside traders or simply the large numbers in some guilds, whose actions were more overlooked than overseen.[16]

Thus the shogunate became successively weaker, relative to lower social classes, during the Tokugawa period. Shogunal decrees were continuously repeated, an indication that they could not be enforced. Merchants loaned to the shogun, to *daimyo* and their retainers (*hatamoto*), and to the warrior class (samurai) and successfully insisted on repayment. The borrowers did not normally pull rank to demand forgiveness of their loans because they feared that if they did, no more would be forthcoming. The famous exclusion of foreigners was repeatedly violated, with smuggling in particular in the western provinces, where the shogun had little influence. Attempts of the shogun to establish a gold or bimetallic standard repeatedly failed because merchants preferred to trade in silver. When the shogun ordered a new coin in gold, merchants refused to use it. The shogun declared many price controls but they were repeatedly ignored.

The further development of village organizations also indicates the weakening of the shogunate.

During the Edo (Tokugawa) era, both the *daimyo* and the shogun accepted and endorsed the village autonomy of the previous era. Thus the trend away from centralized and toward village decision-making continued. Village officials handled local affairs and settled disputes. Villages had corporate powers – to contract, to sue and be sued – and they were collectively responsible for enforcing criminal law. Village matters were decided by consensus. 'It took tact, patience, and compromise to bring opinion to the desired consensus, but once that was achieved the headman spoke on behalf of all' (Smith 1970: 61). Land was managed by the peasant; he took his own risks, earned his own profits and suffered his own losses. We have seen that the central government attempted restrictions on peasant mobility and land sales as well as on the behaviour code of the farmers. Groups of five households became jointly responsible for taxes and for preventing violation of domain laws. However these were matters that the government could not enforce over time.[17]

Japan continued decentralized after the end of the Tokugawa shogunate, as the army was submerged and political organizations arose. Unfortunately Japan's isolation from the rest of the world during the 1920s and 1930s, due to high tariffs in other countries, trade restrictions and sanctions accompanying the Japanese war effort in China, led to new power for the Japanese army and a recentralization of government. At the end of the war the army was destroyed, and decentralized Japan became reinvigorated. This was the period (roughly 1945 to 1990) when Japan took on the reputation of a world economic leader.

NOTES

1. Hurst (1974: 39).
2. Jacobs (1958: 80).
3. Fairbank et al. (1978: 337).
4. Jacobs (1958: 129).
5. Asakawa (1916: 314).
6. Mass (1974: 171–7).
7. Powelson (1988: 179).
8. Powelson (1992), with reference to Asakawa (1914: 109), Duus (1969: 63), Hall (1970: 193), Wintersteen (1974: 211–20).
9. Mass (1974: 165–6).
10. Najita (1982: 9).
11. Davis (1974: 221–47).
12. Powelson (1992: 20).
13. Davis (1974: 226–7).
14. Takekoshi (1930, vol. 2: 489).
15. T.C. Smith (1970: 160).
16. Takekoshi (1930, vol. 3: 253). This paragraph draws on Powelson (1992: 37).
17. This paragraph draws on Powelson (1988: 185).

REFERENCES

Asakawa, Kanichi (1914), 'The origin of the feudal land tenure in Japan', *The American Historical Review*, **20** (1), 1–23.

Asakawa, Kanichi (1916), 'The life of a monastic Sho in medieval Japan', *Annual Report of the American Historical Association for 1916*, Washington DC.

Davis, David L. (1974), 'Ikki in medieval Japan', in John W. Hall and Jeffrey P. Mass (eds), *Medieval Japan: Essays in Institutional History*, New Haven, CT: Yale University Press.

Duus, Peter (1969), *Feudalism in Japan*, New York: Alfred A. Knopf.

Fairbank, John K., Edwin O. Reischauer and Albert M. Craig (1978), *East Asia: Tradition and Transformation*, Boston, MA: Houghton Mifflin Company.

Hall, John W. (1970), *Japan: From Prehistory to Modern Times,* New York: Dell.

Hurst, G. Cameron (1974), 'The structure of the Heian court: some thoughts on the nature of "Familial authority" in Heian Japan', in John W. Hall and Jeffrey P. Mass (eds), *Medieval Japan: Essays in Institutional History*, New Haven, CT: Yale University Press.

Jacobs, Norman (1958), *The Origin of Modern Capitalism and Eastern Asia*, Hong Kong: Cathay Press.

Mass, Jeffrey P. (1974), 'Jito land possession in the thirteenth century', in John W. Hall and Jeffrey P. Mass (eds), *Medieval Japan: Essays in Institutional History*, New Haven, CT: Yale University Press.

Najita, Tetsuo (1982), 'Introduction: a synchronous approach to the study of conflict in Japanese history', in Tetsuo Najita and J. Victor Koschmann (eds), *Conflict in Modern Japanese History: The Neglected Tradition*, Princeton, NJ: University Press.

Powelson, John P. (1988), *The Story of Land,* Cambridge, MA: Lincoln Institute of Land Policy.

Powelson, John P. (1992), *Centuries of Economic Endeavor*, Ann Arbor, MI: University of Michigan Press.

Smith, Thomas C. (1970), *The Agrarian Origins of Modern Japan,* Stanford, CA: Stanford University Press.

Takekoshi, Yosiburo (1930), *The Economic Aspects of the History of the Civilization of Japan*, vols 1, 2 and 3, New York: Macmillan.

Wintersteen, Prescott B. (1974), 'The Muromachi Shugo and Hansei', in John W. Hall and Jeffrey P. Mass (eds), *Medieval Japan: Essays in Institutional History*, New Haven, CT: Yale University Press, pp. 210–20.

Table 5.1 Number of eminently creative individuals in the history of Japan

Dean Keith Simonton

Generation	Medicine	Philos.	Poetry	Non-fict.	Fiction.	Drama	Sculpture	Painting	Ceramics	Sword	Total
500	0	0	0	0	0	0	0	0	0	0	0
520	0	0	0	0	0	0	0	0	0	0	0
540	0	0	0	0	0	0	0	0	0	0	0
560	0	0	0	0	0	0	0	0	0	0	0
580	0	0	0	0	0	0	1	0	0	0	1
600	0	0	0	0	0	0	0	0	0	0	0
620	0	0	0	0	0	0	0	0	0	0	0
640	0	0	1	0	0	0	1	0	0	0	2
660	0	0	1	0	0	0	0	0	0	0	1
680	0	0	5	0	0	0	0	0	0	0	5
700	0	0	8	1	0	0	0	0	0	1	10
720	0	0	6	0	0	0	0	0	0	0	6
740	0	0	3	0	0	0	0	0	0	0	3
760	0	0	2	1	0	0	0	0	0	0	3
780	0	0	0	0	0	0	0	0	0	0	0
800	0	0	1	0	0	0	0	0	0	0	1
820	0	0	0	0	0	0	0	1	0	0	1
840	0	0	3	0	0	0	0	1	0	0	4
860	0	0	4	1	0	0	0	0	0	0	5
880	0	0	2	1	0	0	0	0	0	0	3
900	0	0	4	0	0	0	0	0	0	0	4

Table 5.1 continued

Generation	Medicine	Philos.	Poetry	Non-fict.	Fiction.	Drama	Sculpture	Painting	Ceramics	Sword	Total
920	0	0	0	0	0	0	0	0	0	0	0
940	0	0	3	0	0	0	0	0	0	0	3
960	0	1	3	0	0	0	0	1	0	1	6
980	0	0	2	1	0	0	0	0	0	1	4
1000	0	0	2	1	1	0	0	1	0	1	6
1020	0	0	1	1	0	0	1	0	0	0	3
1040	0	0	0	1	1	0	0	1	0	0	3
1060	0	0	0	0	0	0	0	1	0	0	1
1080	0	0	4	1	0	0	0	1	0	0	6
1100	0	0	1	0	0	0	0	0	0	0	1
1120	0	0	1	0	0	0	1	0	0	0	2
1140	0	0	4	0	0	0	0	1	0	0	5
1160	0	0	3	0	0	0	2	1	0	0	6
1180	0	0	4	0	0	0	4	1	0	1	10
1200	0	0	3	0	0	0	3	0	0	3	9
1220	0	0	1	0	0	0	3	0	0	3	7
1240	0	0	2	0	0	0	2	0	0	3	7
1260	0	0	2	0	0	0	0	1	0	3	6
1280	0	0	2	0	0	0	0	1	0	3	6
1300	0	0	3	0	0	0	0	1	0	4	8
1320	0	0	4	1	0	0	0	2	0	3	10
1340	0	0	3	0	0	1	0	1	0	1	6
1360	0	0	4	0	0	0	0	1	0	1	6
1380	0	0	1	0	0	0	0	4	0	0	5

Year											Total
1400	0	0	0	0	0	1	0	2	0	0	3
1420	0	0	2	0	0	0	0	2	0	0	4
1440	0	0	3	0	0	1	0	2	0	0	6
1460	0	0	1	0	0	0	0	6	0	0	7
1480	1	0	3	0	0	0	0	1	0	1	5
1500	0	0	2	0	0	0	0	3	0	1	7
1520	2	0	0	0	0	0	0	1	0	0	1
1540	0	0	0	0	0	0	0	4	0	0	6
1560	0	0	2	0	0	0	0	3	0	1	6
1580	0	1	0	0	0	0	0	4	0	1	5
1600	0	3	3	0	0	0	0	7	3	1	15
1620	0	4	3	0	0	0	0	7	3	0	16
1640	1	4	3	1	1	0	1	6	3	2	21
1660	0	6	3	2	0	0	2	5	0	1	17
1680	2	8	11	1	0	1	1	6	0	0	27
1700	3	2	5	1	3	2	0	5	1	1	26
1720	5	3	0	2	0	3	0	7	0	0	16
1740	3	3	8	3	0	0	0	88	0	0	105
1760	2	5	5	3	3	3	0	19	8	1	53
1780	3	6	5	8	0	3	0	28	1	0	53
1800	3	6	4	5	5	0	0	15	2	2	39
1820	5	2	4	6	2	0	0	17	2	1	41
1840	2	4	4	2	0	3	0	8	1	0	25
1860	5	2	2	57	0	0	0	11	3	0	79
1880	5	3	1	6	4	1	3	68	5	0	96
1900	14	78	28	45	28	3	36	19	1	0	252
1920	83	11	45	15	59	46	15	66	10	0	350

Note: Dean Keith Simonton used, but did not publish, these data in his 1996 article on creativity in the history of Japan.

6. India

Deepak Lal

A major materialist hypothesis that political and military competition among states and decentralization promotes institutions which lead to economic freedom, innovation and development is belied by the case of India. I had used this counter-example to argue in my recent book *Unintended Consequences* (1998) that purely materialist explanations were insufficient to explain the differing economic outcomes in Eurasia over the last millennium.

In this chapter I first set out the similarities between India and 'Europe' in terms of being areas of Eurasia with cultural unity but political disunity. I then outline the reasons, based on my earlier book *The Hindu Equilibrium* (1988), why these similar initial conditions did not lead to the same institutional developments in India as in 'Europe'. In the final section I argue that, to understand the divergence in institutional developments, one has to bring in the role of what I have labelled 'cosmological beliefs', and show that even in this respect there were initially greater similarities between the cosmological beliefs of these two Eurasian civilizations, and that they only diverged because of two great Papal revolutions in the sixth to eleventh centuries initiated by the two Popes Gregory (the Great and the VII).

In this context it is worth noting that, the reason I have written 'Europe' is because as Michael Mann (1986) has rightly noted: 'Why is Europe to be regarded as a continent in the first place? This is not an ecological but social fact. It has not been a continent hitherto . . . Its continental identity was primarily Christian. It was known as Christendom rather than Europe' (p. 407). And when making civilizational comparisons the relevant civilization to be compared with Hindu India's is not even Christendom as a whole but Western Christendom.

I

Following in the footsteps of Kant (1784), Gibbon (1787) and Weber (1923), Eric Jones (1981) has based the rise of Western Christendom relative to the other great Eurasian civilizations on the political and institutional competition among the states which comprised a European 'state system'. This competition, apart from making each of the states more contestable and hence limiting the natural predatoriness of the state (see Lal: 1988, 1998 for a model of the predatory state) as emphasized for instance by North (1981), also allowed novelty and unorthodoxy to flourish and for new ideas and techniques to be rapidly diffused.

Why Western Christendom alone was able to create this 'equilibrium' state system was according to Jones due to the geography of the region. It had 'core areas' defined as pockets of alluvium on which intensive agriculture based on the plough could be carried out, but which were separated by natural barriers such as mountains, the sea, marshes and dense forests, so that it was difficult after the Romans to combine them into an empire. There was a natural division therefore into states whose basic geographical characteristics allowed them a stable existence.

But, as Jones himself noted of India: 'The matrix of nuclear areas and natural barriers smacks of Europe, especially as the same political divisions recur throughout history. As in Europe, it was costly to try to rule the subcontinent as a single empire. But why, given the makings of a similar set of competing polities, did no state's system emerge? The vessels were there but the brew of history was not poured into them' (p. 194). After a survey of various other explanations for the strength of India's social structure 'and the fluidity of its political and international systems' (Modelski 1964: 559), Jones writes: 'the conclusion seems to be that the structure of Indian society militated against political stability, and the lack of political stability militated against development' (p. 196).

But this only raises the further question: why did the Indian social structure arise and why did it not change if it was dysfunctional? Note also that, once the importance of this social structure is admitted in leading to different political and economic outcomes, despite ecological conditions being similar to 'Europe', the materialist hypothesis that it was the 'European' state system based on the region's ecology which led to economic freedom, innovation and development also collapses. For what has to be explained is why in similar ecological circumstances the differences in social structure arose, which in turn may have led to the 'state system', but certainly did lead to the lineaments of a free economy. That is of course the theme of my *Unintended Consequences*, and part of my explanation is given in section III below. But before that we need an explanation for the Indian social system – why it arose and how it impinged on the polity and thence the economy.

Finally, the lack of an 'equilibrium' state-system in India also meant that unlike 'Europe', political competition and decentralization were not preconditions for innovation and development. For one of the few things Indian historians agree on is that the periods of political stability under dynastic imperial rule – sometimes, though fairly rarely, extending over the whole of the subcontinent

– were also the most prosperous and glorious periods of Indian history, and the periods when innovation and growth took place. When these centralized empires broke down there was a regression, but not as serious as had been previously thought, as is documented in a detailed study by Bayly (1983) of the eighteenth century, when the Moghul empire disintegrated and the British empire was in its infancy. The basic reason for the prosperity of empires was that they provided the subcontinental law and order that allowed long-distance trade to develop, and their demise was usually accompanied by the decline of trade and commerce. As these periods of imperial stability were few and far between (encompassing parts of only eight centuries of the 23 since 300 BC) Indian standards of living probably cycled around a mean established around the second century BC. What we need to explain is the long cultural stability and economic stagnation in India despite its ecological and initially 'cosmological' similarities with Europe, and for this the origins of its unique social structure are crucial.

II

The three pillars of the Indian social system were: the relatively autarchic village communities, the caste system and the joint family. While modernization has undermined the first, the other two pillars stand firmly to our day. In my *Hindu Equilibrium* I provided an explanation for the origins of the caste system and the disjunction between state and society that it engendered, which in part explains the paradox about India that Jones and others have noted. Chapters 2 and 3 of the book may be consulted for the evidence on which the following assertions I shall be making are based.

Caste

I argued that the caste system arose once the nomadic Indo-European tribes, collectively labelled Aryans, who had entered the subcontinent through the northwest passes, spread along the Himalayan foothills towards Eastern India (modern-day Bihar) where they discovered the mineral deposits required to produce the implements they needed to clear the forests which covered the vast Indo-Gangetic plain, and to cultivate this vast alluvial plain with iron ploughs. Being nomadic pastoralists this new highly labour-intensive agricultural form was probably taught to them by the original inhabitants of parts of the plain who they initially enslaved and called Dasas. However they were faced by a number of problems.

Once the vast plain had been cleared it became the battle ground for various feuding monarchies. Though it formed a natural 'core area' in Eric Jones's sense, for an Indian state, given its size and the available military and transport technology, its domination by a single state has been episodic. Though its control and the dream of creating a subcontinental empire has been the lodestone of every Indian chieftain, these centripetal tendencies have been counterbalanced by the centrifugal forces flowing from geography.

This endemic political instability posed a problem in securing a stable labour supply for the relatively labour-intensive plough agriculture the Aryans came to practice. For it meant that various alternative methods of tying labour down when it was scarce relative to land (a common problem faced by Eurasian agrarian civilizations – see Domar 1970) were not available.

The most obvious is slavery. But in the absence of a centralized administrative system to register and enforce slave 'contracts' – which was precluded by the endemic political instability – a necessary condition for slavery to persist is the ease with which slaves can be distinguished from free men by some attribute such as pigmentation or language, the former being more inescapable than the latter. Slavery, apart from some domestic slaves, was unknown in India, though it seems that the original inhabitants, the Dasas – who were distinct from the Aryans in appearance and spoke a different language – were originally enslaved and then emancipated, largely because they had the agricultural skills, which the nomadic pastoralist Aryans did not, to work the plain. As agricultural techniques are notoriously imprecise and would also depend upon the willingness of the Dasas to demonstrate them, an incentive compatible solution was to emancipate them and give them autonomy in decision-making and control over agricultural operations, and incorporate them into the caste system at the lowest rung as Shudras, below the other three 'twice-born' Aryan castes (*varnas* – namely, *Brahmins* (priests), *Kshatriyas* (warriors) and *Vaishyas* (merchants)).

Other forms of tying labour down to land, like poll taxation, indenture or limitations on migration were also not feasible in the absence of a powerful centralized state and its attendant bureaucracy which was precluded by the endemic political instability.

The caste system provided a more subtle and enduring answer to the Aryans' problem of maintaining their rural labour supply. It established a decentralized system of control which did not require any overall (and larger) political community to exist for its survival and it ensured that any attempt to start new settlements outside its framework would be difficult if not impossible. The division of labour by caste and its enforcement by local social ostracism were central to the schema.

The endogamous specialization of the complementary services required as inputs in the functioning of a viable settlement meant that any oppressed group planning to leave a particular village to set up on its own would find – if it were confined to a single caste group – that it did not have the necessary complementary skills (specific to other castes) to start a new settlement. They would need to recruit members of other complementary castes to join them in fleeing the Aryan settlement. This would have been unlikely. For some of these other complementary castes would already have a high ritual and economic status, with little incentive to move to the more uncertain environment of a new settlement.

Neither could the oppressed lower castes (or individuals) acquire the requisite complementary skills themselves and thereby overcome the difficulty of putting together the required coalition to form a new settlement from within a single oppressed caste. This was unlikely to happen because of the social ostracism embedded in the caste system. It would not be profitable for other groups to impart the knowledge of these complementary skills, in as much as the ostracism involved in breaking the caste code, either as a consumer or producer (at each level of the caste hierarchy) would entail higher costs than any gains from performing any profitable arbitrage in the labour market that breaking the castewise segmentation of labour might entail.

Moreover, through the process of 'preference falsification' modelled by Kuran (1995), the system could continue even in the presence of 'hidden dissent'. For the system discourages open protests and disagreements; it uses open voting rather than secret ballots at meetings of caste councils to resolve disputes and it has sanctions against disagreements with the judgement of these councils. Thus a climate of opinion could be maintained that made it virtually impossible for dissenters to reveal themselves and thereby organize caste-breaking coalitions.

Group (but not individual) social and occupational mobility was allowed within the system, which allowed it to take account of changing balances in the demand and supply of different types of labour. Such mobility did occur within the inter-caste or intra-caste status hierarchy. This vertical mobility was dependent on the whole caste moving up the social hierarchy. This was usually done by adopting a different occupation, possibly migrating to a new region and demanding a higher ritual status. The very complicated vertical hierarchy of castes also made it easier to absorb new ethnic groups who arrived in successive waves throughout Indian history. Their place in the hierarchy was determined partly by their occupation and sometimes by their social origin.

That the caste system arose after the Aryans had begun to colonize the Indo-Gangetic plain is supported from the Vedic texts, where in the earlier Vedas going back to the time the Aryans were moving from the Indus along the foothills towards modern-day Bihar, it appears that their society was still organized on tribal lines. The caste differentiation of society only appears in the later Vedic texts which correspond to the later period when they had to clear the forests and cultivate the vast Indo-Gangetic plain and had to tie labour down to land.

Further support for this 'materialist' explanation for the caste system is provided by the different political and social organizations to be found in the foothills along which the Aryans initially travelled, and the plains. The former maintained the republican and tribal nature of the original Aryan tribes. Also, as a less labour-intensive form of agriculture apart from their traditional pastoralism was practised by the Aryans in these foothills, they did not need to tie down labour through the caste system. As such, even after the casteist monarchies were established on the plains, the republics in the foothills remained anti-casteist strongholds where two of the 'Protestant' anti-casteist religions of Buddhism and Jainism arose. These republics also provided a refuge for various groups – particularly the merchants (whose economic power was not matched by political power) – seeking to escape the casteist monarchies. The resulting conflict between tribe (in the foothill republics) and caste (in the monarchical plains) was only settled in the fourth century AD when Samudragupta destroyed the Licchavi republics, marking the final triumph of caste over tribe.

Thus caste only became part of Hindu cosmology after the Aryans had to colonize the plain, while various other aspects of the cosmology like reincarnation go back to the earlier period of the Rig Veda. Hence my argument that caste became part of Indian culture for the instrumental reason of tying labour down to land on the vast Indo-Gangetic plain.

Autarchic villages

The other decentralized element of the Hindu socio-political system were the relatively autarchic village communities which had the tradition of paying a certain customary share of the village output as revenue to the current overlord. The autarchy was the result of the endemic political instability which meant that long-distance trade was highly risky. The tradition of paying a fixed portion of output to the current overlord meant that any political victor had a ready and willing source of tribute already in place.

The caste system's vocational segmentation meant that war was a game for professionals, which saved the mass of the populace from being inducted into the deadly disputes of their changing rulers.[1] For the latter however, the ready availability of revenue from the customary local arrangements greatly reduced the effort required to finance their armies and courts. The village communities for their part bought relative peace and quiet and could carry on their daily business more or less undisturbed by the continuing aristocratic conflict. But this, together with the cosmological beliefs which placed the priest (*Brahmins*) above the rulers (*Kshatriyas*) meant that there was a complete disjunction between state and society.

This system yielded a fairly high standard of living from an early date (ca second century BC), but it stagnated at that level for virtually the following two millennia. But if some heroic estimates are to be believed, this stagnation was at the level of per capita income only achieved by Britain in the reign of Elizabeth I (Maddison: 1971).[2] So for a very long time, from about 350 BC, Indian living standards were probably much higher than in other Eurasian civilizations. India was in a 'high equilibrium trap', but given its relative success there was little pressure to change it from within and the foreigners who have ruled India during the last millennia – the Muslims and the British – far from succeeding in changing this system, most often succumbed to it.

Thus it would seem that the social system established in India did put India on a different political and socio-economic trajectory than the West, and given its resilience and functional success there was no chance of the 'European' state system being established in the northern plain.

South India

This still leaves South India, which according to Jones's map of Eurasian core areas in early modern times shows that this was a region of a multiplicity of alluvium areas which were separated by various natural barriers and should again have provided the ecological conditions for a system of stable states. But this did not happen. Why?

Stein (1980) has argued that the South developed a distinctive polity which he calls a 'segmentary state'. This consists of virtually independent local units which at times recognize the moral (but not real) overlordship of a sacred ruler. (See also Kulke 1995 for alternative views on the nature of the Indian state.) The most distinctive feature of the region 'was that of numerous and scattered peasant localities separated by large and small tracts of inhospitable land' (p. 73). These natural barriers between the localities would have made the unification of the region under one ruler problematic. Nor was there a South Indian equivalent of the constantly feuding *Kshatriya* kingdoms of the North. These local units which were composed of a number of large and densely populated villages – the segments of the segmentary state – were governed by assemblies (*sabhas*) of the local Brahmin and dominant landed *Shudra* castes. The constituents governed by these assemblies inhabited a single territorial unit.

There was no massive migration of Aryans from the North. The Aryans moving into the southern peninsula from about the sixth century BC were initially traders in search of the metals which were essential for providing the instruments of the Aryan colonization of the Gangetic plain – swords and ploughshares. The Gangetic supply of these metals had started drying up by the time of Ashoka (268–31 BC). Hence the Aryan thrust to the South. But no attempt was made at active colonization. Instead under the aegis of *Brahmin* migrants a gradual process of Sanskritization took place, which by the ninth century had created a distinct Hindu-Dravidian society and polity in this macro-region.

These *Brahmins*, by the time of Ashoka, had become the spearhead for the spread of Indian caste society in undeveloped areas all over India (Kosambi 1981): 'They first brought plough agriculture to replace slash and burn cultivation, or food gathering. New crops, knowledge of distant markets, organization of village settlements, and trade also came with them. As a result kings or kings-to-be invited *Brahmins*, generally from the distant, Gangetic basin, to settle in unopened localities' (p. 172). For this, they were given land grants which led to the distinctive *Brahmin* villages (*brahmadeyas*) of the South. With this direct control over the land and those dependent on land, the *Brahmins* in the South came – unlike their northern brethren – to have secular authority in addition to their sacerdotal ones.

The caste society in the South came to be based on a tripartite division of society. At the top were the *Brahmins* in a secular alliance with respectable (*sat*) agricultural *Shudra* castes and the rest of the lower castes – also designated as *Shudras* in terms of *varna* – who in turn were subdivided into left-hand and right-hand castes, with the latter being associated with agricultural production and local trade in agricultural commodities and the former with artisan production and trade in non-agricultural production. The *Vaishya* castes of the North seemed to be merged into the two bifurcated lower castes of *Shudras*.

The *Kshatriya* caste is notable for its absence, in part because as the *Brahmins* did not come to the South in the wake of a martial conquest, they would not have required any warrior class to maintain their position in the secular order (as they did in the North). 'Collaboration with would-be *Kshatriya* warriors could not strengthen, but only weaken, *Brahmin* secular authority' (Stein 1980: 71). They only needed to maintain their alliance with the dominant landed castes in their locality – groups which were probably responsible for inviting them as technical and ideological experts in the first place.

For the landed upper castes, the *Brahmins* provided the form of social organization and ideology (the caste system) to tie down relatively scarce labour to land (as in the North) in these 'core' areas where labour-intensive plough agriculture – also probably brought from the North – was feasible. The *sabhas* and the corporatist nature of the institutions for defence and governance of the localities in the segmentary state could have been an adaptation by the *Brahmins* of the caste system to the older forms of government – with the difference that these were now controlled by the local dominant groups, the *Brahmins* and the upper-caste landlords.

Once established, by about the ninth century AD, this peasant 'ecosystem' remained virtually unaltered up the nineteenth century (see Stein 1980: 24–5).

Thus, even though it had ecological similarities with 'Europe', by the time of the Islamic invasions of North India (AD 1000), the whole of the subcontinent was in the grip of that equilibrium marked by cultural stability (albeit with variations between the North and the South) and economic stagnation which I have labelled the 'Hindu equilibrium'.

III

If ecological conditions did not differ markedly between India and 'Europe', we need to look elsewhere for the Great Divergence between the Eurasian civilizations. In my *Unintended Consequences*, like Weber and more recently Landes (1998), I argued that material differences cannot provide the answer and that cultural differences must be taken into account. As culture is a murky concept which is as a result highly suspect in the eyes of economists, I provided a definition which I hope is both rigorous and useful.

The definition adopted by ecologists is particularly useful (see Colinvaux 1983). They emphasize that unlike other animals, the human one is unique because its intelligence gives it the ability to change its environment by learning. It does not have to mutate into a new species to adapt to the changed environment. It learns new ways of surviving in the new environment and then fixes them by social custom. These social customs form the culture of the relevant group, which are transmitted to new members of the group (mainly children) who do not then have to invent these 'new' ways *de novo* for themselves.

This definition of culture fits in well with the economists' notion of equilibrium. Frank Hahn describes an equilibrium state as one where self-seeking agents learn nothing new so that their behaviour is routinized. It represents an adaptation by agents to the economic environment in which the economy 'generates messages which do not cause agents to change the theories which they hold or the policies which they pursue'. This routinized behaviour is clearly close to the ecologists' notion of social custom which fixes a particular human niche. On this view the equilibrium will be disturbed if the environment changes and so, in the subsequent process of adjustment, the human agents will have to abandon their past theories, which would now be systematically falsified. To survive they must learn to adapt to their new environment through a process of trial and error. There will then be a new social equilibrium, which relates to a state of society and economy in which 'agents have adapted themselves to their economic environment and where their expectations in the widest sense are in the proper meaning not falsified'.

It is useful to distinguish between two major sorts of beliefs relating to different aspects of the environment. These relate to what I labelled the material and cosmological beliefs of a particular culture. The former relate to ways of making a living and concerns beliefs about the material world, in particular about the economy. The latter are related to understanding the world around us and mankind's place in it which determine how people view their lives – its purpose, meaning and relationship to others. There is considerable cross-cultural evidence that material beliefs are more malleable than cosmological ones (see Hallpike 1986, Boyd and Richerson 1985). Material beliefs can alter rapidly with changes in the material environment. There is greater hysteresis in cosmological beliefs, on how, in Plato's words, 'one should live'. Moreover, the cross-cultural evidence shows that rather than the environment it is the language group which influences these worldviews.

This distinction between material and cosmological beliefs is important for economic performance because it translates into two distinct types of 'trans-actions costs' (Lal 1999, Chapter 11). Broadly speaking, transactions costs can be distinguished usefully as those costs associated with the efficiency of exchange, and those which are associated with policing opportunistic behav-iour by economic agents. The former relate to the costs of finding potential trading partners and determining their supply–demand offers, the latter to enforcing the execution of promises and agreements. These two aspects of transactions need to be kept distinct. Douglass North (1990) and Oliver Williamson (1985) have both evoked the notion of transactions costs and used them to explain various institutional arrangements relevant for economic performance. They are primarily concerned with the cost of opportunistic behaviour, which arises for North with the more anonymous non-repeated transactions accompanying the widening of the market, and for Williamson from the asymmetries in information facing principals and agents, where crucial characteristics of the agent relevant for measuring performance can be concealed from the principal. Both these are cases where it is the policing aspects of transactions costs which are at issue, not those concerning exchange.

Cosmological beliefs are part of the culture which seeks to constrain basic human nature to minimize these policing transactions costs. Evolutionary anthropologists and psychologists maintain that human nature was set during the period of evolution ending with the Stone Age. Since then there has not been sufficient time for any further evolution. This human nature appears darker than Rousseau's and brighter than Hobbes's characterizations of it. It is closer to Hume's view that 'there is some benevolence, however small . . . some particle of the dove kneaded into our frame, along with the elements of the wolf and serpent'. For even in the hunter-gatherer Stone Age environment the supremely egotistical human animal would have found some form of what evolutionary biologists term 'reciprocal altruism' useful. Cooperation with one's fellows in various hunter-gatherer tasks yields benefits for the selfish human which can be further increased if he can cheat and be a free rider. In the repeated interactions between the selfish humans comprising the tribe, such cheating could be mitigated by playing the game of 'tit for tat'. Evolutionary biologists claim that the resulting 'reciprocal altruism' would be part of our basic Stone Age human nature.

Archaeologists have also established that the instinct to 'truck and barter', the trading instinct based on what Sir John Hicks used to call the 'economic principle' – 'people would act economically; when an opportunity of an advantage was presented to them they would take it'– is also of Stone Age vintage (see Ridley 1996, Chapter 10, esp. pp. 209–10 and references). It is also part of our basic human nature.

With the rise of settled agriculture and the civilizations that evolved around them, however, and the stratification this involved between three classes of men – those wielding the sword, the pen and the plough – most of the Stone Age basic instincts which comprise our human nature would be dysfunctional. Thus with the multiplication of interactions between human beings in agrarian civilizations, many of the transactions would have been with anonymous strangers whom one might never see again. The 'reciprocal altruism' of the Stone Age which depended upon a repetition of transactions would not be sufficient to curtail opportunistic behaviour.

Putting it differently, the 'tit for tat' strategy for the repeated Prisoners' Dilemma (PD) game amongst a band of hunter-gatherers in the Stone Age would not suffice with the increased number of one-shot PD games that will arise with settled agriculture and its widening of the market. To prevent the resulting dissipation of the mutual gains from cooperation, agrarian civilizations internalized restraints on such 'antisocial' action through moral codes which were part of their 'religion'. But these 'religions' were more ways of life, as they did not necessarily depend upon a belief in God.

The universal moral emotions of shame and guilt are the means by which these 'moral codes' embodied in cultural traditions are internalized in the socialization process during infancy. Shame was the major instrument of this internalization in the great agrarian civilizations. Their resulting cosmological beliefs can be described as being 'communalist'.

The basic human instinct to trade would also be disruptive for settled agriculture. For traders are motivated by instrumental rationality which maximizes economic advantage. This would threaten the communal bonds that all agrarian civilizations have tried to foster. Not surprisingly most of them have looked upon merchants and markets as a necessary evil, and sought to suppress them and the market which is their institutional embodiment. The material beliefs of the agrarian civilizations were thus not conducive to modern economic growth.

There were greater similarities in the 'communalist' cosmological beliefs of the great Eurasian agricultural civilizations than differences. Nowhere was this more so than between Hinduism and Christianity. First, in both there was a disjunction between power and status, where the priests were subject to the king but considered themselves to be religiously or absolutely superior. Second, both – as well as the Greeks – were to an extent individualistic. But this individualism as Dumont (1986) has emphasized was 'out-worldly' rather than the 'in-worldly' individualism that has come to define modern individualism, of the individual in the world. Although for the Greeks, Christians and Hindus salvation was ultimately personal, and they allowed for a role for the individual renouncer, as among the Greek Stoics, the form of individualism was 'out-worldly'. For, as Dumont states: 'the renouncer is self-sufficient, concerned only with himself. His thought is similar to that of the modern individual, but for one basic difference: we live in the social world, he lives outside it' (p. 26).

That this 'out-worldly' individualism was not of the 'in-worldly' type now associated with the West is brought out clearly by Gellner (1988). He tries to picture a Hindu Robinson Crusoe, a polyglot called Robinson Chatterjee. 'A Hindu Crusoe,' he writes, 'would be a contradiction. He would be destined for perpetual pollution: if a priest, then his isolation and forced self-sufficiency would oblige him to perform demeaning and polluting acts. If not a priest, he would be doomed through his inability to perform the obligatory rituals' (p. 121).

The Great Divergence arose in my view because the West alone departed from this 'out-worldly' individualism common to many of the great agrarian Eurasian civilizations. Uniquely for Eurasian agrarian civilizations, whose common cosmological beliefs can be broadly categorized as 'communalist', medieval Europe departed from the pattern and became individualist (Dumont 1986). This was due to the reinterpretation of Pauline Christianity by St Augustine in the fifth century in his 'City of God' which converted the 'otherworldly' individualism of the Christian Church (a trait which it shares with Hinduism) into an in-worldly one by demanding the Church be put above the state (Dumont 1986) a demand that Pope Gregory VII fulfilled in the eleventh century with his injunction 'Let the terrestrial kingdom serve – or be the slave of the celestial', and which led to the so-called Papal legal revolution.

This change in cosmological beliefs is of course the factor which Max Weber and more recently David Landes have identified as the cause of the Great Divergence, but as both base it on the Protestant Ethic, they have got their dates wrong. For as Hicks (1969) noted, an essential element in the rise of capitalism was: 'the appearance of banking, as a regular activity. This began to happen long before the Reformation; in so far as the "Protestant Ethic" had anything to do with it, it was practice that made the Ethic not the other way round' (pp. 78–9).

By contrast I have argued in *Unintended Consequences* that the change in cosmological beliefs was mediated by the Catholic Church in the sixth–eleventh centuries, through its promotion of individualism, first in family affairs by Pope Gregory the Great, and later in material relationships which included the introduction of all the legal and institutional requirements of a market economy as a result of Gregory VII's Papal revolution in the eleventh century (see Berman 1983). These twin Papal revolutions arose because of the unintended consequences of the Church's search for bequests – a trait that goes back to its earliest days.

But this is another story and this is not the place to retell it. Suffice it to say that I hope I have said enough by comparing the similarities in the initial material conditions and cosmological beliefs of India and 'Europe' to show first, that ecology alone cannot explain the rise of the state system in 'Europe', and second, that it is the changes in cosmological beliefs in 'Europe' which must also be included in the 'package' of explanations as Needham (1969) has called it that explains the great divergence of the civilizations of Eurasia.

NOTES

1. I would accept the point made by Erich Weede in his comments on this chapter that this led to the disarming of the population which could not then directly threaten the rulers to obtain various rights. This was a crucial difference from the system used in European manorial feudalism – to tie scarce labour down to land. I would also accept his point that the Muslim centuries perpetuated the economic stagnation because of 'sultanism'. But neither point contradicts my main argument that it was the Indian socio-economic system created over the Hindu millennia which provided cultural stability and economic stagnation in India.

2. The only relative comparisons of standards of living in India and other countries are based on impressionistic travellers' accounts. Amongst them are those by the Greek Megasthenes (ca. 315 BC), the Chinese travellers Fan Hsien (AD 405–411), and Huan Tsiang (AD 630–644) and the Arab Alberuni (AD 1030). These suggest that Indian standards of living were certainly a match for and probably higher than those of these contemporaneous civilizations.

REFERENCES

Bayly, C. (1983), *Rulers, Townsmen and Bazars*, Cambridge: Cambridge University Press.

Berman, H.J. (1983), *Law and Revolution*, Cambridge, MA: Harvard University Press.

Boyd, R., and P.J. Richerson (1985), *Culture and the Evolutionary Process*, Chicago, IL: University of Chicago Press.

Colinvaux, P. (1983), *The Fates of Nations*, London: Penguin.

Domar, E. (1970), 'The causes of slavery or serfdom: a hypothesis', *Journal of Economic History*, **30**, 18–32.

Dumont, L. (1986), *Essays on Individualism*, Chicago, IL: University of Chicago Press.

Gellner, E. (1988), *Plough, Book and Sword: the Structure of Human History*, London: Collins Harvill.

Gibbon, E. (1787), *The Decline and Fall of the Roman Empire*, reprinted 1985, London: Penguin Classics.

Hahn, F. (1973), *On the Notion of Equilibrium in Economics*, Cambridge: Cambridge University Press.

Hallpike, C.R. (1986), *The Principles of Social Evolution*, Oxford: Clarendon Press.

Hicks, J.R. (1969), *The Theory of Economic History*, Oxford. Oxford University Press.

James, Eric L. (1981), *The European Miracle*, Cambridge: Cambridge University Press.

Kant, I. (1784), 'Idea of a universal history from a cosmopolitan point of view', reprinted in P. Gardner (ed.) (1959), *Theories of History,* New York: Free Press.

Kosambi, D.D. (1981), *The Culture and Civilization of Ancient India*, New Delhi: Vikas.

Kulke, A. (ed.) (1995), *The State in India 1000–1700*, New Delhi: Oxford University Press.

Kuran, T. (1995), *Private Truths, Public Lies*, Cambridge, MA: Harvard University Press.

Lal, D. (1988), *The Hindu Equilibrium*, Oxford: Clarendon Press.

Lal, D. (1998), *Unintended Consequences*, Cambridge, MA: MIT Press.

Lal, D. (1999), *Unfinished Business*, New Delhi: Oxford University Press.

Landes, D.S. (1998), *The Wealth and Poverty of Nations*, New York: Norton.

Maddison, A. (1971), *Class Structure and Economic Growth: India and Pakistan Since the Moghuls*, London: Allen and Unwin.

Mann, M. (1986), *The Sources of Social Power*, Vol 1, Cambridge: Cambridge University Press.

Modelski, G. (1964), 'Kautilya: foreign policy and international system in the ancient Hindu world', *American Political Science Review,* **58**, 549–60.

Needham, J. (1969), *The Grand Titration: Science and Society in East and West*, London: Allen and Unwin.

North, D. (1981), *Structure and Change in Economic History*, New York: Norton.

North, D. (1990), *Institutions, Institutional Change and Economic Performance*, Cambridge: Cambridge University Press.

Ridley, M. (1996), *The Origins of Virtue*, London: Viking.

Stein, B. (1980), *Peasant State and Society in Medieval South India*, New Delhi: Oxford University Press.

Weber, M. (1923), *General Economic History*, reprinted 1961, New York: Collier.

Williamson, O.E. (1985), *The Economic Institutions of Capitalism*, New York: Free Press.

COMMENT

Dietmar Rothermund

Deepak Lal, like many other scholars, wants to explain the 'Great Divergence' between Europe and Asia. The causes as well as the starting point of this divergence are debated, and the respective arguments are interrelated. Since the recent work of Kenneth Pomeranz (2000) who argues that at least parts of China were as 'developed' in the eighteenth century as Western Europe and that the 'divergence' obviously manifested itself fairly late, the explanation of its causes have also to be re-examined. If one opts for differences in 'cosmological beliefs', as Deepak Lal does, one would tend to prefer patterns of causation which go far back into ancient history – and in some respects he does that by outlining the evolution of the caste system and the relation between state and society. He claims that there was 'a complete disjunction between state and society' in India. He seems to agree with Eric Jones and quotes his conclusion that 'the structure of Indian society militated against political stability, and the lack of political stability militated against development'. For Jones competition within a fairly stable but decentralized state system was the secret of European development. But Lal then doubts the 'materialist' arguments with which Jones supports the specific characteristics of the European state system.

In his subsequent discussion of the 'state system' Lal wavers between acknowledging similarities of the European and the Indian state systems and stressing their differences. As far as the differences are concerned he mentions repeatedly 'political instability' in India. But except for asserting that this instability led to a decline of long-distance trade, he does not mention any criteria by which one could measure it. In discussing long-distance trade one should distinguish between trade in bulk commodities like grain and valuable commodities such as precious stones, textiles, metal and so on. The latter trade was well developed in all periods of Indian history. The trade in bulk commodities on overland routes involved high costs of transportation. Pack animals were the usual means of transport and the cost of their maintenance had to be taken into consideration. Grain was thus rarely transported on overland routes unless it was required for the support of armies. It was however transported overseas, and the Portuguese noted with amazement that rice from Gujarat would even reach the coasts of Africa or Hormuz in the Persian Gulf.

As far as 'political instability' is concerned, medieval India was probably at least as stable as medieval Europe. But the massive expenditure on warfare in the late medieval period – a factor not touched upon by Lal – so to speak pre-empted development in other spheres. This will be discussed later on.

After the demise of the last ancient empire of India, the Vakataka-Gupta empire, regional kingdoms emerged throughout India which copied more or less the court culture, the methods of administration and warfare and so on, of the Guptas. Whereas Buddhism had been of great political importance from the days of the Maurya empire, it declined in the regional kingdoms of medieval India. Buddhist monks were highly mobile messengers of imperial culture. They were also not tied down by the caste system. But there was a strange paradox which finally led to the decline of Buddhism. The individual monk spurned private property, but the Buddhist order (*sangha*) established great monasteries supported by land grants and donations. This is how Buddhism became too 'expensive' in the course of time. *Brahmins* required only small land grants for their families. They were ready to settle anywhere at the invitation of kings and they played an important role in the extension of royal culture. I do not think that one could speak of 'a disjunction of state and society' in this context. On the contrary, *Brahmins* were agents of state formation. But they also articulated social relations in terms of the caste system, and elevated and legitimized the king with their rituals. The model of Indian kingship was so successful that it could be even transferred to South East Asia – by invitation and not by conquest.

The medieval kingdoms formed a fairly stable system of states. In keeping with the means of warfare and political power at their disposal, their actual control was limited to a radius of about 200 km around their capital. But their range of military intervention could go beyond 1000 km. There was considerable interregional trade carried on by guilds of traders. There was also a fairly free 'international' maritime trade. There were occasional interventions in this arena too, as the Chola king showed with his maritime expedition against Srivijaya (on Sumatra) at the beginning of the eleventh century. Srivijaya had obviously tried to interfere with the China trade of the Cholas.

Competition among the medieval kingdoms led to cultural innovation in the styles of literature, sculpture, construction of temples and so on. Literatures in the regional language emerged which absorbed many elements of Sanskrit. But this 'system' prevailing until about 1200 was upset when conquerors from West Asia swept through North India and established the Delhi sultanate. Literally the 'kingpin' of this new system was the 'man on horseback', usually a slave trained from his childhood as an expert cavalryman. The new type of cavalry warfare had an enormous range of swift intervention, but it was also very expensive. Good war-horses did not flourish in India and had to be imported from western and central Asia at very high prices. The sultans established a system of military feudalism for the maintenance of their huge cavalry contingents. The man on horseback was also a good revenue collector. The share of agrarian surplus amassed by these people was very high. All Hindu states which wanted to survive the onslaught of the sultans had to adopt the same system of cavalry warfare. It was characteristic that Krishnadevaraya, the greatest king of Vijayanagar in the early sixteenth century, once called himself a 'Hindu sultan'.

The cavalry system also had an impact on the functions of urban centres and the structure of local government. Earlier institutions of local government were wiped out, the cavalry captain was not only the commander of the garrison, but also the 'district officer'. The town in which he resided was first and foremost a military headquarter accommodating large numbers of troops and horses; it was also a market place, and the centre of 'civil' administration. Since their functions were similar all over India, such towns looked alike everywhere. Military urbanization was very different from the type of urbanity prevailing in earlier times. The Mughal empire did not change this style very much. It only introduced the field artillery as an even more expensive type of armament which assured the central control of the Great Mughal over a vast empire.

The 'Hindu equilibrium' which Deepak Lal has stressed was maintained under this oppressive weight of military feudalism. The Hindus retained their identity but became introvert. It is only under such conditions that one could speak of a 'disjunction of state and society'. This was continued under British colonial rule. The British took over the prevailing structure of the state as a going concern. They also introduced new methods of infantry warfare and conquered India with Indian soldiers drilled and employed by them at the expense of the Indian taxpayer. They continued the old methods of revenue collection, but collected the revenue much more efficiently. They replaced the military district officer with a civilian. They finally spent less on warfare in India but transferred a great deal of the revenue abroad.

The British had been attracted to India by the flourishing trade in Indian cotton textiles. In the seventeenth and eighteenth century India was one of the greatest producers of such textiles worldwide and its products were in great demand. Cotton textiles conquered the European market with amazing speed in the seventeenth century. In 1700 legislation was passed in Great Britain which debarred printed Indian cotton goods from the British home market, but this led to a surge of activities of London cotton printers who imported white Indian cloth as a semi-finished product which then became the most important stock in trade of the East India Company, before Chinese tea challenged its position.

With the London cotton printers, some of whom employed 400 workers in their 'proto-industrial' workshops in the early eighteenth century, started a chain of import substitution which led to the industrial revolution. Compared to the manufacture of woollens, the cotton industry was a marginal one in Great Britain and economic historians have wondered why it became the vanguard of the industrial revolution. There is a simple explanation: the scarcity of labour. When import substitution had reached cotton spinning, it soon turned out that this became a bottleneck. One weaver requires yarn spun by six to eight spinners. Contrary to the usual complaints of the woollen industry, it prospered throughout and was in fact driven to profitable innovations by competition with the cotton textiles. There was no chance that spinners and weavers would leave a 'decaying' woollen industry and shift to the cotton industry. Mechanical equipment for increasing productivity in cotton spinning thus became the vanguard of the industrial revolution. This equipment was rather cheap and could have been easily reproduced in India, but since there was no scarcity of labour in India, neither the spinning-jenny nor any of the subsequent machines were needed in India. The first half of the nineteenth century was then characterized by a long deflation as the British pumped the silver out of India which they had earlier injected into it when buying cotton textiles. As long as food and raw materials were cheap due to the decline in prices, Indian spinners and weavers could make both ends meet – maintaining a low-level equilibrium. These conditions changed when silver once more poured into India for the investment in railways. The silver started to depreciate in the world market and India absorbed great quantities of it. There was a slow but steady inflation. Spinners and weavers were at a disadvantage now and a modern Indian textile industry could take off, greatly encouraged by British manufacturers of textile machinery who were eager to sell their machines.

But Indian industry remained one without any internal linkages because the opening of the Suez Canal and steamer traffic lowered freight rates and India lost its locational advantage. Even British coal was cheaper in Bombay than Indian coal (mined in the hinterland of Calcutta). I cannot outline the economic history of British India in detail. I only wish to add that the sequence war–depression–war contributed to a process of decolonization. India emerged from the Second World War as a creditor rather than as a debtor of Great Britain. In the course of that war the colonial state had been turned into an interventionist one. The instruments of this interventionism were inherited by independent India and used for the promotion of rapid industrialization based on import substitution behind protective tariff walls. India did build up internal industrial linkages in this way, but at the price of opting out of competition in a growing world market – a decision whose unintended consequences still impair India's industrial progress.

The interventionist Indian state stressed centralization and eliminated competition which was thought to imply the wasting of scarce resources. Under the Government of India Act of 1935, industry had been a provincial subject; it should have reverted to the provinces (federal states) of India after the Defence of India Act, which had introduced central control, had lapsed. But Nehru saw to it that central control was not only maintained but further strengthened in independent India. This was a natural reaction to the industrial impotence of India induced by colonial rule. It was successful in the short run but had unfortunate effects in the long run.

In concluding my comments I should like to stress that I am less inclined to stress 'cosmological beliefs' or the 'caste system' in explaining the impediments to Indian development. I would tend to agree with Pomeranz that the Great Divergence originated in the eighteenth century rather than much earlier. In earlier centuries the South Asian subcontinent was blessed with a surplus of arable land. The subcontinent covers about 4 million square kilometres. Half of this area is cultivable, but probably only a quarter of it was actually cultivated before the eighteenth century. There were still vast tracts of forest at that time. With the exception of witnessing occasional regional famines, foreign visitors generally attested to the higher living standard of South Asia as compared to contemporary Europe. But I would rate the long period of military feudalism as a negative influence which dampened local initiatives in India. Colonial rule then extended the methods of control of this earlier regime, made India a passive appendage of the British imperial system, then introduced a wartime interventionist regime which was taken over by independent India for good reasons but with negative consequences for its further development.

References

Pomeranz, Kenneth (2000), *The Great Divergence: Europe, China and the Making of the Modern World Economy*, Princeton, NJ: Princeton University Press.

COMMENT

Erich Weede

Lal's chapter includes some criticism of Jones's (1981) explanation of the rise of the West and stagnation in Asia. Since I have accepted most of Jones's explanation in my own work (Weede 2000), I want to defend the defensible parts of Jones's analysis. I also want to amend Lal's analysis from a fairly orthodox Weberian perspective.

One may reduce the core of Jones's (1981) analysis to a causal chain:

1. The ecological characteristics of a region make either an empire or an interstate system likely.
2. Interstate competition, as in Europe, helps to limit the natural predatoriness of the state.
3. Overcoming the predatory state contributes to economic development and growth.

I do accept the second and the third part of this causal chain, but I reject the first proposition. The unification of much of Europe by the Roman empire in itself calls the ecological predestination of the European state system into question. Having extensively travelled in China, I find an ecological predestination of empire quite implausible for China.

Without the ecological proposition, Jones's (1981) 'materialist' explanation of freedom, property rights and development becomes a kind of 'geopolitical' explanation. Whatever the label, I agree with Lal that immaterial factors, like religion and the caste system, have to be included in an explanation of economic stagnation in India.

Before turning to those issues one should consider whether the geopolitical circumstances of Europe and India were as similar as Lal seems to contend. In my view there was the similarity of the existence of multiple polities most of the time in both areas. But there was also the dissimilarity in unit persistence between both areas. Lal recognizes this by his reference to the 'endemic political instability' in India. Whereas many European political units, like England, France, Castille-Spain, Austria, the Netherlands, Brandenburg-Prussia-Germany, Denmark or Sweden, lasted for centuries even where frontiers have been shifted, political unit survival was more precarious in India. Only in an interstate system, where polity and dynastic persistence is the rule rather than the exception, did rational rulers face an incentive to limit their natural predatoriness and to recognize the property rights of some of their subjects. The less stable or persistent polities and dynasties are, the less reason there is for rulers to limit their confiscatory inclinations.

Concerning the effects of the caste system I am inclined to give much more credit to the 'orthodox' Weberian (1921/1978) analysis of India than of either the West or of China. In Weber's analysis, the spirit of Hinduism and the caste system reinforced a flight from this world rather than attempts to improve it. Moreover, the caste system came close to preventing individual mobility, thereby making a wealth-maximizing division of labour impossible. And the caste system deterred innovation because of magical beliefs, according to which innovation might not only be incompatible with caste obligations, or *dharma*, and therefore damage one's prospects of upward mobility in one's next life, but according to which forgetting one's caste obligations also harms other members of the caste. So conformity pressure within castes made the introduction of new working techniques extraordinarily difficult in Hindu India.

In Weber's (1921/1978) account the political characteristics of Hinduism also matter. For orthodox Hindus, war-making and ruling others is a right and a duty of a special caste. Lal also refers to this fact in the following observation: 'The caste system's vocational segmentation ... saved the mass of the populace from being inducted into the deadly disputes of their changing rulers.' As a statement of fact I do not want to dispute it. Building on Weber (1921/1978), Andreski (1968) and to a lesser degree Pipes (1999), however, I offer a different interpretation. Where the mass of the population is excluded from war-fighting, there is little reason for rulers to grant rights, including property rights, to the disarmed population. In India not only Hinduism and the caste system contributed to the disarmament of most of the population, but the heterodox offspring of Hinduism, that is Jainism and Buddhism did so too. By teaching *ahimsa*, or pacifism, they made the assertion of rights by subjects impractical.

Finally, I regard all explanations of India's stagnation as incomplete which neglect the fact that most of India was ruled by Muslims for centuries. Muslim rule in India has been patrimonial rather than feudal, in Weberian (1922/1964) terms even 'sultanistic'. Sultanism prevails where the ruler recruits his staff largely from foreigners or slaves, that is he rules with the assistance of people who are extremely dependent upon him and who therefore are reliable tools of arbitrary rule. Whereas feudalism in the West prepared for the later rule of law, sultanism in India had no comparable positive impact. Moreover, the practice of polygyny among the ruling Muslim classes of India implied too much reproduction at the top of society and too little at the bottom of it. This reduced the prospects of upward mobility and thereby contributed to political instability as well as economic stagnation.

References

Andreski, Stanislav (1968), *Military Organization and Society*, 2nd edn, Berkeley, CA: University of California Press.

Jones, Eric L. (1981), *The European Miracle*, Cambridge: Cambridge University Press.

Pipes, Richard (1999), *Property and Freedom,* New York: A.A. Knopf.

Weber, Max (1921), *Gesammelte Aufsätze zur Religionssoziologie.* 2nd vol, reprinted 1978, Tübingen: Mohr.

Weber, Max (1922), *Wirtschaft und Gesellschaft*, reprinted 1964, Köln: Kiepenheuer and Witsch.

Weede, Erich (2000), *Asien und der Westen. Politische und kulturelle Determinanten der wirtschaftlichen Entwicklung*, Baden-Baden: Nomos.

7. Islamic statecraft and the Middle East's delayed modernization

Timur Kuran

Pre-modern states that ruled in the name of Islam are often characterized as absolutist. The implication is that they exploited their subjects and menaced foreigners with formidable strength and that their initiatives emanated largely from one powerful man. A famous variant of this thesis belongs to Max Weber (1925 [1947]: 347), who used the term 'sultanism' to describe the exercise of unlimited and arbitrary Islamic authority. Another famous variant, Karl Wittfogel's *Oriental Despotism*, portrays the early Islamic states as merciless systems of exploitation. Drawing on Marx, Wittfogel (1957: 49–80, 173–82) suggests that each of these states gained strength through its strategic role in administering integrated irrigation networks.[1] Various political movements of our own era have propagated similar interpretations for self-serving reasons: colonizers to justify foreign rule, secular nationalists to appear benevolent by comparison, Islamists to make moral corruption seem eradicable through religious discipline.

All versions of the 'absolutist Islamic state' thesis make the mistake of projecting state control in the modern sense to distant periods when social control technologies were still primitive. Like other pre-modern states, from the Prophet Muhammad's polity and the Arab caliphates to the Ottoman empire and Safavid Iran at their peak, states legitimized through Islam had difficulty regulating markets, controlling production, directing food supplies, manipulating household decisions and appropriating resources. Although some Muslim rulers may have wanted to manage their economies in a manner akin to Soviet-style central planning, they surely recognized their limits. In any case, the wish to micro-manage individual economic choices was hardly the norm. Conscious of the obstacles to counting heads, measuring output, assessing taxable capacity and monitoring employees, competent rulers understood that much economic activity would escape their notice, that regulations would often be evaded and that production would fluctuate unpredictably. Nor do the observed government policies support the absolutist state thesis. Leaders prepared to punish any challenger left many economic variables undisturbed. The image of the absolutist Islamic state has coexisted with that of the 'Islamic conquest state' – a Muslim-dominated state that prospered and expanded by subjugating its neighbours and looting their properties. It is true that the earliest Islamic state, headed in succession by Prophet Muhammad (622–32) and the Madinan caliphate of the first four caliphs who succeeded him (632–61), extracted enormous resources from the territories they conquered. Also true is that Arab-Muslim conquerors of the seventh and eighth centuries formed an ethnically more or less exclusive ruling caste that lived in opulence by imposing onerous taxes and relying on native bureaucracies.[2] The numerous bloody uprisings of this period testify to the resentments generated by huge resource transfers forced on the conquered peoples. As in other conquest states, the distribution of booty formed another steady source of conflict. Despite measures to bring order to this redistribution, it stimulated feuds among the ruling Arabs. Significantly, three of the four Madinan caliphs were assassinated in the course of power struggles.[3]

The Islamic states of subsequent centuries, like other pre-modern states, benefited from plundering foreign or newly conquered lands. This does not mean that looting was a major source of prosperity over the long run. Looting can only be a temporary source of income. A state that relies on looting alone for revenue will inevitably lose strength and succumb to challengers, if only because the exploited territories will lose productivity. So the view that the long-lasting states of the Islamic world, for instance the Abbasid empire (750–1258) and the Ottoman empire (1299–1922), financed themselves mainly through conquests is simplistic. Although conquests lubricated the wheels of government during the expansions of these empires, their successes and failures ultimately rested on the incentives they created for wealth creation. In sum, the characterization of a conquest state applies less to the Islamic states of later centuries than to those of the initial century or so.

To speak of an 'Islamic state' is not to invoke a static construct. There were important differences between, say, the Ottoman state and that headed by the founder of Islam. Part of the reason is that the Ottomans admitted two categories of law in addition to religious law (*Şeriat*, Turkish for *Shari'a*): customary law (*örf*) and state law (*kanun*). Instituted through pronouncements of the sultan, state law was meant to cover matters not addressed by religious or customary law. So in practice, secular legislation played a role in day to day administration. Nevertheless certain key organizing principles of the Ottoman state were grounded in Islamic law. For example Islamic judges and teachers (*qadis* and *hojas*) played important administrative roles. They regulated markets, collected taxes, organized security, adjudicated disputes, supervised charities and even maintained roads.[4] All such functions were justified through religious means; and although they changed over time, later interpretations were constrained by perceived Islamic precedents, including understandings of how the Islamic state had operated in seventh-century Arabia. It is thus meaningful to explore the consequences of Islamic statecraft – provided one recognizes its variations. The variations themselves are of interest in their own right as well. Whether and how successive states adapted to changing circumstances is critical to understanding why the Middle East, like the rest of the Islamic world, remains economically underdeveloped.

The chapter focuses first on the economic governance of the Ottoman Empire at its prime. This is appropriate because from the late eighteenth century onward, the Ottoman empire, as a state stretching into Europe, was at the forefront of efforts to modernize, and in many respects also to Westernize, its administration in a hurry. An examination of the means by which the Ottoman government stimulated or hindered economic growth in earlier centuries will provide clues as to why it eventually faced a deep crisis that resulted in fundamental structural reforms. I shall go on to link the Ottoman economic record to its core principles of economic governance and, in turn, these principles to key characteristics of Islamic law, as they took shape during Islam's first few centuries. An effect of these characteristics, I will argue, was that the economically productive class gradually lost political influence to the state bureaucracy. The consequent political weaknesses of the productive class limited the pressures that might have propelled the modernization of economic rules established in Islam's early centuries.

The huge literature on the links between political governance and economic development would make one expect political centralization to have harmed the economic performance of Islamic states. Yet the Ottoman state was highly centralized during the period considered its Golden Age. It united a vast area spread over three continents, admitted no separation of powers, and allowed the sultan to get involved in the simplest of appointments. There is no systematic relationship between the degree of Islamic political unity and the Middle East's economic success.

The form of unity that was directly relevant to political success, I shall argue, was not political but legal. Almost from the beginning, Islamic states allowed legal pluralism. In principle therefore, competition among legal jurisdictions might have served as an engine of legal modernization, as in the West. If legal modernization had to await Western influences of the nineteenth century, the reason is that only some subjects of the Middle East, specifically the non-Muslim minorities, were entitled to choice of law. The Muslim majority was required to abide by Islamic law and to adjudicate all its disputes in Islamic courts. This asymmetry in legal choice affected the evolution of each of the available legal systems. In particular it caused the legal practices of the minorities to resemble those of Muslims on matters of financial and commercial significance. Thus the form of legal pluralism practised in the Islamic world blocked the legal modernization observed in medieval and early modern Western Europe. In sum, the economic divergence between the Islamic world and Western Europe has less to do with political unity or disunity than with opportunities for legal experimentation and flexibility.

SHALLOW ECONOMIC GOVERNANCE

'Ottoman government,' writes S.E. Finer (1997: 1170), author of a comparative trilogy on the history of government, 'was conspicuously shallow in its penetration of everyday life – more so than most agrarian empires. Its role was to make war, acquire plunder, slaves, and revenues, raise taxes, and keep order. It was, in short, predator, revenue-pump, and policeman.' There were several exceptions, he notes. The state took better care of its roads than any state in Europe since the fall of the Roman empire; it ran great naval yards; and it built an impressive school system to train religious scholars (*ulama*). But the Ottomans provided few other public goods, making their rule conspicuously superficial. In advancing these observations Finer relies on his extensive knowledge of coeval European states and on the judgements of leading Ottomanists, including H. Gibb and H. Bowen, Halil İnalcık, and Stanford Shaw.

What sorts of public goods did the Ottoman state provide inadequately, if at all? In contrast to modern states, it sought practically no direct role in such areas as productivity, sanitation, health, welfare and mass education. Nor did it assist merchants directly, except in giving them physical protection and maintaining the roads they used. Before about 1500, when the commercial practices of Western merchants began to differ sharply from those of Ottoman merchants, their respective states were pursuing palpably different mercantile policies. The Italian port cities that dominated the cross-Mediterranean trade organized commercial diasporas, which they protected through force. They also posted consuls all over the Islamic world, whose duty was to assist the merchants they represented and to coordinate their activities. Over time these consuls became increasingly efficient at lobbying local authorities, collecting commercial intelligence, keeping records on business reputations and publishing periodic bulletins on market conditions. For its part, the Ottoman government took no major steps to strengthen its own trading communities in the Mediterranean or elsewhere, to say nothing of organizing or running them.[5] Ottoman officials did not consider it necessary or useful to solve commercial coordination problems by collecting and disseminating economic information.[6]

Another public good notably absent from the Ottoman state's menu of services was the organization of commercial fairs. True, the Ottoman government continued to its dying days to administer and protect the world's greatest commercial event of pre-modern times, the fair held in Mecca during the annual pilgrimage. In the sixteenth century, it has been estimated 200 000 people gathered in Mecca for the traditional prayer meeting, many of them merchants who financed their pilgrimages, even made a living, by buying and selling at the pilgrimage fair and on the journeys to and from Mecca.[7] But nothing in Ottoman economic history resembles the periodic non-religious fairs established after 1350 in Germany, the Low Countries, France, Spain and Italy. Various European states assisted these fairs by providing political security, enforcing contracts in courts, granting toll franchises and helping to disseminate commercial information. The economic significance of the fairs lies largely in the challenges they posed to local, town-based monopolies.[8]

It is often asserted that the fairs of pre-modern Europe were responses to the rising transaction costs that accompanied commercial expansion. However it is not obvious why the solution to mounting transaction costs had to be fairs; with their well-established service sectors, towns offered significant advantages.[9] What made fairs preferable in the eyes of European states is precisely that they promoted allocational efficiency by undermining the market power of the towns. Over the long run, an even greater benefit of the European fairs lay in their capacity to respond more flexibly than urban guilds to changing technologies and market conditions. In the Ottoman empire, by contrast, the state supported the privileges of urban guilds. Why the difference? Whereas the towns of Western Europe enjoyed considerable autonomy, those of the Ottoman empire, including their guilds, were controlled by the central authorities. So whereas the regimes of Western Europe promoted fairs as a means of consolidating power at the expense of their cities, Ottoman administrations had no such incentive. What is critical is that the states of the West tried harder to extend commercial networks and stimulate commercial economies of scale.

Not only was the Ottoman state less inclined, for one reason or another, to supply public goods conducive to private prosperity but it was willing under certain circumstances to adopt measures bound to weaken its own subjects *vis-à-vis* outsiders. At the height of their political and military power, the Ottoman government provided European merchants increasingly broad trade concessions, which worked against Ottoman merchants. While geopolitical considerations played a role here, it is significant that these were allowed to trump the interests of private traders.[10]

A more specific case comes from the early eighteenth century. At this time, the cloth dyers of Aleppo began facing increasing competition from French sellers of cloth dyed in vibrant colours that were new to the region. But they kept themselves in business by developing local substitutes. In the course of this adjustment process the Ottoman government extended no help. On the contrary, it undermined the survival of domestic enterprises by burdening them with new taxes. The new colours they had introduced, announced the authorities, were innovations not covered by existing regulations, which exempted from taxation only traditional dyes – red, crimson and light yellow.[11] Apart from shortsightedness, the new taxes point to a striking disregard for private economic prosperity. They show that officials could pounce on new sources of revenue even if this would endanger the local economy – and eventually extinguish the revenues themselves. The example is all the more significant because the empire's trade with the West had fallen under the overwhelming domination of foreigners, who were beginning to make inroads into domestic trade as well.

The Ottomans were equally shortsighted when they imposed price ceilings (*narh*) that distorted market signals. But it would be wrong to treat this interventionism as evidence of deep economic governance. Although the reign of Mehmed II (1444 and 1451–81) may be characterized as a period of comprehensive market interventionism, subsequent rulers, recognizing that binding price ceilings cannot be enforced indefinitely, opted for a policy of selective interventionism. Thereafter they generally let markets function unhindered, intervening only during crises generated by war, monetary instability or major supply shocks.[12]

Implicit in the foregoing interpretations is the observation that good governance is critical to wealth creation and economic development. One of the clearest statements of this observation has come from Mancur Olson (1996).[13] Along with most economists, Olson recognizes that market efficiency ordinarily depends on voluntary exchanges based on full information about demand and supply conditions. He adds that the rules securing voluntariness and the dissemination of information are not found in nature. Rather, market participants, or a third party representing their interests, must develop and enforce the appropriate rules. Such a third party, which improves markets by providing supporting collective goods, including appropriate laws, is what Olson labels a 'market-augmenting government'. Among the collective goods supplied by all market-augmenting governments are clear property rights, protection against theft, freedom of contract and contract enforcement. Depending on market conditions they may also include institutions that facilitate information flows. All such collective goods enhance the benefits of freely negotiated exchanges.

Against this background the posting of consuls in commercial centres abroad, assisting commercial fairs, and resisting calls for price controls may be seen as acts of market-augmenting government. By contrast the imposition of new taxes on struggling producers or of price controls that prolong shortages appear as acts of 'market-diminishing government'. Taxation *per se* is not necessarily harmful to markets, for the generated revenue may support services critical to disseminating information, coordinating bids and offers, providing security and enforcing agreements. The Western consuls posted in Ottoman cities were supported through fees paid by the merchants they served.

But taxation is often motivated by redistribution rather than market augmentation. The cloth dyers of Aleppo were not taxed to enhance their competitiveness. The motive was to redistribute resources to causes state officials considered more important.

Government failures to pursue market-augmenting policies, Olson argues in a work with Martin McGuire (2003), fall into three categories. There are 'failures of redistribution' exemplified by the taxes on Aleppo's dyers. There are also 'failures of representation' which arise when certain market participants, for example producers, are excluded from government. The cloth dyers had no representation in government so it was relatively easy to burden them with new taxes. Finally, there are 'failures of implementation' which entail the neglect of policies to augment markets. These may be driven by corruption on the part of fully informed officials who happen to be interested in lining their own pockets. To these three categories I would add a fourth: 'failures of ideology'. Officials may be ignorant about the workings of markets or about the determinants of commercial success. They may also subscribe to a worldview that limits their interest in market augmentation or makes them interpret this goal in ways harmful to certain groups.

The failures of Ottoman economic governance were driven in part by an ideology whose persistence was facilitated by Islamic law, more precisely by certain critical elements of the Islamic legal heritage. As a prelude to developing this thesis it is necessary to give a fuller account of economic governance in the Ottoman empire, with an emphasis on its inadequacies.

OTTOMAN MARKET-AUGMENTING POLICIES

Like every long-lasting state, the Ottoman state strove to protect its subjects and their properties against brigands, pirates and foreign armies. Accordingly, it maintained a military presence across the empire and funded policing services. It also supported an Islamic judicial system whose functions included the adjudication of commercial disputes, the determination of liability and the interpretation of contracts. So the notion of market augmentation was hardly alien to the Ottoman concept of governance. Yet Ottoman policies designed to facilitate production and trade were not uniformly or consistently successful. The types of equity contracts acceptable to the Islamic courts remained, with only minor changes, those in use in the Arab-governed states of classical Islam. As late as the nineteenth century the concept of an enterprise enjoying juridical personality and able to issue transferable shares was alien to the Islamic legal system; equally significant, the Islamic partnerships developed almost a millennium earlier remained in use. For another example, the Islamic courts accepted the notion of limited liability for the sleeping member of a commercial partnership, but they never developed the legal apparatus to support formal commercial insurance. Consequently Ottoman merchants subject to Islamic law had to take risks that, from the fourteenth century onward, their Western counterparts could shift on to specialized insurers. The critical point is that at a time when the corresponding infrastructure in the West was undergoing revolutionary developments, the Ottoman empire's economically relevant legal infrastructure improved only marginally. As I have argued elsewhere (Kuran 2001b), this legal rigidity set the stage for the Middle East's later economic woes.[14]

For another such failure, consider the Ottoman policies concerning private property. To its credit, the Ottoman judicial system regularly enforced the property rights of individuals. But ordinarily there were limits to what an individual outside the governing class could accumulate. While high state officials were permitted to become enormously wealthy, private producers and traders who achieved affluence were liable to see their assets confiscated. Moreover an official who got fired or even demoted could lose most of his assets overnight. In any case, wealth acquired through official privileges generally could not be bequeathed to one's descendants. The heir of a prosperous official was the state, which used the estates of former officials to support the treasury or to reward its current officials. By these means the Ottomans prevented the creation of large and durable accumulations of wealth. The intention of course was to block the emergence of power bases capable of upsetting the political status quo.[15] Among the by-products of this policy was that commercial and productive enterprises remained small, simple and ephemeral at a time when their European counterparts were growing in size, complexity and durability. Because of this stagnation, Ottoman private enterprises did not pressure the legal system to produce, as their Western counterparts did, innovations to increase the efficiency of large economic operations.[16]

Although the Ottoman system of government limited private enrichment, it allowed the preservation of wealth within the framework of Islamic trusts known as *waqfs*. A *waqf* is an unincorporated trust established under Islamic law by a living person for the provision of a designated social service in perpetuity. It emerged in the early Islamic centuries, I have suggested elsewhere, as a credible commitment device to give dignitaries economic security in return for social services. The founder of a *waqf* could maintain control over at least some of his wealth by appointing himself its paid manager-trustee (*mutawalli*) for life. He could also confer lasting benefits on his descendants by bringing them into the *waqf*'s administration and designating them as his successors. What made the *waqf* an especially convenient wealth shelter was that it acquired legitimacy as an Islamic institution. Its religious identity made it more or less immune to confiscation, for rulers were loathe to develop a reputation of impiety. From the standpoint of a *waqf* founder, this security came at a price, however. It required him to dedicate a significant portion of the *waqf*'s revenues to some social or charitable service. Although the Ottoman state rarely tried to influence the functions of the smaller *waqfs*, it took a keen interest in those of the largest ones. It required large *waqfs* to provide services to broad social groups and to advance the state's own objectives. Many of the largest Ottoman *waqfs*, including most of those established by high officials, were located within or near a strategically important city.[17]

The previous section characterized Ottoman economic governance as shallow. This is certainly an accurate designation insofar as it refers to direct state involvement in the economy. But it ignores the state's indirect participation in decisions relevant to mass economic welfare. Not only did the Ottoman state influence the decisions of major *waqfs* but it pressured officials to use the wealth they amassed partly to provide social services. The sorts of social services expected of high officials included public goods such as mosques, schools, roads and water fountains as well as essentially private goods such as poor relief and retirement pensions. It is clear then that the shallow economic governance thesis requires qualification. Yet the Ottoman state's indirect mode of governance drastically curtailed its capacity to manage society's economic resources. At least in principle, a *waqf*'s deed of establishment fixed its mission in stone; not even the founder of a *waqf* was authorized to alter its purpose. This rule constrained the state's ability to shift resources across sectors or regions. Although enterprising officials sometimes managed to circumvent the restrictions, they had to avoid the appearance of impiety – hardly an easy task when vested interests had every incentive to castigate reformers as violators of sacred law. In times of rapidly changing opportunities, like the nineteenth century, the rigidities of the *waqf* system were bound to seem a nuisance to a growing segment of society. Not surprisingly, that period witnessed massive and largely successful drives to confiscate *waqf* properties.

JURISDICTIONAL HOMOGENEITY

Over and beyond the specific policies they pursue and the legal systems they administer, states affect economic outcomes through the room they allow for experimentation. Leading economic historians observe that around the fifteenth century Western Europe's political disunity and jurisdictional fragmentation stimulated creativity and productivity. The existence of many states allowed entrepreneurs to escape burdensome conditions simply by moving somewhere else. As such, this condition constrained rent-seeking on the part of rulers. It also gave them reasons to permit, facilitate and even encourage legal improvements. 'The ubiquitous competition among the evolving nation-states was a deep underlying source of change,' writes Douglass North (1995: 26, 30), 'and equally a constraint on the options available to rulers within states ... Competition among states offered constituents alternatives – states to which they might flee or send their movable wealth, thus constraining the ruler's options.' Some of the alternatives proved superior to others; as England and the Netherlands became economic powerhouses, Spain and Portugal stagnated. The multiplicity of legal jurisdictions increased the likelihood that one or more of these would generate self-sustaining economic growth.[18]

The West's jurisdictional fragmentation was obviously related to its political disunity. Yet these two conditions had distinct effects. The growth-enhancing benefits of its political disunity are symbolized by Christopher Columbus's search for funding to find a sea route to India. Columbus's request for patronage was turned down by three rulers until the king and queen of Spain finally agreed to sponsor his attempt to cross the Atlantic.[19] Columbus's legendary fleet set sail precisely because Europe was highly fragmented. Had Europe been united under any one of the first three rulers, its discovery of America would have been delayed. All the states in question, including the three that refused to extend assistance, could have had identical legal systems. In fact, the laws, regulations, customs and norms that affected investment and accumulation decisions varied greatly even within individual states. For example there existed a huge variety of inheritance systems. Some places allowed primogeniture, which is the practice of leaving an entire estate to one's oldest son; in other places estates had to be divided more or less equally among surviving family members.[20] Insofar as inheritance practices mattered to institutional evolution, and thus to economic growth, the variety of inheritance systems afforded the West multiple opportunities for starting down the path to economic modernization. Against this background, consider the degree to which the Islamic world was politically unified and legally homogeneous during the long period before it started to show signs of underdevelopment. In the sixteenth century, at its zenith, the Ottoman empire was politically unified. Moreover there were few other Islamic states; two of them were Safavid Iran and Mughal India, whose capitals stood much farther away than those of any two neighbouring states in Western Europe. This mean that a seventeenth-century Turkish visionary who was denied patronage in Istanbul had little chance of finding an alternative sponsor. He could conceivably have moved to Iran or India. Yet his funding choices would have been far more limited than those available to a French entrepreneur. Accordingly, his hopes of finding a sympathetic wealthy patron would have been slimmer.

Subsequently of course, Ottoman territories in the Balkans, the Middle East and North Africa fell under the control of local leaders. This political fragmentation was not accompanied by a period of institutional innovation. By itself, then, political disunity proved to be no panacea for growth. The Arab

Middle East was also politically fragmented before it fell to the Turkish armies in 1516, and this period was one of economic stagnation for the region; its economic performance appears to have improved, at least for a while, after the Ottomans reunited it.[21] These patterns confirm the absence of a direct empirical link between political unity and economic retardation. The reason why no such connection exists is that, along with the harmful economic effects stemming from lack of competition, political unity can have beneficial effects. It facilitates technological diffusion, lowers coordination costs, promotes trust and simplifies the enforcement of contracts. Moreover it enlarges markets, which stimulates competition.

If the Ottoman empire lacked the creative tension observed in the West, the reason lies in its jurisdictional homogeneity. The inheritance rules followed and enforced throughout the Ottoman empire were the Islamic rules based on the Qur'an. Although they could differ across Islam's schools of law, the variations were minor. Likewise, the rules of partnerships and *waqfs* differed minimally across regions. What matters here is that the legal infrastructure of commerce and finance was strikingly homogeneous as compared with its counterpart in the West. Consequently the various regions of the Islamic world spawned similar pressures concerning institutional innovation. Thus the institutional trajectory that caused Turkey to become underdeveloped was essentially identical to that of Egypt, Syria and Iraq – not to mention the Balkans, most of which remained under Turkish rule up to the final decades of the Ottoman empire. True, except on criminal matters the religious minorities of the Islamic world were always entitled to choice of law. They were free for example to follow the inheritance practices of their own religions. Likewise they had the option of forming partnerships at odds with Islamic prescriptions. However the very privileges that permitted the existence of multiple legal jurisdictions gave non-Muslim individuals the right to demand adjudication before an Islamic court. The daughter of a deceased man who had bequeathed all his wealth to his oldest son could appeal to an Islamic judge for an Islamic settlement, under which she would receive half as much as any of her brothers. This possibility induced the courts of the minorities to make pragmatic adaptations to ensure their own survival. These adaptations made the law they enforced increasingly similar to the dominant law of the land, namely Islamic law. By contrast the Islamic courts made no such adjustments, for Muslims were denied the choice of law granted to Christians and Jews.

At least on matters of financial significance, then, the legal jurisdictions of the Islamic world displayed far less heterogeneity than was possible in principle. Until the late eighteenth century, when vast numbers of non-Muslims moved to Western legal jurisdictions, the Middle East's Christians and Jews were subject to business rules similar to those of the Muslim majority. As such, their legal institutions did not produce an evolutionary dynamic fundamentally different from that generated by the Islamic legal system. The formally independent jurisdictional units of the Islamic world functioned as a single, highly interconnected legal system.[22]

The jurisdictional homogeneity of the Islamic world, including the Ottoman empire, dampened pressures for raising the economic sophistication and efficiency of the law. Had it harboured multiple and equally unprotected jurisdictions that differed in economically important ways, the ensuing competition would have produced adjustments that enhanced the efficiency of production and trade. Just as modern states compete for foreign investment by trying to make their laws hospitable to business, so each jurisdiction would have had to make improvements in the interest of remaining competitive. Whatever the static benefits of Ottoman jurisdictional homogeneity, they came at the expense of dynamic efficiency. Unlike the competing polities of Western Europe, the Ottoman legal system did not fuel internal pressures to offer producers and traders an ever-expanding menu of markets, contractual forms, insurance devices and instruments of economic security. It is the external pressures generated by the rise of the West that eventually forced the Ottoman empire to undertake far-reaching legal reforms.

THE PRINCIPLES OF OTTOMAN ECONOMIC GOVERNANCE

Every historical process that culminates in a deep crisis demands an explanation. In the case of the crisis involving Ottoman legal stagnation, one wonders why state officials did not promote jurisdictional competition as a means of stimulating economic growth. For one thing, the economic advantages of jurisdictional variety, obvious in hindsight, were not appreciated. For another, economic development in the modern sense of the term was not among the goals of the Ottoman state or, for that matter, of any other state bound by Islamic law. Until the nineteenth century Ottoman economic policies reflected objectives that were often indifferent to continuous economic development and sometimes deliberately opposed to it. In several celebrated articles, Mehmet Genç observes that three basic principles defined the Ottoman 'economic mind': provisionism, fiscalism and traditionalism.[23] Provisionism refers to the emphasis given to securing steady supplies of critical commodities. In the case of Aleppo's cloth dyers, Ottoman officials did not consider limiting imports, for that would diminish total supply. If locals went out of business that would be regrettable, but no reason to change course; the French were there to take their place. The second principle, fiscalism, signifies the relentless drive to raise revenue from an economy considered subservient to the needs of the treasury. In the example at hand this principle is evident in the opportunism exhibited through the use of a change in styles – new colours – as a pretext for imposing new taxes. Finally, traditionalism entails a preference for preserving the political status quo, with a consequent aversion to economic innovations disruptive to established social patterns. In the episode under consideration here, traditionalism manifests itself in the expressed rationale for new taxes. The dyers were told that they themselves had invited the reassessment of their tax obligations by choosing to modify their established production pattern.

However clear the logic of these interpretations, we must be careful before accepting Genç's three principles as a general explanation for the Ottoman pattern of economic governance. In and of themselves, they imply nothing about the specifics of the Ottoman state's market augmentation policies. Only under special conditions, which Genç implicitly assumes to hold, do these three principles provide clues to the causes of Ottoman underdevelopment.

Fiscalism

To start with fiscalism, this principle is certainly compatible with market-augmenting policies. Where rulers have long planning horizons, it may be used to support policies that limit tax revenue over the short run in order to raise them permanently over the longer run. As a case in point, fiscalism could have been used to justify tax reductions for the Aleppo dyers. Such reductions, the tax collectors might have reasoned, would enhance the competitiveness of the local dyers, thus augmenting the state's future tax base. One of two conditions could imply opportunistic taxation of the kind imposed on Aleppo's dyers. The first is a time horizon short enough to make the immediate returns trump all long-term benefits. High turnover among officials, promoted by rulers eager to keep their functionaries from acquiring local influence, must have contributed to keeping tax policies focused on the near term. The other condition that would justify opportunistic taxation, more subtle than the first, has to do with perceptions of foreign capabilities. A ruler who considers Western producers more efficient than their Ottoman competitors and attributes the difference to Western institutions resistant to emulation, will consider protectionism doomed to failure.[24] As such, he will judge the downside of burdening local producers with new taxes to be dominated by immediate fiscal advantages. The two conditions – short horizons and perceptions of obstinate institutional handicaps – are not mutually exclusive. In fact the second would accentuate the first. If it took decades for reforms to bear fruit, short horizons would definitely override any concerns about harming local production.

Provisionism

On the face of it, there is nothing unusual about provisionism *per se*. Throughout history, all states – certainly all successful ones – have sought to prevent shortages of critical commodities, especially of food. The main motivation has been the prevention of violent uprisings. What is striking about Ottoman provisionism is not the principle itself but that it fuelled anti-mercantilist policies. During the centuries preceding the industrial revolution, when Western governments were pursuing mercantilist policies for the benefit of their own producers and traders, the Ottomans consciously encouraged Western imports and discouraged exports to Europe. Moreover they gave foreign merchants increasingly broad privileges that had the effect of putting the cross-Mediterranean trade almost exclusively in foreign hands. As Genç himself recognizes, the link between the anti-mercantilism of the Ottomans and their provisionist mentality rested critically on two economic observations: the productivity of the relevant sectors was low, and attempts to improve matters could make matters worse.

I would add that Ottoman policy makers of the fifteenth and later centuries were aware of the superior capabilities of European merchants. Although no Ottoman policy-maker understood the institutional sources of these advantages in a manner that would satisfy a modern institutional economist, the advantages themselves became self-evident as European market institutions gained sophistication. Given the realization that Westerners were more efficient at trade than locals, the principle of provisionism made it reasonable to tolerate, even to encourage, Western control of the bilateral trade between the Ottoman empire and Western Europe. Under the prevailing circumstances mercantilism would have amounted to bestowing privileges on relatively inefficient merchants. By contrast, provisionism required favouring those who were more efficient. From a provisionist standpoint it hardly mattered that the merchants being pushed aside were Ottoman subjects. The overriding goal was to entrust the provision of major cities to the most reliable, if not also the cheapest, suppliers.[25]

If Ottoman officials recognized the inefficiencies of their own mercantile class, they might have sought to identify the secrets of the West's commercial ascendancy. Not until the end of the eighteenth century were systematic efforts made to understand Western institutions, and it took even longer for economic institutions to receive serious attention. As late as the seventeenth century, when resident European consuls could be found in every major commercial centre of the Middle East and the Balkans, there was not a single permanent Ottoman representative in any Western capital. As already mentioned, the Ottoman administration did not feel compelled to keep informed about Western economic conditions or trends – to say nothing of disseminating information to merchants.[26] To anyone familiar with modern economic policy-making, this will seem puzzling. Most economic officials of today's underdeveloped countries make a point of learning about the economic institutions of the developed world, and a common measure of their success lies in their adeptness at performing institutional transplants. Yet from a provisionist perspective no institutional transplants were necessary as long as strategically critical cities remained well-stocked with essential commodities. Western merchants were doing an admirable job carrying goods to and from the empire. The global trading system was serving the empire adequately. Why risk supply disruptions by seeking to alter the balance of trade or the composition of merchants?

Traditionalism

The third member of Genç's trio, the principle of traditionalism, is also consistent with the passivity of the Ottoman regime in the face of revolutionary changes in European economic capabilities. The formal expression of this principle, which undergirded all reform (*Islahat*) projects of the sixteenth to eighteenth centuries, was that 'nothing be done that upsets what has existed since the distant past'.[27] In accordance with this principle, a common response to economic problems was to look for policy changes rooted in human error or corruption and then seek to restore the old order in its pristine purity. This pattern made analysts look inward rather than outward, at the prevailing system as opposed to the global environment. Of course no one treated the outside world as absolutely fixed; if nothing else, the Ottomans were aware of the West's growing military might. However within the traditionalist frame of mind the goal was not to analyse the sources of the West's strengths. It was to learn how to resist Western advances. Whatever the West's ways of doing things, if the Ottoman empire was losing ground in one domain or another, the reason had to lie in Ottoman degeneration rather than in Western improvements.

Traditionalism has been used as a blanket explanation for a host of Ottoman policy rigidities. Yet the very same principle could have served to justify major adaptations. As a case in point, the goal of preserving the economic *status quo* could have been invoked in defence of protectionist policies to maintain the market shares of Aleppo's dyers. In particular a plausible case could have been made that the local dyers were victims of foreign challenges to a long-established economic pattern. In the event, the principles of fiscalism and provisionism favoured an interpretation partial to free international trade. So the content of traditionalist state policies depended on the framing of economic outcomes. Objectives other than traditionalism itself inevitably coloured the meaning of stability.

Whatever the uses of traditionalism, it obviously shifted attention from economic efficiency, growth and market augmentation to competing definitions of the *status quo*. So its net effect would have been to distort policies in the interest of whatever group gained the attention of the authorities. This distortive potential was not lost on Western functionaries eager to serve their own constituents. As their influence increased, they managed to make Ottoman authorities restore traditional patterns upset by the adaptations of Ottoman subjects. In the eighteenth century for example, a French ambassador in Istanbul frequently invoked Ottoman traditionalism in his struggles against local forays into French-dominated markets.[28] As such he turned traditionalism into a weapon against domestic competition.

We have seen repeatedly that the economic principles of Ottoman statecraft were used in conjunction with each other and with other considerations. They were not necessarily mutually supporting. Groups capable of posing trouble could, and invariably did, invoke traditionalist argumentation in objecting to fiscalist tax increases prompted by rising prosperity. In such situations traditionalism undermined fiscalism. Could the principles themselves be used, then, to justify practically any policy? Did they serve merely as window dressing? These three principles constrained economic debates within the ruling hierarchy, and they invariably influenced how problems were approached. By the same token they contributed to popular expectations of official policies and constrained opposing arguments. Neither individually nor as a group did they predispose the Ottoman state to make market augmentation a central objective. On the contrary, they legitimized a broad array of market-diminishing policies and blocked the consideration of alternative policies that might have given Ottoman economic institutions greater dynamism.

ISLAMIC PRECEDENTS

The three economic principles of Ottoman statecraft were not Ottoman creations. Each directed policy-making, or served to rationalize selected policies, in earlier Islamic states as well as in pre-Islamic and non-Islamic states of the Eastern Mediterranean. Centuries before the founding of the Ottoman dynasty in 1299, Arab statesmen were invoking fiscal needs to justify new taxes and arbitrary expropriations. Early Islamic rulers imposed price controls and carried out forced sales to keep strategic regions supplied with cheap food. They also restricted mobility on the ground that uncontrolled migration disrupted traditional balances. Although the surveyed Ottoman principles were not the inexorable results of such precedents, pre-Ottoman history offered abundant grounds for treating them all as integral components of the Islamic administrative tradition.

From the period of the first four caliphs strenuous efforts were made to rationalize various administrative practices as Qur'anic mandates. For their part, the critics of these practices sought to justify their opposition through sacred teachings, including verses of the Qur'an. It was not difficult to concoct Islamic arguments against common practices. Nowhere does the Qur'an authorize arbitrary taxation. Its verses on *zakat*, the tax incumbent on all Muslims of means, could plausibly be interpreted as fixing and limiting the individual's obligations to the state.[29] For another example, the remembered words and deeds of the Prophet and his companions, known collectively as the *Sunna* and considered a supplementary source of Islamic guidance, harbour positions inimical to provisionism. According to one recollection (*hadith*), the Prophet rejected price controls on the ground that only God can fix prices. According to another, he required commodities intended for sale to be brought to market for general inspection and exposed to competition before the start of transactions. On the basis of the latter, widely believed precedent, forced official purchases could have been ruled out as illegal. As for traditionalist approaches to economic policy-making, they conflict with the institutional dynamism of the earliest Islamic centuries. In developing what became the Islamic administrative tradition, the early caliphs, especially the Umayyad caliphs who ruled from Damascus (661–750) and their Abbasid successors, exhibited remarkable openness to change.

The Ottomans had ample ground, then, for rejecting as un-Islamic the fiscalist, provisionist and traditionalist policies of the Islamic regimes that immediately preceded, or overlapped with, their own. Likewise these other regimes – the Fatimid caliphate and the Seljuk, Ilkhan, Mamluk and Safavid empires – could have made a point of invoking Islam in support of property rights, market freedoms and institutional flexibility. Why then did Genç's trio of principles solidify their identification with Islam while other elements of Islamic statecraft lost influence?

The answer lies in two broad historical patterns, both rooted in classical Islamic law. The first pattern is the gradual but unmistakable decline in the Islamic world's commercial competitiveness. As already mentioned, even as the Ottoman empire reached its zenith its trade with the West was largely under the control of Western merchants and financiers; also, the Ottoman government contributed to this pattern through policies that favoured foreign traders over locals. These patterns did not originate with the Ottomans. They can be traced to certain developments of the seventh to ninth centuries, when economically critical elements of Islamic law took shape. The Islamic inheritance system raised the costs of keeping mercantile and financial wealth intact across generations. It also kept the contractual partnerships formed under Islamic law small and ephemeral by raising the cost of dissolution in the event of a partner's death. This outcome had momentous consequences for the evolution of the Islamic social system. Merchants could not build increasingly large and ever more complex enterprises. Nor therefore could they increase their political power. And no pressures emerged, as they did in the West, to develop more advanced business enterprises or, for that matter, to make the legal system conducive to new organizational forms. In short, the Islamic world found itself in an equilibrium trap that kept financial and mercantile institutions essentially frozen.[30] The persistent political weakness of the Ottoman commercial sector continued a pattern established well before the Ottoman state came into existence.

The second historical pattern pertinent to the durability of Genç's trio of principles is that Islamic law, as it emerged by the ninth century, precluded corporations. As surely as Islamic law gave every individual standing before the courts, it denied such standing to organizations. It also failed to accommodate corporations, which are social structures entitled to make and remake their internal rules and able to outlive their members. Not even the *waqf*, whose existence was assumed perpetual, enjoyed corporate status. It lacked juridical personality as well as the ability to restructure itself. Over time this anti-corporatism limited the growth of civil society, in other words of intermediate organizations capable of asserting and defending the interests of groups outside the state apparatus.[31] In Western Europe, meanwhile, the corporate form of organization spread to religious orders, universities, cities, guilds and eventually also to commercial enterprises.[32] Within the Islamic world, one finds no parallel to this organizational development. Although the cumulative effects of Islam's legal constraints did not turn into pressing problems until the nineteenth century, they stunted the development of intermediate organizations from the beginning.

Together these two patterns made the state bureaucracy expand at the expense of the private sectors of the economy. This transformation is reflected in statistics concerning the division of labour in the mainly Arab part of the Islamic world. Data collected by Maya Shatzmiller from medieval chronicles and documents show that the number of unique occupations in the extractive and manufacturing sectors of the Arab Middle East fell from 477 between the eighth and eleventh centuries to 428 between the twelfth and fifteenth centuries. In these two sectors, she thus finds, there were fewer unique occupations in the period immediately preceding the region's fall to the Turks than there had been in the period when Islamic law took shape. Between these two periods, the number of occupations in the service sector rose from 522 to 883. Particularly revealing are figures regarding the state bureaucracy. The occupations that formed the bureaucracy more than tripled, jumping from 130 to 483. The lion's share of the new bureaucratic titles concerned the public treasury, especially tax collection. Meanwhile the number of distinct commercial occupations fell slightly, from 233 to 220.[33] The significance of these comparisons lies in the fact that division of labour is a prime indicator of economic development. Apparently in the centuries after Islamic law took shape the most vibrant part of the economic system was the state sector. Equally important, the commercial and productive sectors seem to have lacked dynamism.

If the state sector expanded and gained complexity while private sectors underwent no major structural transformations, the reason, I have suggested, is that the legal system limited the flexibility of private actors. Because of barriers created through unanticipated and unintended interactions among Islamic laws, civil society did not develop enough clout to shape the evolution of the social order. Under the circumstances, the military, the civilian administration and religious corps – the three branches of the state sector – were able to advance their own interests, control the content of education and dominate public discourse. These politically privileged groups tended to view the world from the perspective of the state's own needs. They were also socialized to consider fiscalism, provisionism and traditionalism as essential to keeping the state strong and stable. In every period the state apparatus would have included independent thinkers and nonconformists. But anyone who sought to develop a counter-ideology conducive to commercial development and political decentralization would easily have been eliminated from positions of influence.

A striking feature of classical Islamic thought is the absence of an expectation that the state should commit itself to continuous development, defined as steadily growing national prosperity. Today, by contrast, it is taken for granted that states should foster conditions favourable to rising living standards, if not that they should actively bring about such conditions. Whatever its economic philosophy, every modern government promises better days ahead. Such a promise is implicit in the concept of a 'market-augmenting government'. By contrast, pre-modern Islamic governments did not aim to provide ever higher living standards for their constituents as a whole. There would be good times and bad times, and rulers were to minimize the latter by preventing invasions, maintaining order and securing justice. But they were not expected, and did not promise, to achieve what we now call economic development. Of course neither they nor their subjects lacked an interest in material accumulation or considered it impossible to improve their own living conditions. However they could not imagine that steady economic development was possible for society as a whole.

This zero-sum mentality was common, it has been observed, to all medieval civilizations.[34] The idea of economic development emerged in Europe after the Renaissance, and it became a hallmark of economic thinking only during the industrial revolution. Two key points deserve recognition here. First, economic development never became an objective of governance in pre-Ottoman Islam, and the Ottoman empire itself discovered the concept quite late, in coming to realize that Europe had surged ahead economically. Second, the lack of an Islamic commitment to steady growth supported Ottoman traditionalism. Had Islamic thought spawned a notion of economic development, Ottoman statecraft would probably have been more innovative as well as more hospitable to the needs of producers, traders and financiers. And had Islamic law not blocked the evolution of commercial institutions, the Ottoman empire might have transformed its economic worldview and discovered the idea of development through its own internal dynamics.

The foregoing explanation for the rigidity of Ottoman and other Islamic institutions implicitly rejects the view, disturbingly common to studies of modernization, that institutional development is spearheaded by enlightened and altruistic state officials.[35] Treating rulers and their functionaries as essentially selfish agents interested primarily in self-preservation and advancement, I have posited that institutions favourable to economic development, whether commercial contracts or property rights, are created in response to pressures that private economic agents exert on the state. Therefore our challenge has been to explain why in the pre-modern Islamic world such pressures failed to emerge. The legal system kept producers, merchants and financiers weak, I have argued, thus limiting political pressures to create new and more sophisticated institutions; and it is the feebleness of these pressures that kept the Islamic world from modernizing its economic system without outside assistance.

RELIGIOUS DISCRIMINATION

One might expect a state committed to upholding Islamic law and controlled almost exclusively by Muslims to have made religious discrimination one of its guiding principles in all spheres of government, including economics. We have already encountered an example of confessionally differentiated rules: the granting of choice of law only to non-Muslims. Recall that this differentiation shielded Islamic law against pressures to make competitive adjustments, and it caused the legal practices of religious minorities to resemble those of the majority. Why then does religious discrimination not appear among Genç's principles of Ottoman economic governance?

Discrimination in favour of Muslims could be considered so basic a characteristic of all Islamic statecraft as to render its mention superfluous in any particular context. The reservation of practically all high government positions for Muslims, even if many were converts, is itself a form of religious discrimination, if only because until the industrial age a vastly disproportionate share of the wealthiest people were state officials. Also, Muslim subjects were supposed to be taxed relatively lightly.

Early on, during Islam's first few decades, taxes were heavier on non-Muslims, who paid a poll tax (*jizya*) in return for exemption from military service. Non-Muslims also paid a special agricultural tax (*kharaj*) in lieu of the agricultural levy that Muslims paid under one name or another, sometimes as *zakat*. The consequent discrimination prompted large-scale conversions to Islam, with adverse effects on tax revenues. In response, already at the end of the seventh century, measures were taken to discourage, in some places even to prohibit, further conversions to Islam. Moreover the aggregate tax obligations of Muslim farmers were raised by burdening them with often geographically or ethnically specific new taxes from which non-Muslims were exempt.[36] The upshot was that the nature and extent of religious tax discrimination came to depend on numerous variable factors. What allowed this transformation is that the fundamental sources of Islam leave most specifics of taxation to the judgement of the Muslim community. The practical meaning of this delegation was to empower rulers to modify tax rates in accordance with evolving state priorities. It left them free, in other words, to tax groups as heavily or as lightly as they wished. The system of tax farming, which decentralized the process of tax collection, like the tax treaties that various Islamic governments made with newly conquered communities, contributed to the variability of taxation both across and within religious, ethnic, geographic and occupational groups.[37]

The resulting precedents of opportunistic taxation legitimized later efforts to tax groups according to their taxable capacities. They thus facilitated the adoption of fiscalism as a major principle of governance. In itself, fiscalism did not call for religious discrimination. Requiring rulers to raise revenue wherever possible, it allowed any particular group, regardless of faith, to be taxed heavily. Where convenient, Islam's discriminatory traditions could be used to justify making any given Christian or Jewish community pay onerous taxes. But the motivation was usually not religious discrimination *per se* but fiscalism. Muslim communities within the large servile class were no less vulnerable to being singled out for special taxes. Where the treatment of Muslims differed is that their taxes were rationalized differently and sometimes collected under different names.

Genç is right, then, to have excluded religious discrimination from the main principles of Ottoman economic statecraft. A basic reason why such discrimination did not become a primary Ottoman economic objective is that Islamic history provided abundant precedents for modifying tax rates on a case by case basis. Not that other forms of religious discrimination were unimportant. Confessionally differentiated political and social rights remained an explicit state policy until the nineteenth century, when such institutionalized inequality was formally abolished, partly under European pressure, during the first wave of Westernization. But confessionally based economic discrimination did not necessarily work against non-Muslims.

There is a form of discrimination that was eventually abandoned after serving as a defining feature of Islamic statecraft. Its basis was the distinction between non-Muslim subjects of Islamic states and foreign non-Muslims. According to rules adopted by Islamic polities of the seventh and eighth centuries, the former were to enjoy privileges denied to the latter. Thus local non-Muslims, for example Armenian merchants based in Syria, were to pay lower tariffs than Western non-Muslims such as Venetian or French merchants. Within a few centuries however, Islamic governments, including Mamluk Egypt, the Seljuk principalities and the Ottoman empire, entered into treaties that ended the customary discrimination against foreigners. The tariffs paid by Westerners thus fell below those imposed on local non-Muslims, eventually even below the rates applied to Muslims. What would explain these blatant violations of the early Islamic principle of pro-local discrimination? This principle became untenable as local merchants failed to remain competitive against Western merchants, for Islamic rulers then took to offering foreigners inducements to use their ports, pass through their cities and finance their trade. As noted above, local merchants lost competitiveness because of the evolutionary consequences of Islamic laws adopted without any thought of blocking organizational development. These laws, including the Islamic inheritance system, thus undermined the relegation of foreign non-Muslims to the lowest category of protection, below local non-Muslims.

In theory, discrimination against foreign non-Muslims was supposed to be accompanied by non-discrimination against the Muslim subjects of other Islamic states. The underlying logic was that the Muslim community (*umma*) is inseparable, and the only legitimate political boundaries are those between the 'House of Islam' (*Dar al-Islam*), where Muslims rule and Islamic law prevails, and the 'House of War' (*Dar al-Harb*), comprising the rest of the world.[38] Within the House of Islam, boundaries between states had no legal status. Accordingly, the Abbasid rulers of twelfth-century Baghdad had to treat Muslim merchants from the Seljuk principalities in Turkey exactly as they treated local Arabs. Neither the Abbasids nor any other Islamic state adhered to this equality principle consistently; from the beginning Muslim rulers even practised ethnic discrimination among their own subjects.[39] Nevertheless to one degree or another all Islamic states upheld this principle even as non-Muslim foreigners gained increasingly valuable privileges. And as the Islamic world expanded, the resulting economic unit grew correspondingly. Just as the rise of Islam turned Western Arabia into a trading area within which commerce took place more freely than before, so in subsequent centuries the entire Islamic world became a giant trading emporium within which Muslims could generally travel without encountering new official demands at every turn.

Islam served the same purpose also through legal standardization. Although understandings and applications of Islamic law could differ among localities, the variations were minor compared to those between say Islamic law and Germanic law. A twelfth-century merchant could travel from Baghdad to Granada, or an eighteenth-century merchant from Sarajevo to Delhi, without encountering significant differences in the dominant commercial code.

We see again that the Islamic legal system could serve as an instrument of market-augmenting governance. Nevertheless over many centuries Islamic law became a source of inefficiency by blocking organizational advances and also by nurturing a governance ideology incompatible with what economic historians call 'modern economic growth'. Both these observations treat Islamic law as a critical determinant of Islamic statecraft. They thus suggest that to pinpoint the mechanisms by which Islamic statecraft affected economic performance one must examine Islamic law, including not only its substance but also its enforcement and capacity for responding to evolving needs.

Such an investigation would fit naturally, one might observe, within Islamic political thought. The starting point of classical Islamic political theory is not the state, or state policies, or the economic principles of statecraft. Rather, it is the law, which is considered God's revealed command. The state is simply a vehicle for discovering, interpreting, implementing and enforcing the law, which is presumed to be fixed as well as comprehensive.

THE FLEXIBILITY OF ISLAMIC LAW

By tradition, the ultimate authority on Islamic law is the Qur'an. Although the Qur'an contains legal verses that are much longer than the typical non-legal verse, it is not a legal manual. Rather, it is a compilation of moral prescriptions. Moreover as a source of guidance it presents ambiguities, even apparent inconsistencies. Consider verse 16:67: 'And of the fruits of the date-palm, and grapes, whence ye derive strong drink and also good nourishment. Lo! therein, is indeed a portent for people who have sense.' And now turn to 5:90: 'O ye who believe! Strong drink and games of chance and idols and divining arrows are only an infamy of Satan's handiwork. Leave it aside in order that ye may succeed.' Taken together, these verses lead to confusion over the permissibility of consuming alcohol. Other ambiguities stem from a lack of specificity. If one must pray (2:43), how often? If 'power' is given to the 'heir' of someone 'slain wrongfully' (17:33), what does that entail? Does it include a right to pardon? If the 'needy' are to be on the receiving end of the *zakat* system (2:177), who qualifies as 'needy'? Is neediness an absolute concept or a relative one? Clearly, a person intending to abide by Qur'anic dictates will encounter many situations requiring clarification and elaboration.[40] By Muslim tradition, the required supplementary guidance is to come, above all, from the *Sunna*. But the *Sunna* harbours contradictions of its own. In any case, the remembered words and deeds of Muhammad and his close companions could not have addressed every possible contingency in the lives of later Muslims.

The evolution of the *Sunna* itself is indicative of the need felt for clarification and interpretation. It became obvious to the earliest Muslims that the Qur'an does not legislate in all domains or anticipate every future problem. Prominent among the areas in which the need for new rules and proposals became acute was leadership. The Qur'an says nothing specific about how the Islamic community should be governed after the Prophet, and he himself did not formulate a procedure for political succession. Another area requiring fresh thinking was economics. The Qur'an contains no specifics about commercial contracts, adjudicating financial disputes or coordinating demands and supplies. Early Muslims committed to operating within an explicitly Islamic framework sought to resolve such issues by appealing to the Prophet's remembered utterances and actions, or by reasoning analogically from cases covered in authoritative texts (*qiyas*), or by deferring to the general agreement of the community about how one should proceed (*ijmā*).[41] In time, there also emerged writings on the theory and practice of statecraft.[42] All these endeavours shaped the development of various institutions through increasingly refined legal rulings that served to interpret, complete and expand the message of the Qur'an. Those involved in this legislation process undoubtedly realized that the bulk of the resulting body of Islamic law was human-produced. Still, they continued to call the ever-changing corpus God's law (*Shari'a*) and to perpetuate the notion that this law is fixed and comprehensive. In other words, even as they were implementing change, they refrained from admitting that Islam allows flexibility, novelty and reform. Why this lack of transparency? For one thing, rulings gained force when cloaked in timeless religion. For another, the practice allowed the powerful to conceal their personal agendas behind a façade of divine origin.

At least initially, the process of Islamic jurisprudence was quite responsive to the needs of key economic players. The Islamic law of contractual partnerships, which specified procedures for the orderly conduct of business, developed over a period stretching from the seventh to the tenth centuries to meet the evolving needs of investors and merchants. Jurists active in finance and commerce played a leading role in this process. Like the practising traders who produced Europe's 'law merchant',[43] they looked for enforceable rules and principles to govern transactions between regions separated by distance, language, culture and political allegiance.[44] Remarkably, right up to the eighteenth century there was a close match between the resulting commercial law and its practice.[45] This was so precisely because the interpretation of Islamic law was not tied to a closed sacred book. Among the tangible benefits of the observed responsiveness to market realities was that, by the global standards of the early Islamic era, contracting parties enjoyed remarkable flexibility.[46]

Like every legal system, that developed by Muslims restricted certain contractual freedoms. Many restrictions appear to have been intended to balance the interests of buyer and seller, and to keep one or both parties from feeling cheated. Consider the ban on selling a pregnant animal. However quaint this old prohibition now seems, it offered the advantage of channelling trade toward assets (specifically, non-pregnant animals) whose market value was relatively easy to ascertain. As with the Islamic law of partnerships, such restrictions were drawn from sources other than the Qur'an. They, and the morality they supported, were promoted by jurists keenly aware of the most common commercial disputes and eager to promote harmony by blocking situations liable to fuel perceptions of injustice.

It is clear that during Islam's first few centuries Islamic law was conducive to market-augmenting governance. The significance of the consequent wealth creation is evident in the spread of Islam over a vast geographical area. Where this expansion was driven by force, the economic successes of the early Islamic regimes created some of the necessary wealth. In any case, Islam's formidable expansion did not always involve military campaigns. Parts of sub-Saharan Africa and South East Asia joined the Islamic fold as Muslim traders familiarized their peoples with a legal code that was advanced for the time in many respects, including the organization of economic exchange.

LEGAL BARRIERS TO SUSTAINED DEVELOPMENT

Yet it would be sheer Panglossianism to assert that Islamic jurisprudence generated every institution that might have fuelled economic development, or that it was equipped for permanent economic success. From the beginning Islamic law prescribed limitations on the ruler's authority and also on the subject's duty of obedience; but it created no apparatus and established no procedures for enforcing these limitations. Nor for that matter did it develop constitutional procedures for an orderly transition of power or for removing an incompetent or crooked ruler.[47] In the Islamic world the first constitutions meeting these needs were promulgated in the nineteenth century, in the course of broad Westernization movements.[48] Insofar as this long delay restrained the strengthening of property rights and gave rulers greater opportunities to prey on their subjects, it must have reduced incentives for investment and harmed economic growth.

This brings us back to the claim of Islamic absolutism, which I characterized as simplistic. As Bernard Lewis (1988: 31ff.) observes, the notion that Muslim sovereigns had unlimited and unrestrained authority is false in both theory and practice. Islamic law never conceded absolute power to rulers, who were supposed to obey God's commands as strictly as their weakest subjects.

By the same token, any ruler who appeared to be skirting the law was liable to be overthrown, typically under the leadership of a challenger posing as more virtuous. Therefore while formal constitutional bounds on the exercise of power were absent, rulers had to appear as though they were upholding Islamic law. The easiest way to appear committed to the rule of Islamic law is of course to rule in a manner considered properly Islamic. The consequent political constraints would have included matters of economic relevance. Rulers seeking to appear pious would have avoided challenges to institutions strongly identified with Islam. One such institution was the law of inheritance spelled out in the Qur'an. Another was the form of individualism practised by the Islamic court system, which precluded the recognition of corporate entities. So if the main reason for the Islamic world's delayed economic modernization was an equilibrium trap that limited the influence of the productive classes, a secondary reason lay in religious constraints on rulers' market-augmenting activities.

To be constrained is not, of course, to lack options. A budget-constrained person has choices to make within his constraints, and these include the allocation of resources to relaxing the constraints themselves. So it is with politics. Political players who are sensitive to public opinion will often strive to manipulate their constituents' perceptions and preferences. In the pre-modern Islamic world the objects of such manipulation included the interpretation of Islamic law and of properly Islamic statecraft. During Islam's first two centuries, a key instrument of manipulating moral standards was the invocation of selected *hadiths* and the fabrication of new ones.

Not all Muslim-run political regimes have been equally driven to give their policies an Islamic façade. During the first two centuries of Ottoman rule, the fourteenth and fifteenth centuries, the Ottomans scarcely tried to discharge authority according to Islamic law. Precisely because they did not seek to ground their decisions in Islam, Arabs tended to consider the expanding Turkish state, at the time limited to Anatolia and the Balkans, a heretical entity. The Ottoman dynasty's disinterest in Islamic legitimation reflected, it has been observed, the religious composition of the population they ruled, mostly Christian and heterodox Muslim.[49] All this changed in the sixteenth century when much of the Arab world fell under Turkish rule, turning the Ottoman empire into the world's largest and most populous Muslim power. From then on, and especially after the empire's European expansion came to a halt, Ottoman sultans sought to put the weight of Islam behind their rulings. Thus it became customary to ground state policies in religious principles; Islamic scholars gained increasing prominence in administration; and the state started seeking to legitimize its acts through the approval of the chief Islamic officer, the *Şeyhülislam*.[50]

As in the past, and as in previous and coeval Islamic regimes, the state continued to legislate. The longest-reigning Ottoman sultan, known to Westerners as Suleiman the Magnificent (r. 1520–66), is known to Turks as Kanunî Sultan Süleyman – Süleyman the Lawgiver, a promulgator of laws rather than merely the top enforcer of an inherited sacred code. But in principle Islamic law remained the law of the land, so even rulings enacted by the state (*kanuns*) were incorporated into the evolving corpus of Islamic law. Thus scores of terms, concepts, interpretations and policy preferences without precedent in early Islam began to appear in Ottoman legal opinions (*fatwas*) ostensibly based on Islamic law.[51] The Ottoman religious establishment managed to produce Islamic justifications for cash *waqfs* (which violated the age-old rule restricting *waqf* assets to immovables), tax farming systems that side-stepped traditional Islamic taxes, the confiscation of properties, interest ceilings, the execution of defaulters (a penalty more severe than the hardships ancient Arabian defaulters endured under the institution of *ribā* banned by the Qur'an), and even the practice of killing a new sultan's siblings as a precaution against disunity.[52] Some of these rulings extended or updated Islamic law; others amounted to major reinterpretations. To prohibit interest charges above a certain rate amounts to legalizing rates below the adopted ceiling; hence it conflicts with the view, shared through the ages by many Islamic scholars, that all interest is illegal.

In its high period, then, the Ottoman approach to law struck a balance between deference to the principle of a fixed religious law and the supply of new rulings to accommodate evolving social conditions. Achieving a symbiosis between religious and human-produced laws, it endowed the latter with the sacredness of the former. Religious and secular law thus coexisted harmoniously, each recognized in its own domain, and neither considered illegitimate. Moreover religious officials rarely challenged the principle of coexistence. If they objected at all, they criticized specific rulings that infringed on religious laws, rather than the prevailing legal duality.[53] Formally, therefore, the supreme law of the land remained Islamic law. Until modern times judicial cases were almost always handled through Islamic courts, and litigants considered themselves participants in a process governed by religion.[54]

Where does this leave the claim that the persistent weakness of the merchant class and the corresponding strength of the state bureaucracy stemmed primarily from Islamic law? Throughout the Islamic world, and right up to modern times, inheritance matters were always handled by the Islamic courts; largely because of their articulation in the Qur'an, they fell squarely within the domain of religious law. Private contract law, though not anchored in the Qur'an, had emerged through a process considered integral to Islamic jurisprudence; as such it enjoyed strong identification with Islam. The Islamic courts that adjudicated contracts remained averse to the concept of a corporation, thus closing one of the paths by which large and durable Middle Eastern enterprises might have developed under the rubric of Islamic law. So the legal elements that blocked the legal features responsible for blocking the Islamic world's commercial modernization lay well within the domain of religious law. In principle the merchants of the Islamic world could press for the secularization of commercial law. But the elements of Islamic law that left them handicapped also kept them politically weak. A by-product of the resulting institutional stability was the perpetuation of an economic ideology that subordinated private commercial interests to objectives of the state.

CONCLUSION

A salient division within the broad literature on links between statecraft and economic development concerns the fixity of the institutional web within which private transactions occur. One tradition treats the structure and objectives of the state as given; another considers these features as dependent on economic outcomes, including the evolving distribution of wealth among social groups. By the first tradition, a basic reason why the economic fortunes of the West and the Islamic world diverged is that these two regions started off with fundamentally different state structures. The counter-tradition, endorsed here, seeks to identify the processes responsible for the observed state structures. In the West, I have proposed, medieval structures of governance proved self-destroying and self-renewing; they gave rise to new structures conducive to increasingly complex business relations. In the Islamic world, by contrast, key structures of governance turned out to be self-enforcing, even self-*rein*forcing. In particular, Islamic laws of critical importance to enterprise growth and continuity restrained the emergence of incentives to challenge and modify those laws. The feebleness of those incentives also contributed to thought patterns that discounted the requisites of commercial and financial development.[55]

All arguments centred on the presumed absolutism of the Islamic state provide incomplete explanations insofar as they neglect to elucidate the persistence of that absolutism at a time when Western states were providing merchants and financiers the freedom to develop the organizational infrastructure of modern capitalism. The evolutionary paths of the two civilizations differed not because one offered greater freedoms at the start. Rather, there were critical differences in the laws governing organizations and the intergenerational transmission of wealth. Those differences put the two civilizations on their respective paths, making one take the lead in developing the institutions of capitalism and democracy while the other became one of the laggards.

In and of itself the Islamic world's degree of political unity fails to explain why it fell behind the West. Its political centralization varied over time in ways that correlate poorly with the observed institutional creativity. The critical difference is not that one of these civilizations was more fragmented than the other in a political sense, but that laws critical to organizational development were relatively less flexible, and therefore more homogeneous, in the Islamic world. Greater homogeneity implied less institutional experimentation and fewer opportunities for starting down the path to modern capitalism.

The legal homogeneity that produced momentous consequences was not a planned institutional feature. The Christian and Jewish minorities of the Islamic world were allowed to operate legal systems of their own, and they enjoyed choice of law. Had that choice of law been extended to Muslims, the instituted legal pluralism might have spawned competitive pressures capable of generating revolutionary structural transformations. Because Muslims were denied choice of law the legal adjustments that mattered to the pace and substance of organizational development were ones that enhanced legal homogeneity. The upshot is that the pre-modern Islamic world enjoyed less institutional diversity than had been planned.

NOTES

1. Marx's scattered writings on the subject are critiqued by Lichtheim (1963: 90–100).
2. McGraw Donner (1981: 75–82, 251–71), Hodgson (1974, vol 1: 187–230).
3. Most accounts ascribe this political instability to such factors as personal ambition, regional rivalry and fanaticism. However, distributional matters were never far from the surface. See Hodgson (1974, Vol. 1: 146–230), Shaban (1971, Vol. 1, Chapters 1–4), Finer (1997, Vol. 2: 665–704). On the struggles over the distribution of booty, see also Løkkegaard (1991, Vol. 2: 1005–6).
4. Starr (1992, Chapter 2); İnalcık (1973, Chapter 10); Ortaylı (1999, Chapter 5).
5. Curtin (1984: 115–16). On the economic role of the Italian city states, see also Lane (1973).
6. Toprak (1995: 87–97). See also Lewis (1982), esp. Chapter 7.
7. Peters (1994: 180–83, 291–3); Faroqhi (1994), esp. Chapter 1, Barbir (1980, Chapter 3). The estimate comes from the second source, pp. 46–7, where several additional first-hand estimates may be found.
8. Epstein (2000, Chapter 4). See also Pirenne (1937: 96–102).
9. Epstein (2000: 83–4).
10. On these concessions and the conventional wisdom about their rationale, see İnalcık (1994, Chapter 9: 188–95).
11. Masters (1988: 211).
12. Pamuk (2000: 13–15). The reason why many economic historians have mistakenly considered the Ottoman policy toward markets to have been heavily and systematically interventionist is that they have failed to allow for the unrepresentative nature of their data. Whereas each government intervention was documented, no records were kept of countless occasions when markets were left alone. Price lists, Pamuk finds, were not a regular feature of Ottoman governance.
13. Olson's followers develop these ideas in Azfar and Cadwell (2003).
14. On the evolution of commercial law in pre-modern Europe, see Harris (2000), esp. Chapters 1–2.

15. İnalcık (1969: 97–140), esp. 135–8.
16. For an expanded version of this argument, see Kuran (2001b).
17. On the emergence and functions of the *waqf* system, see Kuran (2001c: 301–57).
18. For further insights into the advantages of Europe's political and legal fragmentation, see Jones (1987, Chapters 6–7), Mokyr (1990: 206–8), Rosenberg and Birdzell, Jr. (1986: 60–62).
19. Fernández-Armesto (1991, Chapter 3).
20. Platteau and Baland (2001: 27–67), esp. sections 2–3.
21. Hodgson (1974, Vol. 2).
22. For the details of this argument, see Kuran (2002b).
23. Genç (1989: 175–85); further refinements may be found in a collection of Genç's articles (2000, Chapters 2–4).
24. Such perceptions were not without foundation. For evidence of the growing institutional handicaps Middle Easterners faced *vis-à-vis* their Western competitors, see Kuran (2001b).
25. Not all cities merited equal attention; the needs of the capital overrode those of others. Goffman (1990: 21–3, 33–45) shows how Izmir's food trade was regulated to meet the provisioning needs of Istanbul.
26. Mercantilist ideas were not entirely absent from Ottoman discourse. The eighteenth-century historian Naima urged his fellow Ottomans to buy local products as a means of preventing trade deficits and outflows of coinage. But as Sayar (1986: 84–104) observes, Naima's position lay outside the intellectual mainstream of his society.
27. 'Kadimden olagelene aykırı iş yapılmaması.' See Genç (2000: 49, 333–42).
28. Eldem (1999: 273). This book, especially its tenth chapter, provides many additional insights into the impact of Ottoman economic philosophy.
29. In modern times this interpretation has been defended by Rahman (1974: 32–3). On the origins of *zakat* and its applications through time, see Kuran (2002a).
30. For the details of this argument, see Kuran (2001b).
31. Mardin (1969: 258–81).
32. On the legal developments that sustained this evolution, see Berman (1983: 10–12). The emergence of commercial corporations is examined by Harris (2000), esp. Chapters 2 and 5.
33. Shatzmiller (1994), Tables 5.1, 5.6, 5.8 and p. 293. Shatzmiller's definition of the state bureaucracy includes the civilian administration and the military as well as educational, legal, and religious functionaries.
34. Arndt (1987: 10–14). See also Rostow (1975, Chapter 1).
35. For a shining exception, see Shleifer and Vishny (1998), esp. Chapters 1 and 11.
36. Abu Yusuf (1969: 82–3, 100–101), Dennett, Jr. (1950: 40, 87, 114–15), Tritton (1970, Chapter 13). For more details on the interpretation offered here, see Kuran (2001a).
37. On tax treaties, Dennett (1950: 116–19); on tax farming, Morimoto (1981: 222–57); İnalcık (1994: 55–76); Darling (1996), esp. Chapters 4–6.
38. On the origins and ramifications of these distinctions, see Lewis (1988, Chapter 4).
39. Crone and Cook (1977), especially Chapter 12, show that salient precedents for discrimination against non-Arab Muslims were set by seventh-century efforts to depict Muhammad as the founder of a community parallel to that of Moses. These efforts included the treatment of the Prophet's Arabia as the only legitimate source of culture and the rejection of all cultural achievements that could not be Arabized. Because Islam presented itself as a universal religion, these efforts sowed massive confusion as to social standings of non-Arab converts. On the one hand it was widely accepted, partly on the basis of the Qur'an (49:13), that no person has more merit over another except through piety. On the other, various statements attributed to the Prophet turned Arab identity into a source of special distinction. The tensions between these two positions remain unresolved. Even in the non-Arab parts of today's Islamic world, notably the Indian subcontinent, there exist dignitaries who enjoy a special status on the basis of presumed descent from the Prophet.
40. For many additional examples, see Hallaq (1997: 3–7, 42–58).
41. Rahman (1979, Chapters 3–4), Coulson (1969), Rosen (1989, Chapter 3), and Tibi (1990).
42. Lambton (1981, Chapters 3–16).
43. Benson (1989: 644–61).

44. Udovitch (1970).
45. Çizakça (1996), Gedikli (1998).
46. See Kuran (2001b).
47. Lewis (1988), Chapter 5, esp. p. 113; Lambton (1981), esp. Chapters 2, 4 and 11.
48. The first constitution of the Islamic world, that of Tunisia, was proclaimed in 1861. Drafted in French, with the assistance of the French consul in Tunis, it represents a milestone in the process of Westernization. The next two constitutions, those of Turkey and Egypt, were promulgated in 1876 and 1882, respectively. See Caldwell et al. (1966: 2, 11, 26).
49. Farah (1993: 1–4), Barkan (1975: 50–55). For more details, see Kafadar (1995).
50. Gerber (1994, Chapters 2–3), Barkan (1975: 70–83).
51. Gerber (1999, Chapters 2–3).
52. Barkan (1975: 50–55, 57, 65–6, 74). For complementary insights, see Repp (1988: 124–45); İnalcık (1969: 105–38).
53. Repp (1988: 128).
54. Gerber (1999), esp. Chapter 2. See also al-Nahal (1979).
55. The concepts of self-destroying, self-renewing, self-enforcing and self-reinforcing institutions are developed by Greif, 'Historical Institutional Analysis', unpublished chapter of a book manuscript to be published by Cambridge University Press.

REFERENCES

Abu Yusuf (c. 790), *Kitab al-Kharaj*, translation by A. Ben Shemesh 1969 as *Taxation in Islam*, vol 3. Leiden: E.J. Brill.

Al-Nahal, Galal H. (1979), *The Judicial Administration of Ottoman Egypt in the Seventeenth Century*, Minneapolis, MN: Bibliotheca Islamica.

Arndt, H.W. (1987), *Economic Development: The History of an Idea*, Chicago, IL: University of Chicago Press.

Azfar, Omar, and Charles Cadwell (2003), *Market-Augmenting Government: The Institutional Foundations for Prosperity*, Ann Arbor, MI: University of Michigan Press.

Barbir, Karl K. (1980), *Ottoman Rule in Damascus, 1708–1758*, Princeton, NJ: Princeton University Press.

Barkan, Ömer Lütfi (1975), 'Türkiye'de din ve devlet ilişkilerinin tarihsel gelişimi'; in *Cumhuriyetin 50. Yıldönümü Semineri*, Ankara: Türk Tarih Kurumu, pp. 50–55.

Benson, Bruce (1989), 'The spontaneous evolution of commercial law', *Southern Economic Journal*, **55**, 644–61.

Berman, Harold J. (1983), *Law and Revolution: The Formation of the Western Legal Tradition*, Cambridge, MA: Harvard University Press.

Caldwellö J.A.M. et al. (1966), *Dustūr: A Survey of the Constitutions of the Arab and Muslim States*, Leiden: E.J. Brill.

Coulson, Noel J. (1969), *Conflicts and Tensions in Islamic Jurisprudence*, Chicago, IL: University of Chicago Press.

Crone, Patricia, and Michael Cook (1977), *Hagarism: The Making of the Islamic World*, Cambridge: Cambridge University Press.

Curtin, Philip D. (1984), *Cross-Cultural Trade in World History*, New York: Cambridge University Press.

Çizakça, Murat (1996), *A Comparative Evolution of Business Partnerships: The Islamic World and Europe, with Special Reference to the Ottoman Archives*, Leiden: E.J. Brill.

Darling, Linda T. (1996), *Revenue-Raising and Legitimacy: Tax Collection and Finance Administration in the Ottoman Empire, 1560–1660*, Leiden: E.J. Brill.

Dennett, Jr., Daniel C. (1950), *Conversion and the Poll Tax in Early Islam* Cambridge, MA: Harvard University Press.

Eldem, Edhem (1999), *French Trade in Istanbul in the Eighteenth Century*, Leiden: Brill.

Epstein, S.R. (2000), *Freedom and Growth: The Rise of States and Markets in Europe, 1300–1750*, London: Routledge.

Farah, Caesar E. (1993), 'Introduction', in Caesar E. Farah (ed.), *Decision Making and Change in the Ottoman Empire*, Kirksville, MO: Thomas Jefferson University Press, pp. 1–4.

Faroqhi, Suraiya (1994), *Pilgrims and Sultans: The Hajj Under the Ottomans, 1517–1683*, London: I.B. Tauris.

Fernández-Armesto, Felipe (1991), *Columbus*, Oxford: Oxford University Press.

Finer, S.E. (1997), *The History of Government from the Earliest Times*, vol 2. Oxford: Oxford University Press.

Gedikli, Fethi (1998), *Osmanlı Şirket Kültürü: XVI.–XVII. Yüzyıllarda Mudârebe Uygulaması*, Istanbul: Iz Yayıncılık.

Genç, Mehmet (1989), 'Osmanlı iktisadî dünya görüşünün ilkeleri', *Sosyoloji Dergisi*, 3rd ser. 1, 175–85.

Genç, Mehmet (2000), *Osmanlı İmparatorluğunda Devlet ve Ekonomi*, Istanbul: Ötüken.

Gerber, Haim (1994), *State, Society, and Law in Islam: Ottoman Law in Comparative Perspectiv*, Albany, NY: State University of New York Press.

Gerber, Haim (1999), *Islamic Law and Culture, 1600–1840*, Leiden: Brill.

Goffman, Daniel (1990), *Izmir and the Levantine World*, Seattle, WA: University of Washington Press.

Hallaq, Wael B. (1997), *A History of Islamic Legal Theories: An Introduction to Sunnī usūl al-fiqh*, Cambridge: Cambridge University Press.

Harris, Ron (2000), *Industrializing English Law: Entrepreneurship and Business Organization, 1720–1844*, Cambridge: Cambridge University Press.

Hodgson, Marshall G.S. (1974), *The Venture of Islam: Conscience and History in a World Civilization*, Chicago, IL: University of Chicago Press.

İnalcık, Halil (1969), 'Capital formation in the Ottoman Empire', *Journal of Economic History*, **19**, 97–140.

İnalcık, Halil (1969), 'Suleiman the Lawgiver and Ottoman law', *Archivum Ottomanicum*, 1, 105–38.

İnalcık, Halil (1973), *The Ottoman Empire: The Classical Age 1300–1600*, translation by Norman Itzkowitz and Colin Imber, London: Weidenfeld & Nicolson.

İnalcık, Halil (1994), 'The Ottoman state: economy and society, 1300–1600', in Halil İnalcık and Donald Quataert (eds), *An Economic and Social History of the Ottoman Empire, 1300–1914*, New York: Cambridge University Press, pp. 188–95.

Jones, E.L. (1987), *The European Miracle: Environments, Economies, and Geopolitics in the History of Europe and Asia*, Cambridge: Cambridge University Press, 2nd edn.

Kafadar, Cemal (1995), *Between Two Worlds: The Construction of the Ottoman State*, Berkeley, CA: University of California Press.

Kuran, Timur (2001a), 'Opportunistic taxation in Middle Eastern history: Islamic influences on the evolution of private property rights', unpublished paper, supplied by author at University of Southern California.

Kuran, Timur (2001b), 'The Islamic commercial crisis: institutional roots of economic underdevelopment in the Middle East', unpublished paper, accessed at www.papers.ssrn.com.

Kuran, Timur (2001c), 'The provision of public goods under Islamic law: Origins, impact, and limitations of the waqf system', *Law and Society Review*, **35**, 301–57.

Kuran, Timur (2002a), 'Islamic redistribution through zakat: Origins and early functions', in Michael Bonner, Mine Ener, and Amy Singer (eds), *Poverty and Charity in Middle Eastern Contexts*, Albany, NY: State University of New York Press, pp. 275–93.

Kuran, Timur (2002b), 'The economic ascent of the Middle East's religious minorities: the role of legal pluralism', unpublished paper.

Lambton, Ann K.S. (1981), *State and Government in Medieval Islam: An Introduction to the Study of Islamic Political Theory*, London: Oxford University Press.

Lane, Frederic C. (1973), *Venice: A Maritime Republic*, Baltimore, MD: Johns Hopkins University Press.

Lewis, Bernard (1982), *The Muslim Discovery of Europe*, New York: W.W. Norton.

Lewis, Bernard (1988), *The Political Language of Islam*, Chicago, IL: University of Chicago Press.

Lichtheim, George (1963), *Marx and the 'Asiatic Mode of Production'*, London: Chatto & Windus.

Løkkegaard, F. (1991), 'Ghanima', *Encyclopaedia of Islam*, vol 2, Leiden: E.J. Brill, 2nd edn.

Mardin, Şerif (1969), 'Power, civil society and culture in the Ottoman Empire', *Comparative Studies in Society and History*, **11**, 258–81.

Masters, Bruce (1988), 'The origins of Western dominance in the Middle East: mercantilism and the Islamic economy of Aleppo, 1600–1750', New York: New York University Press.

McGraw Donner, Fred (1981), *The Early Islamic Conquests*, Princeton, NJ: Princeton University Press.

McGuire, Martin C. (2003), 'Failures in governance: restrictions on the dominion of markets', in Azfar Omar and Cadwell Charles (eds), *Market-Augmenting Government: The Institutional Foundations for Prosperity*, Ann Arbor, MI: University of Michigan Press.

Mokyr, Joel (1990), *The Lever of Riches: Technological Creativity and Economic Progress*, New York: Oxford University Press.

Morimoto, Kosei (1981), *The Fiscal Administration of Egypt in the Early Islamic Period,* Kyoto: Dohosha.

North, Douglass C. (1995), 'The paradox of the West', in R.W. Davis (ed.), *The Origins of Modern Freedom in the West*, Stanford, CA: Stanford University Press, pp. 26–30.

Olson, Mancur (1996), 'Distinguished lecture on economics in government: Big bills left on the sidewalk: why some nations are rich, and others poor', *Journal of Economic Perspectives*, **10**, 3–24.

Ortaylı, İlber (1999), *İmparatorluğun En Uzun Yüzyılı*, 4th edn, Istanbul: İletişim.

Pamuk, Şevket (2000), *A Monetary History of the Ottoman Empire*, Cambridge: Cambridge University Press.

Peters, F.E. (1994), *The Hajj: The Muslim Pilgrimage to Mecca and the Holy Places*, Princeton, NJ: Princeton University Press.

Pirenne, Henri (1937), *Economic and Social History of Medieval Europe*, 1st edn 1933, San Diego, CA: Harcourt Brace.

Platteau, Jean-Philippe, and Jean-Marie Baland (2001), 'Impartible inheritance versus equal division: a comparative perspective centered on Europe and Sub-Saharan Africa', in Alain de Janvry, Gustavo Gordillo and Jean-Philippe Platteau (eds),

Access to Land, Rural Poverty, and Public Action, Oxford: Oxford University Press, pp. 27–67.

Rahman, Fazlur (1974), 'Islam and the problem of economic justice', *Pakistan Economist*, August, 32–3.

Rahman, Fazlur (1979), *Islam*, Chicago, IL: University of Chicago Press, 2nd edn.

Repp, C. (1988), 'Qānūn and sharī'a in the Ottoman context', in Aziz Al-Azmeh, *Islamic Law: Social and Historical Contexts*, London: Routledge, pp. 124–45.

Rosen, Lawrence (1989), *The Anthropology of Justice: Law as Culture in Islamic Society*, Cambridge: Cambridge University Press.

Rosenberg, Nathan, and L.E. Birdzell Jr. (1986), *How the West Grew Rich: The Economic Transformation of the Industrial World*, New York: Basic Books.

Rostow, W W. (1975), *How It All Began: Origins of the Modern Economy*, New York: McGraw Hill.

Sayar, Ahmet Güner (1986), *Osmanlı İktisat Düşüncesinin Çağdaşlaşması*, Istanbul: Der Yayınlari.

Shatzmiller, Maya (1994), *Labour in the Medieval Islamic World*, Leiden: E.J. Brill.

Shleifer, Andrei, and Robert W. Vishny (1998), *The Grabbing Hand: Government Pathologies and Their Cures*, Cambridge, MA: Harvard University Press.

Tibi, Bassam (1990), *Islam and the Cultural Accommodation of Social Change*, translation by Clare Krojzl, first edn. 1985, Boulder, CO: Westview Press.

Tritton, A.S. (1970), *The Caliphs and Their Non-Muslim Subjects: A Critical Study of the Covenant of Umar*, first edn 1930, London: Frank Cass.

Shaban, M.A. (1971), *Islamic History: A New Interpretation*, vol 1, Cambridge: Cambridge University Press.

Starr, June (1992), *Law as Metaphor: From Islamic Courts to the Palace of Justice*, New York: State University of New York Press.

Toprak, Zafer (1995), *Milli İktisat – Milli Burjuvazi*, Istanbul: Tarih Vakfı.

Udovitch, Abraham L. (1970), *Partnership and Profit in Medieval Islam*, Princeton, NJ: Princeton University Press.

Weber, Max (1925 [1947]), *The Theory of Social and Economic Organization*, translation by A.M. Henderson and Talcott Parsons, New York: Free Press.

Wittfogel, Karl A. (1957), *Oriental Despotism: A Comparative Study of Total Power*, New Haven, CT: Yale University Press.

COMMENT

Peter Bernholz

Introduction

Timur Kuran has provided an interesting analysis of the importance of political, legal, institutional and economic competition in the Islamic world. Though his analysis is mainly concerned with the Ottoman empire, he also touched on other periods and regions of the Islamic World. However, Islamic Spain is not mentioned by him. This is understandable for several reasons. First, it is impossible even to sketch all developments in the huge Islamic World over a period spanning about 1300 years. Second, Islamic Spain was on the Western periphery of this world. And finally, when the Ottoman empire moved towards its zenith after conquering Constantinople in 1453 and moving towards Vienna in 1529, Muslim Spain had already shrunk to the kingdom of Granada, which fell in 1492.

Still, historians seem to agree that al-Andalus was a flourishing community during most of its existence. Moreover, it was no longer under any control of the caliphs after 756, when the Abbasids had taken over the Caliphate. Also, Muslim Spain is especially interesting from the vantage point of the hypothesis examined in this book because it was during most of its existence not only in strong political competition with Christian rulers, but also with the Muslim states of the Maghreb. It seems, therefore, rewarding to take a look at the developments in al-Andalus as a kind of extension of Kuran's chapter.

When studying the developments in Muslim Spain the following periods have to be distinguished:

1. The time from the conquering of Spain by the Arab invaders in AD 711 to the establishment of the Umayyad emirate in 756 (the dependent emirate, that is dependent on the Umayyad caliph in Damascus).
2. The Umayyad emirate (founded by 'Abd ar-Rahman I) and caliphate of Cordoba from 756 to 1031.
3. The period of the *Muluk at-Tawa'if,* of the small *ta'ifa* kings from 1031 to 1086 (or 1110).
4. The rule of the Almoravids, who were Berbers and, at least for most of the time, Islamic fundamentalists coming from the south of Morocco, from 1086 (1110) to about 1144.
5. The return to small kingdoms until about 1155.
6. The rule of the Almohads, who were also Berbers and Islamic fundamentalists coming from Morocco, from about 1155 to 1212.

7. The loss of the Baleares in 1229, of Valencia 1238 and of Seville in 1248. Only the Islamic kingdom of Granada remained until 1492.

For our analysis it is important to explore whether more or less innovation and development took place during these different periods. In doing so we have to be aware that the periods were rather short, except for the period mentioned under 2. This is especially true for period 5. Also, it has to be kept in mind that there existed even during the more centralized periods military and political competition with Christian rulers and under the Umayyad emirate and caliphate also with Muslim rulers in North Africa.

From the Dependent Emirate and the Emirate and Caliphate of Cordoba to the Small Kingdoms

We learn from historians that in the years immediately following the conquest, that is in the eighth century, the cultural level was not higher than that attained by the Mozarabs, that is the Arabized Christians, who lived among the Arab conquerors. In this period popular works of medicine, agriculture, astrology and geography were translated from Latin into Arabic.

During the following two centuries, Islamic culture seems to have been original in many respects, for instance in inventing new arches (which can still be admired in the great mosque of Cordoba) and of strophic poems with an often complicated metric. But on the whole it remained provincial. This is also witnessed by the great reputation enjoyed by oriental Islamic scholars (Grunebaum 1963). The latter development may have been caused by the many Andalusians, who followed the rule of their religion to undertake a pilgrimage to Mecca at least once in their lifetimes, and who took advantage of their stay in those regions to enhance their knowledge and to bring it back to Spain.

With the decline and finally the fall of the Umayyad dynasty in 1031 many small kingdoms, the *ta'ifas*, developed. This dispersion of political power 'did, however, not mean the end, but a greater extension of cultural life: Seville, Granada, Valencia and other cities became centres of spiritual life besides the old Cordoba' (Cahen 1968: 234; my translation).

A similar conclusion is drawn by Grunebaum:

The Spanish-Islamic culture gains her real independence and discovers itself during the 11th century. This development is embodied in the great politicians and writers of prose Ibn Shuhaid (992–1034) and Ibn Hazm (994–1064). Ibn Hazm, moreover, excelled as a jurist and as a historian of comparative religion, especially of Islamic heresies. It is as if the political disintegration had set free energies and as if the manifold small centres had offered greater space to the diversity of talents. . . . The cultural interests were not only furthered by the mostly short-lived dynasties but also transformed into durable accomplishments by prudent patrons (Grunebaum 1963: 117, my translation).

Finally, Vernet Gines and Viguera (1994–98) remark that:

The highest peak in Islamic literature in Spain was attained during the era of the ta`ifas, when the poet-king al-Mu'tamid established an embryo of an academy of belles lettres, which included the foremost Spanish intellects as well as Sicilians who emigrated from their native land because of its conquest by the Normans. Other petty kings in the peninsula endeavoured to compete with al-Mu'tamid but did not succeed in assembling a constellation of writers of comparable stature.

It seems that the sciences and medicine also flourished during this period. In the field of lexicology the blind Ibn Sida of Denia (d. 1066) was eminent in this field and also wrote a kind of 'dictionary of ideas'. In history, the first known chronicles in Muslim Spain, for instance the *History of the Conquest of Spain* by Ibn al-Qutiyyah, were written in the tenth century. During the era of the *ta'ifas* the pre-eminent Spanish historian is Ibn Hayyan of Cordoba (d. 1076) who wrote an anthology of historical texts collected from the works of his predecessors. He also wrote an original chronicle, the *Matin*. Of great interest are also the *Memoirs* of King Ziri 'Abd Allah who was deposed by the Almoravids and who tried to justify his deeds as a statesman in his memoirs.

An important handbook of the history of science, which contained much information on technical subjects, was written in mid-eleventh century by Sa'id, a *qadi* of Toledo. In mathematics Maslama al-Majriti (d. 1008) should be mentioned. This scholar probably took part in the translation of Ptolemy's *Planispherium,* besides contributions to pure mathematics.

Some scholars sought to simplify the astrolabe, and finally az-Zarqali (Azarquiel; d. 1100) succeeded in inventing an apparatus called the *azafea* (Arabic: *as-safiha*) which was widely used by navigators until the sixteenth century. Abu 'Ubayd was an outstanding geographer, as was al-Bakri (d. 1094), who composed the *Book of Highways and of Kingdoms.*

Especially interesting is the dominance of the Jews in the kingdom of Granada, where Samuel ibn Nagrada (ca 1030–1066), a Talmud scholar, grammarian, poet, and since 1027 leader of the Jewish community, became chief administrator of the king. Even though his *de facto* position as vizier, which was not permitted by Muslim law, later cost the lives of his son Joseph and of many other Jews during a pogrom, it shows the tolerance of rulers during this period.

Almoravids, Almohads and the Last Period of Muslim Rule

The existence of many rulers had, however, negative consequences because of the many wars they fought against each other and the increasing pressure from the Christian kingdoms to which they often had to pay tribute to maintain their independence. Added to these expenses were those for mercenaries and the extravagance of the small courts. Finally, when Alfonso VI of Castile conquered Toledo in 1085, the princes of Seville, Badajoz and Granada felt threatened and asked the Almoravids for help. This help was granted and led to the defeat of Alfonso near Badajoz in October 1086, but also in time to the subjugation of the small Muslim kingdoms by the Almoravid King Jusuf ibn Tashfin. The last independent kingdom of Saragossa was incorporated in 1110.

The Almoravids (*al-Murabitum*) had been soldiers stationed, like religious orders, in fortified garrisons at the extreme Muslim borders from Mauritania to the Senegal and Niger rivers. They had become Muslims not long ago, were recruited among the Berber tribes and adhered to a rather simple and militant Islam. Given these conditions it was not difficult for Ibn Yasin, a fundamentalist propagandist, to win a growing number of followers among them with the aim of literally following the doctrines of Islam, renewing it and leading a 'Holy War' against the 'bad' Muslims. The commander of these soldiers and believers, Yusuf ibn Tashfin, soon succeeded in conquering Morocco and central Maghreb. In 1062 the newly founded Marrakesh became his capital.

With the rule of the Amoravids a spirit of intolerance against non-Muslims, who were suspected of collaboration with the Christian enemy, came to Spain, and ended four centuries of profitable cooperation in a 'holy war'. As a consequence, it was easy for Alfonso VI to force thousands of Mozarabs to move into depopulated Christian territory. The deportation of Christians to Morocco demonstrates the feeling of crisis after the Muslims had been defeated at Arminsol near Granada in 1125. True religious life even of Muslims was hindered by the dictates of narrow-minded Muslim jurists who wanted to preserve people from moral corruption.

But the rule of the Almoravids did not last very long. The mistakes of the regime led to the evolution of another fundamentalist Islamic movement, the Almohads (*al-Muwahhidun*, 'those who believed in the One'), among the mountain population of the Atlas. Their religious leader was the 'Mahdi' Ibn Tumart (d. 1130), and his student 'Abdalmu'min (1130–63) became their political organizer. The Almohads soon conquered the whole Maghreb, including Tunisia, in a 'holy war' against the Almoravids. Opposition was eliminated in a massacre. Even after the final victory it 'proved necessary' to exterminate opposing tribes in a second *tamfiz* ('distinction'). And the princes of the small kingdoms of Spain, which had emerged once more from the decline of Almoravid rule, called as before for assistance against the Christian *reconquista*. The Almohads saved the Muslim territories again for some time by defeating Alfonso VIII of Castile at Alarcos in 1195. They subjugated the small Muslim kingdoms and made Seville their capital in Spain.

The Almohads also followed a policy of intolerance. The Jews were weakened economically by high taxes. The Arabized Christians were not only driven into opposition by all kinds of harassment but many of them emigrated to territories reconquered by the Christian kingdoms. As a further consequence, many Jews emigrated to the Near East, among them the great scholar Maimonides. All these measures taken by the Almohads led to a hardening of religious divisions and an impatience felt by a broad segment of the population to become Castilian subjects.

In spite of this intolerance, the deeper understanding of the Almohads for a vital religion favoured within Islam a greater freedom of spiritual developments and of science, as witnessed by the great names of Spanish-Islamic poets and philosophers. Among other outstanding poets of the twelfth century were Ibn Khafaja of Alcira and his nephew Ibn az-Zaqqaq in eastern Andalusia. In spite of their limited interest in the physical sciences, the Andalusians excelled in astronomy. Az-Zarqali anticipated Kepler by suggesting that the planetary orbits were ovoid and not circular, and Jabir ibn Aflah criticized the Ptolemaic system in the twelfth century. And in the field of the arts the time of the Almohads is one of the great, perhaps even the greatest epoch of Western Islam (Cahen 1968: 310).

It has been mentioned that soon after the decline of Almohad rule only the kingdom of Granada remained as the last Muslim state on the Iberian peninsula. It was able to maintain a highly developed culture, of which the Alhambra still bears evidence. For instance, during the great days of Granada, 'Ali al-Qalasadi did important work on fractions. The vizier-historian Ibn al-Khatib (d. 1375) was an important mathematician. Ibn al Baytar (d. 1248) described the medicinal properties of more than 1400 plants, following in the steps of Dioscorides and of several Andalusian countrymen who had extended his work. In 1323 the first Arabian nautical map appeared, which stemmed probably from Granada. The poets Abu al-Baqa of Ronda and Ibn Sa'id belonged to the era of the greatest decadence in the thirteenth century. Three poets at the court, Ibn al-Jayyab, Ibn al-Khatib and Ibn Zamraq, preserved their verses by having them inscribed in the Alhambra in the fourteenth century. But many Muslims already felt that the position of the kingdom of Granada was rather precarious so that those who were able to do so preferred to emigrate to the Maghreb, or even better to Egypt or Syria.

The Economic Development

There can be no doubt that Muslim Spain flourished economically though we seem presently not to be able to draw a clear line between the economic situations in the different periods. When the Muslims had successfully invaded the peninsula, they divided the conquered lands and generally cultivated them through tenant farmers. The raising of sheep and Arabian horses occupied a central position in the peninsular economy as did the use of woodland. Irrigation was encouraged by the development of favourable rules which were operated, at least in well-known examples of the countryside around Valencia, Murcia and Orihuela, and Alicante, by self-governing bodies related to or controlled by landed proprietors (Ostrom 1990: 69–82, Glick 1970, Maass and Anderson 1986).

Muslim Spain was noted for its windmills and for its manufacture of paper. The government protected plants used in the manufacture of textile (flax, cotton, esparto grass and mulberry for silk) as well as those with medicinal properties.

Similar to the Roman period, lead, iron, gold and mercury were mined. The domestic industry excelled in the production of luxury cloths like silk which was a state monopoly, in the tanning of hides (Cordovan leather) and in the export of ivory objects. But this development never went beyond the handicraft stage. Commerce was selective and concentrated on products of low weight and high value. Far distant trade reached the most remote regions of the known world. There are reports of Andalusian travellers as far as the Sudan, central Europe and even China. Muslim coins were well received most of the times, and Barcelona counterfeited Muslim coins in the eleventh century.

According to some estimates the population reached the following numbers in the urban centres at the end of the tenth century: Cordova 250 000, Toledo 37 000, Almeria 27 000, Granada 26 000, Saragossa 17 000, Valencia 15 000, and Malaga 15 000. The latter cities developed further during the period of the petty kings. Cities enjoyed baths, gardens, markets and mosques. They had a high cultural level and were quite different from and superior to those of Christian Europe though they did not enjoy the independence of the latter.

Chalmeta (1992) reports that the population of Spain during the time of emperor Augustus was estimated to have been 7 to 7.7 million and that it had declined to 3 million until 700, before the Muslims arrived. During the heyday of the Umayyad caliphate it reached about 10.23 million, of which 9.3 million were rural people. For Cordoba, Chalmeta calculates from widely diverging figures an even more numerous population than mentioned above, of about 500 000 (p. 755). He quotes 'Ibn Haciqul:

> The cities vie with one another in their situations and by [the amount of] taxes and their incomes ... There is no town which is not well populated and surrounded by a huge rural district, by a whole province rather, with numerous villages and labourers living in prosperity, owning large and small livestock, good equipment, beasts of burden and fields ... The price of the goods is pretty much that of a region with a good reputation for commerce, prosperous, and rich in resource, where life is easy ...

Chalmeta finally adds:

> ... we must remember that its economy was self-sufficient and enjoyed continuous
> growth over three centuries. For 75 years from ... 1009 [during the time of the
> ta'ifa kingdoms], al-Andalus was also capable of sustaining and (involuntarily)
> financing the development of another, external and parasitical social entity: The
> Christian kingdoms of the North. It would be difficult to provide a better indication
> of the economic situation and importance of al-Andalus from its establishment up
> to the Almoravid seizure of power (pp. 756 ff.).

This last remark seems to suggest that economic welfare at least did not
diminish during the *ta'ifa* kingdoms compared to the heyday of the
Umayyad period. A similar impression can probably be derived from Remie
Constable's (1992) article on merchants: 'Arabic sources show that the final
period of the Umayyad rule in Cordoba was a fertile period for merchant
activity' (p. 763). Concerning the period of the petty kingdoms she
explains: 'The number of references to native Andalusi merchant-scholars
travelling abroad decreased during the ta'ifa and Almoravid regimes, even
in biographical works largely devoted to scholars living in this period' (p.
764).

But she seems to be surprised that:

> In contrast to this paucity of references to Andalusi merchant-scholars travelling
> eastward in the early ... 11th century, there is a relative abundance of biographical
> information on merchant-scholars arriving in Islamic Spain between the years ...
> 1023 and ... 1041 ... (p. 764).
>
> The time frame is intriguing, because these twenty years span the gap between
> the final years of the Umayyad dynasty and the emergence of the early ta'ifa states,
> an era thought to have been troubled by unrest and civil war. One would expect to
> see a decrease in merchant activity in this period, as is suggested by the data on
> native Andalusi traders. In contrast, although the sample is small, tarajim [Arabic
> biographical dictionaries] references indicate that foreign merchants continued to
> arrive in Andalusi markets during this period of political turmoil and weak govern-
> ment control in Islamic Spain.
>
> After this brief heyday of abundant references, biographical information on east-
> ern merchant-scholars suddenly becomes scarce after the middle of the 5th/11th
> century. The apparent decrease in the activities of merchant-scholars should proba-
> bly be attributed to non-commercial causes – perhaps the arrival in Spain of the
> Almoravids and Almohads, since it is not reflected in sources pertaining to the rest
> of the merchant population (p. 765).

The kingdom of Granada, the last remaining Islamic kingdom in Spain
during the 250 years until 1492, seems also to have flourished economically,
and this in spite of incessant manoeuvring, changes of alliances and warfare
with the Christian kingdoms of Castile and Aragon and the Merinid state in
Morocco. As Kennedy (1996) reports:

The meagre evidence suggests that the Kingdom of Granada was both densely populated and comparatively prosperous, although, as Levi-Provencal observed, we know much less about the economic state of the Kingdom of Granada than we do of the caliphate of Cordoba half a millennium earlier. In contrast to Christian Spain, where the production of wool from merino sheep was coming to dominate the agricultural economy, Granada seems to have had a mixed agricultural economy. Silk and dried fruits were exported in significant quantities to Italy and northern Europe. Most of the external trade was in the hands of Genoese merchants who established trading colonies in Malaga, Almeria and Granada. In contrast to earlier periods, commerce with the Muslim east seems to have almost completely dried up, though grain may have been imported from the Maghreb. The city of Granada itself expanded and new quarters like the Albaicin to the north and the Antequeruela (inhabited by people from Antequera which fell to the Castilians in 1410) to the south were developed, partly to house refugees who arrived from Christian-held territories. The population has been estimated at 50 000, perhaps half of that of Cordoba in the tenth century, although the estimates are very speculative. But it is the Alhambra palace itself which survives to give us the fullest impression of the wealth of this last remaining Muslim enclave (p. 277).

Conclusions

Muslim Spain, perhaps except for the first period, was characterized by intense political and military competition. This is even true for the emirate and caliphate of Cordoba and the rule of the Almoravids and Almohads as witnessed by the limited time span during which the latter kingdoms were able to survive. And the Umayyad rulers were not only in competition with their Christian neighbours, which were not too threatening at that time, but more so with their North African Muslim competitors. Nevertheless the military and foreign policy competition was most intense when the Islamic part of the Iberian peninsula was split up among many small kingdoms. It follows from the hypothesis analysed in this volume that innovation and development should have been strongest during this period. Though it is often not possible to assign innovators clearly to one period or the other, either because historians have not examined the evidence until today from the vantage point taken here, or because the lifetimes of innovators overlapped different periods, it seems that there exists evidence to support our hypothesis. As pointed out by Vernet Gines and Viguera (1994–98), 'Arab civilization in the peninsula reached its zenith when the political power of the Arabs began to decline'.

Similarly, von Grunebaum (1963: 119) states:

In contrast to the nationalistic theories of the Arabs of today, but not to the general experience of humanity, the zenith of the Arabian-Islamic culture occurred at a time of political decline in which the rule of small states was self-evident and in which the political centres threatened and fought each other incessantly. The Italian

Renaissance can be offered as a parallel development, also the view transmitted by Justus Moeser to Goethe that a set of small cities is highly desirable for the spread of culture. Moeser presupposed peaceful relationships of the princes and cities belonging to the Reich. The Islamic national states of the High and Late Middle Ages, however, could not expect such a state of affairs [my translation].

Finally, we have seen that religious fundamentalism returned to Islamic Spain with the Almoravids and Almohads. Their repressive and intolerant policies are, besides less foreign policy competition, another possible reason for the smaller degree of the flourishing and development of culture and economy. For we can observe such negative consequences for cultural life and the economy when the Christians became intolerant and oppressive against Jews and Moors after they had conquered Granada in 1492, this quite in contrast to their mostly tolerant policies in the centuries after the fall of Toledo in 1085. The Umayyad rule also knew periods of religious intolerance. Emir 'Abd ar-Rahman II introduced an era of political, administrative and cultural regeneration of Muslim Spain. He imposed the death penalty on Christians who protested against the growing arabization of their co-religionists by blaspheming the Prophet Muhammad. This provocation led to the execution of 53 people before the conflict ended in 860.

In summing up, it seems that innovation and growth of al-Andalus were furthered by political competition among rulers and that they were less pronounced when Islamic Spain was united and subject to religious intolerance. But our knowledge seems still to be limited, and further research is necessary, especially since historical events, among them economic developments, have not been studied from the vantage point of the hypothesis discussed in this book.

References

Cahen, Claude (1968), 'Der Islam. I. Vom Ursprung bis zu den Anfaengen des Osmanischen Reiches', *Fischer Weltgeschichte,* vol 14, Frankfurt: Fischer Buecherei.

Chalmeta, Pedro (1992), 'An approximate picture of the economy of al-Andalus', in Salma Khadra Jayyusi (ed.), *The Legacy of Muslim Spain, Handbuch der Orientalistik, Erste Abteilung, Der Nahe und Mittlere Osten,* vol 12, Leiden, New York, Cologne: E.J. Brill, pp. 741–58.

Glick, T.F. (1970), *Irrigation and Society in Medieval Valencia,* Cambridge, MA: Harvard University Press.

Grunebaum, Gustav Edmund von (1963), 'Der Islam', in Golo Mann and August Nitschke (eds), *Propylaeen Weltgeschichte,* vol 5, Berlin and Frankfurt am Main: Propylaeen Verlag, pp. 21–180.

Kennedy, Hugh (1996), *Muslim Spain and Portugal. A Political History of al-Andalus,* London and New York: Longman.

Maass, A., and R.L. Anderson (1986), . . . *and the Desert Shall Rejoice: Conflict, Growth and Justice in Arid Environments*, Malaba, FL: R.E. Krieger.

Ostrom, Elinor (1990), *Governing the Commons: The Evolution of Institutions for Collective Action*, Cambridge and New York: Cambridge University Press.

Remie Constable, Olivia (1992), 'Muslim merchants in Andalusi international trade', in Salma Khadra Jayyusi (ed.), *The Legacy of Muslim Spain, Handbuch der Orientalistik, Erste Abteilung, Der Nahe und Mittlere Osten*, vol 12, Leiden, New York, Cologne: E.J. Brill, pp. 759–73.

Vernet Gines, Juan, and Maria J. Viguera (1994–98), 'Culture of Muslim Spain', in *Encyclopaedia Britannica*.

COMMENT

Michael Cook

Kuran's chapter is rich, consistently intelligent, and by American standards breathtakingly politically incorrect. But the parts I want to comment on are only those that bear on the hypothesis under discussion in this volume (hereafter 'the hypothesis').

Let me start by taking issue with the account of the balance of political unity and disunity in Islamic history as Kuran sums it up. He says that the Islamic world lost its political unity soon after the Prophet's death, but never became as fragmented as medieval Western Europe. I am not sure about the comparison with Europe – it would depend on which medieval century one chose, and on how one defined a political unit. But leaving that aside, I would give a picture significantly different from Kuran's (and also, I think, from Baechler's if I understand correctly):

First (A), the political unity of the Islamic world was pretty well maintained from the time of the Prophet down to the later ninth century – some two-and-a-half centuries. I leave aside the episodes of quite intense civil war that punctuate this period, sometimes for several years at a stretch; and I also disregard the small independent states that were appearing in peripheral areas towards the end of it, since I do not think them sufficient to make an acceptable federal pattern (cf. p. 29 f. (1)). So this is a period of much greater unity than Kuran's formulation allows for.

Second (B), the period from the later ninth century to the early sixteenth century is one of disunity rather than unity. Of course the balance varies from century to century. Take the case of Iran. There are periods of disunity from the ninth to the eleventh century, from the twelfth to the thirteenth, in the fourteenth, and again in the fifteenth. There are periods of unity in which Iran is the core of a regional empire from the eleventh to twelfth century, from the thirteenth to fourteenth, around 1400, and again around 1500. But even during these imperial periods in Iran, there are still plenty of states elsewhere in the Islamic world, and even in the Near East. So overall this is perhaps a period of rather less political unity than Kuran's formulation allows for.

Third (C), the Ottoman empire of the sixteenth century is a very large and centralized state. There are other states, like Morocco in the west and Iran in the east, and while they are not peripheral, neither are they in the same league as the Ottoman empire. Of course, we are tending to forget about the eastern parts of the Islamic world, but so be it. Here, then, I have no serious disagreement with Kuran.

Fourth (D), the Ottoman empire of the seventeenth and eighteenth centuries is large but not centralized. There is a chaotic period in the first half of the seventeenth century, and when the dust settles in the second half, the balance of power between centre and periphery has shifted: there are now semi-independent centres of regional or local power in much of the empire. This development is not mentioned by Kuran, but it is surely relevant to our concerns.

In short, Islamic history provides quite a varied terrain on which to try out the hypothesis: a unitary period, a plural period, a second unitary period and what might be called a crypto-plural period.

Kuran's prime concern is (C), the high Ottoman period. Here he makes very clear a certain sympathy with the hypothesis. He sees the unity, and especially the legal unity, of the Ottoman empire as having several economic advantages, but also serious disadvantages: thus the absence of inter-jurisdictional competition dampened pressures for raising the economic sophistication and efficiency of the law, and by implication Columbus would have got nowhere had he taken his project to the Ottoman sultan (I base this on one of two possible readings of what Kuran says). In a similar vein Kuran later comes back to the theme of the costs of unity in the wider context of Islamic history, noting that it meant fewer choices of rulers and hence of official patronage; here he suggests that the disadvantages may well have tipped the balance. All this makes good sense, though it is odd against such a background to find that it is precisely in this period that, as Kuran points out, major reinterpretations take place in Ottoman law, some of them in the economic field (cf. p. 29 f. (2)).

On balance, then, the hypothesis provides a plausible way to look at the Ottoman period, or at least that portion of it in which the empire was large and centralized. If we assume that this approach is right, what would it lead us to expect in the other periods I listed above? (note that I use the vague wording 'lead us to expect', not anything as crisply logical as 'imply'.)

The initial period of Islamic unity (A) under the Umayyad and Abbasid caliphs should surely resemble the Ottoman period in the respects that concern us. But this goes against the way historians of the Islamic world think of it. First, they view this period as by later standards one of remarkable cultural creativity and diversity, and it would be hard for them not to – this is a period in which a new civilization takes shape. Second, they think of it as a time more friendly to mercantile interests than what follows; this is a less well-established view but it is not, I think, to be dismissed outright. And indeed Kuran sides with the rest of us. For example he refers to the institutional dynamism of the first few Islamic centuries, and to the openness to change of the caliphs in developing what became the Islamic administrative tradition. Moreover he speaks of Islamic law in its early history as having been quite responsive to the needs of key economic players. I do not disagree with any of this, and I therefore tend to think that the hypothesis is in some kind of trouble for this initial period of Islamic unity (cf. p. 50 (2)) – unless we are defining cultural creativity restrictively (cf. p. 50 ff. (3)).

One very simple point that may help here is that competition between states can only be good for aspects of culture in which states compete. With other aspects, even if competition is relevant (and it probably is), it is not interstate competition that counts. The picture Islamicists have developed suggests that significant aspects of Islamic culture – including in considerable measure Islamic law – developed outside the context of state patronage, in places far from the political centre. In such a situation it may be irrelevant whether there is one state or many. In the same way, though musically illiterate, I tend to assume that interstate competition played a greater role in the development of grand opera than of hard rock. But of course it could be argued that the relative homogeneity of Islamic law presupposes the presence of a single state, at least in appointing judges, and that an Islamic law that had evolved in a period of disunity would, if it had evolved at all, have been much more regionally differentiated.

For the intervening period of disunity (B), the hypothesis leads us to expect good things to happen. Kuran I think is telling us that they did not. He remarks that such dynasties as the Fatimids, Seljuks, and so on could have used Islam to support property rights, market freedoms and institutional change – implying that in fact they did not do so. He quotes figures indicating that the division of labour contracted in the economy but expanded in administration in roughly the period of disunity. So he clearly does not think that this period delivered the kind of goods the idea would lead us to expect. Why did it not? Kuran emphasizes in his chapter the role of broad historical patterns rooted in certain aspects of Islamic law in precluding economic innovation, in this and other periods. In other words, political plurality is not enough (cf. p. 29 f. (1)). Thus Islamic law plays the role in Kuran's analysis that endemic political instability plays in Lal's.

There are two things to take up here, the record (what these dynasties did or did not do) and the explanation (why they did or did not do it).

With regard to the record, I know no reason to doubt what Kuran says about economic matters. If he is wrong, historians of the Islamic world do not seem to have noticed. I am not of course claiming that we Islamic historians are a particularly observant species, but if good things were happening on a large scale, we would surely have registered the fact. Quite the contrary, we tend to think that the military regimes associated with Turkish power from the tenth century onwards were bad for mercantile interests, whether the states concerned were large or small. The picture might look rather different if we turned from the economy to culture in a narrow sense. Historians of the Islamic world would have no difficulty with the idea that the federal pattern is good for some kinds of cultural creativity, or at least cultural variety. The re-emergence of Persian as a literary language within the Islamic world in the tenth century is a clear example: nobody doubts that this was closely connected to the political disunity of the period, which gave new scope for rulers to relate to regional heritages that were not part of the mainstream Islamic cultural tradition.

With regard to the explanation, I would like to pick up Kuran's observation that to be constrained is not to lack options. What I have in mind goes like this. Let us assume that the pressure of competition is strong (as the hypothesis would lead us to expect), and that the period over which it is at work is relatively long (cf. p. 30 (5)). Should it not then be the case that sooner or later, somewhere or other, someone would come up with a way to get round the adverse heritage of Islamic law and reap the attendant rewards?[1] And once one ruler did so, would not others follow suit? This thought inclines me to think that even if Kuran is right about Islamic law, the rewards may not have been all that great, or the competition not all that intense – which does not tend to support the hypothesis.

Another explanation we might want to consider here is Lalian political instability. If this is thought to provide an acceptable explanation for the fact that the idea does not seem to work well in India, could it not do the same for at least some of this disunited period in the Islamic world? But we would then find ourselves entangled in the question how unstable things have to be for the explanation to kick in. And the question would again arise (as it might in the Indian context): why did not some ruler find a way to overcome the political instability and reap the rewards?

Finally, we come to the late Ottoman period of formal unity and effective disunity (D). Historians of the Ottoman empire have, I think, little sense that in this period competition between regional semi-autonomous potentates within the empire was delivering the kind of goods envisaged by the hypothesis (or not at least until Muhammad Ali began to rule Egypt in the early nineteenth century). It is of course no longer considered well-bred to speak of Ottoman decline; but we are not yet committed to seeing the period as one of vibrant and sustained economic growth. It is also noteworthy that we hear remarkably little of regional potentates as patrons; they do not for example seem to have been builders on any scale. So in this period too the hypothesis seems to be in some kind of trouble. Lalian instability would be a plausible alibi here if anywhere.

How does all this stack up? Before I try to answer this question, let me bring the papers on China and India into the discussion.[2]

Mo's central thesis is that the hypothesis is vindicated in the Chinese context. Baechler had adduced the Warring States period and the interval between Han and T'ang to support his argument; Mo now adds the Sung period, with a primarily economic concern that fits well with the title of the conference. What bothers me is (4): Southern Sung is a clear example of the federal pattern, but is Northern Sung really a case of it? However, I leave this question to others. All we need note here is that the hypothesis gets a clear 'yes' from the chapter on China.

Lal's paper on India, by contrast, responds with a clear 'no', in its first paragraph. More precisely, he sees pre-Muslim India as a case in which the federal pattern did not deliver the goods (at least in the rather restrictive sense of placing India at the top of world history (cf. p. 30 f. (3))). Lal's explanation is that the federal pattern is not enough (cf. p. 30 f. (1)); there also has to be a modicum of political stability. This of course would be compatible with a weak form of the hypothesis. I have two queries. First, do we actually know enough about the political history of pre-Muslim India to judge whether or not it was marked by endemic political instability? Second, do we know enough about its economic history to exclude the possibility that there was significant economic innovation short of seizing the high ground of world history? But again I happily leave such questions to the commentator. All we need note here is Lal's clear 'no' to the hypothesis.

So we have the hypothesis being supported in the case of China (usually united, occasionally disunited), and dismissed in the case of India (usually disunited, occasionally mostly united). It seems then to depend on Japan and the Islamic world (sometimes united, sometimes disunited) who wins.

My sense, as will be obvious from what I have said above about the individual periods, is that the hypothesis does not perform as well as one might have expected. More precisely, it works fairly well for the high Ottoman period (C), but is *prima facie* in trouble in one way or another for the other three. I deliberately use the vague phrase 'in trouble', rather than more precise words like 'confirmed' or 'falsified', for the reasons set out in my comment on Baechler. So on balance the Islamic vote probably goes with India rather than China. This leaves me slightly puzzled as to why a hypothesis that seems so intuitively plausible should not fare better – but only slightly, because as a historian I have experienced such disappointment often enough before.

In closing, I would like to stress that what I have attempted above is very limited. I have taken three things and tried to relate them: the hypothesis that is the subject of this volume, the parts of Kuran's chapter that more or less directly bear on it, and my general knowledge as a historian of the Islamic world. It might be very rewarding to comb through the detail of Islamic history for material relevant to the hypothesis, but it would also consume more time than I have had available. Moreover my hunch, for what it is worth, is that the key question is what it was about early modern Europe that makes the hypothesis work there.

Notes

1. Consider the fact that for large numbers of pre-modern Muslims customary law was of far greater practical importance than Islamic law, and that such legal systems could ignore the Islamic law of inheritance and recognize the legal personality of corporations.
2. Distelrath's chapter on Japan was not yet available at the time I composed this comment.

COMMENT

Mark Elvin

Professor Kuran's chapter is a deeply informed analysis of a subject on which I am almost wholly uninformed, the consequences for the workings of the economy of the political structure and policies of the Ottoman empire. My questions are therefore those of an interested outsider.

The fundamental question that the chapter seems to be addressing, though this is not explicitly spelt out, is why the far-flung Ottoman empire at its height did not enjoy what Goldstone has recently called a period of economic 'efflorescence'. That is, a period of enhanced economic vitality based on technological and organizational improvements, Sung-dynasty China being perhaps the paradigm case. The point of this particular term is to avoid prejudging the more problematic issue of a transition to something resembling 'modern economic growth'. Efflorescences characteristically sooner or later come to a close, if only because – without modern science – they cannot sustain the flow of innovations needed to continue.

In the later sixteenth century the Ottoman empire was a polity based on what is present-day Turkey that, broadly speaking, controlled the eastern half of the Mediterranean, the eastern shore of the Red Sea, Mesopotamia, most of the Black Sea, and the Balkans in an extended sense including not only Greece but also Hungary and parts of Austria. It had become, as the author says, a huge internal market. In the chapter it is presented as very much a unity, but some historical maps at least distinguish between the core area and 'tributary states' (for example the area north of Belgrade). These were probably of limited economic importance at the time but it would be analytically useful to know if any political differences associated with tributary status in fact made any difference to their economic functioning.

The title suggests that we might approach the topic along two axes, that of 'Islam' and that of 'statecraft', so let us do so, beginning with the religion.

The first question is to what extent we can reasonably take Islam, considered as a human cultural phenomenon, both intellectual and social, as a historical constant. As a sort of unchanging Weberian 'ideal-type' if you like. There would seem to be at least two reasons for not doing so. The first is that, at least to an outside observer, the impressive intellectual vigour of medieval Islam seems to have declined dramatically just as the Western world was beginning to enter what is commonly, if perhaps misleadingly, known as the 'early modern' period. The reasons for this underlying phenomenon – if you agree that I have identified it correctly, and it is to some extent controversial – need to be addressed, as it defined a context of which the diminished economic vitality on which the chapter focuses was only a part, though an important part.

Let me give but one example that may have some bearing on the chapter's interesting emphasis on the virtual absence of any legal standing for groups or corporations in the Ottoman empire. The late fourteenth-century economic and social historian Ibn Khaldun is famous for his emphasis on the importance of cooperation among people in various ways. This general cooperation among people was basic to civilization, and – relatively unusually for Islamic thought, as I understand it – he also gave a positive twist to the idea of 'group feeling' (*'asabîyah*). More commonly this term was used in a pejorative sense of a biased partisanship, and it is true that it tended to refer to kinship and political association, but in Ibn Khaldun's conception it was one of the foundations – laudable foundations – of success. The reason I mention this is that there would seem to have been potential intellectual resources of this sort that could in principle have been developed, had there been real intellectual vitality, into some sort of limited ideological validation for groups, even if 'Islamic law . . . precluded corporations' (as is stated on p. 167). We may also note in passing in this regard that on p. 167 'universities' are mentioned as being – by implication – one of the distinctive features of Western corporation-based life. I would suggest that the analysis here needs to go a bit deeper. Islam had at least one great university known to non-specialists like me, the al-Azhar in Cairo, and there were certainly other institutions whose names are translated in English as 'colleges', mentioned by Ibn Khaldun, for example [VI. 8], as particularly abundant in Egypt. As with the state universities of T'ang and Sung China, I suspect that what needs focusing on are the more precise differences in their constitutional and administrative structures in contrast with their partial Western counterparts. In the same way, there would seem to be slight but real elements in the Islamic tradition that gave support to the idea of economic and technical progress. The thirteenth-century encyclopaedist ash-Shahraûri wrote that:

> of necessity there must exist a group the members of which co-operate to acquire many different crafts and [technical] skills. In this way, each individual accomplishes something from which his fellow men can profit. Full cooperation will [in this way] materialize, and the life of the human species and of other animal species will reach perfection.

This is not a zero-sum mentality as regards economics (*pace* p. 168). It may be that we should be cautious in stressing this counter-position too strongly. In his book on Ibn Khaldun, for example, Rosenthal has written that in his world, 'it was believed that human intellectual power was always constant and capable of producing the highest civilization at any time', and hence Ibn Khaldun 'could hardly have assumed that steady progress in human civilization was possible or even necessary', and the great historian was of course famous for his theory of cycles. All I am suggesting is that by the rather later time with which the chapter is mainly concerned, a number of what we would see as potentially valuable intellectual trends had been closed off.

The second reason is that several observations in the chapter indicate that early Islamic polities – the Umayyad and Abbasid caliphs for example – were much more open to change than their successors (p. 166). Very importantly, on p. 173 we are told that 'at least initially, the process of Islamic jurisprudence was quite responsive to the needs of key economic players'. Gradually, however, it seems this flexibility was lost, and the tendency to support legislation of human origin with the claim that it was divinely sanctioned froze it into semi-immobility. Here I am of course citing from the chapter to support my suggestion that all our other analytical considerations have to be related, one way or another, to this loss of psychological dynamism within Islamic intellectual culture as the centuries passed. The 'Islamic' context was not unchanging.

This said, the chapter lays weight on one unchanging factor, namely the Islamic laws of partible inheritance that made it hard to accumulate enduring concentrations of wealth in private hands. Other great pre-modern societies, however, have also had laws or conventions of partible inheritance, imperial China being an obvious example. Observing them, and taking into account simple demographic considerations about the likely probability of a middle-aged man dying without at least one surviving son in pre-modern conditions, suggests that this factor would have been important but not altogether decisive. Accumulation through inheritance was in fact certainly possible. Ibn Khaldun notes [IV. 15] that 'the acquisition and accumulation of [real] property . . . may come about through inheritance from one's forefathers and blood relatives, so that eventually the property of many comes to one person, who thus possesses much'. The political vulnerability of private wealth, at least that outside a charitable trust, a point on which the author also rightly lays emphasis, seems to have been more important. Ibn Khaldun asserts that wealthy people in cities need protection ([V. 16]: 'A sedentary person who has a great deal of capital and has acquired a great number of estates and farms . . . competes in this respect with amirs and rulers. The latter become jealous of him . . . They envy him and try every possible trick to catch him in the net of a government decision . . . so as to confiscate his property.'

With this we move into Professor Kuran's often penetrating account of Ottoman statecraft. The crux of his analysis is the absolute indifference of the rulers to fostering in a proactive fashion the economic well-being of its subjects. One obvious contrast here is with the Chinese empire for whom *minsheng*, the 'people's livelihood', was a well-understood Confucian responsibility. He argues that the cause of this indifference was that 'the economically productive class gradually lost influence to the state bureaucracy'

(p. 152), and while this seems perfectly reasonable, it probably cannot be a sufficient explanation in itself as the case of the Chinese bureaucracy – also fairly free from the direct influence of the economically productive class – suggests. The orientation of the political culture was also seemingly significant. The Ottomans were interested in revenue, assured supply, security, social stability and in preventing durable accumulations of independent wealth, even intervening to control to some extent the larger charitable foundations. And there were few if any institutional restraints to stop them preying on their subjects.

This sobering catalogue is a broadly convincing explanation as to why there was no home-grown economic efflorescence, but there is at least one question that still needs raising. The Ottoman empire was a huge trading area, and long-distance trading was beset with problems, above all those of trust. One last quotation from Ibn Khaldun, speaking of course of a somewhat earlier time [V:13]:

> In the attempt to earn the increase [of capital] that constitutes the profit, it is unavoidable that one's capital gets into the hands of traders, in the process of buying and selling and waiting for payment. Now honest [traders] are few. It is unavoidable that there should be cheating, tampering with the merchandize which may ruin it, and delay in payment which may ruin the profit, since [such delay] while it lasts prevents any activity that could bring profit. There will also be non-acknowledgement of obligations, which may prove destructive of one's capital unless [the obligation] has been stated in writing and properly witnessed. The judiciary is of little use in this connection, since the law requires clear evidence.

He notes that it helped to have political power to get legal disputes settled in one's favour. In medieval Europe, as Avner Greif has shown, the problem of trust in transactions over long distances and long periods of time was initially handled by merchants belonging to permanent groups of fellow-regionals with representatives in major centres of transactions, including fairs. Members of these groups knew each other and mutually guaranteed each other, and were capable of pursuing defaulters. Individuals disappeared but the group did not, so there was no temptation to default on the last transaction of a series, and the collectivity had an enduring interest in maintaining the credit standing of its members. If, because of the problems of establishing corporate bodies, there was nothing comparable in the Islamic world, and the law courts were only – if we follow Ibn Khaldun – of much use to people with political clout, how was the question of mercantile trust handled in long-distance trade? The Chinese to some extent used well-established brokers who served as middlemen. Was something like this perhaps the institutional solution? We need to know the answer to this for the picture – well drawn though it is – to be convincingly completed.

COMMENT

Toby E. Huff

The idea that political competition and decentralization would have an impact on scientific development and creativity, as well as economic growth, is a suggestive one. It seems likely that this implied influence of decentralized political competition among states has been variable over the centuries. The expansion and contraction of the 'Islamic lands' over the centuries has been enormous, and rarely (if ever) have all of the domains with large Muslim populations been under the control of a single centralized state. Following the decline of the Abbasids (ca 1258), the Ottoman empire was probably the largest of these, yet it too fell far short of including all of the major Islamic lands that had, by the sixteenth century, nearly encircled the globe. Nevertheless, with the rise of the Ottomans, historians (Dale 1996, Lawrence 1999, Hodgson 1974) identify three additional great Muslim empires, namely the Safavid centred in Iran, the Uzbek (Timurid) empire centred around Bukhara and Samarkand, and the Mughal empire of South East Asia extending from central Afghanistan to southern India (see the accompanying map). Moreover, there was an important and autonomous Mamluk empire (ca 1254–1517) centred in Cairo. Even that leaves out the territories of the Malaccan sultanate and adjacent territories, as well as Morocco in the Maghreb and the somewhat ephemeral Songhay empire that flourished for many centuries in sub-Saharan Africa around Timbuktu. Thus it seems that the Islamic world, and its world expansion after the demise of the Abbasid empire, was an exceedingly polycentric world insofar as political control is concerned. The imagined unity of the *umma*, the 'Islamic community', is a mythology that expresses the great desire of pious Muslims to create a universal religious body. According to our guiding hypothesis this polycentricity ought to have generated considerable competition in the realm of commerce as well as the intellect. Before commenting on Timur Kuran's impressive study of the economic side of this problem, I want to add some further notes regarding science and education in the Islamic lands, areas of Muslim life that might have undergone innovation due to competitive pressures.

The Golden Age of Scientific Creativity

It was during the 'classical' phase of Islamic civilization, from roughly the ninth to the fourteenth century, and especially during the Abbasid Golden Age (ca 750–1258), that scientific thought flowered. It was during this period of time, especially in the tenth and eleventh centuries, that scientific thinkers of many religious persuasions (Christians, Jews and Muslims) developed the

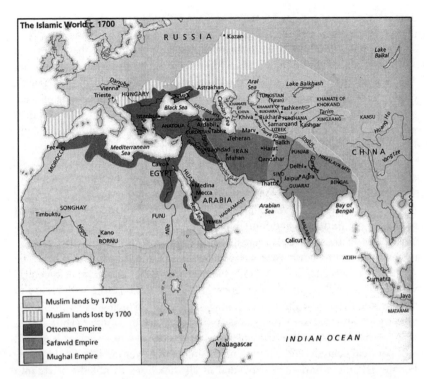

Source: *The Cambridge Illustrated History of the Islamic World*, edited by Francis Robinson, Cambridge University Press, 1996: 66).

Figure 6.1   The Islamic World ca 1700

most advanced intellectual systems in astronomy, medicine, optics and mathematics, as well as pharmacology. Although technical innovations continue to appear in Arab astronomy until the end of the fourteenth century and the death of Ibn al-Shatir in 1375, no further outstanding innovations occurred that would put Arabic science on the path of modern science.

The Abbasid period was, however, one of the more politically stable periods when interstate warfare and rivalry was probably at a minimum. The Abbasid dynasty was a unique creation of imperial power, one that attempted to fuse the Sunni Arab culture of Islam's origins with the Shia and Persian heritage. It was more or less successful in doing this, creating in the process a vast central imperial apparatus that was to see more than three dozen individuals serve as caliph and 'commander of the faithful'. While some historians suggest that al-Wathiq (r. 842–7) was 'the last great Abbasi ruler of a relatively unweakened empire' (Hodgson 1974, Vol. 2: 8), the Abbasid empire was the dominant ruling apparatus for the main Islamic lands of the period, something that no other Islamic political regime could claim subsequently.

Nevertheless, scholars who have studied key figures in the history of Arabic-Islamic science have often pointed out, as Hartner did (Hartner 1957), that most of the major philosophers and scientists of this period required royal patronage, and when they lost it, suffered at the hands of local religious opposition groups. In a word, the scientific enterprise requires minimal levels of stability and continuity for its survival and development. But that is not all.

At the same time one should point out that despite the Mongol conquests and the sacking of Baghdad in 1258, Arabic astronomy continued to develop. This is seen in the construction of the great observatory in Maragha (beginning in 1259), and in the development of various 'non-Ptolemaic' astronomical models in the thirteenth and fourteenth centuries (Saliba 1994). Selected technical parts of these models were later incorporated in Copernicus's revolutionary astronomy, but no one has yet shown a path of transmission from the Arabs to Copernicus, and the Arabs themselves did not adopt the heliocentric view until several centuries after Copernicus. The same is true with regard to modern medicine and the use of human dissection, which was so brilliantly used by Vesalius (1543) when it was forbidden in Islamic circles (Huff 2002).

After the demise of the Abbasid dynasty, no central city – such as Baghdad – or political centre could claim to maintain control over the Islamic domains. For the Islamic world soon expanded in all directions as noted earlier: into sub-Saharan Africa, into Europe (the Balkans), northward and east along the southern border of Russia into Central Asia, into Afghanistan and India, and the Malay archipelago. The expansion of Islam into Europe had already occurred in Spain, but with the fifteenth-century expansion into the Balkans along the Adriatic, still another cultural domain was brought under Islamic control. These new far-flung domains – in the Balkans, Mughal India, Central Asia, and the Malay archipelago, as well sub-Saharan Africa – all had their increasingly separate cultural identities, very different from the Arab heartlands and from the formerly Arabo-Persian territories forming the core of the Abbasid empire.

Islamic Law, *Madrasas* and Universities

To a significant degree the cultural glue that held all this together was the underlying conception of Islamic law, the *Shari'a*, that went wherever Islam spread. No comparative study of the actual practice of Islamic law in the 'Four Corners' of the Islamic territories exists to inform us how it was understood and practised for any significant period of time. The Ottoman empire was the largest and most cohesive political state within this domain from the fifteenth century until the First World War. Timur Kuran's chapter provides an especially useful account of the role that Islamic law played in the delayed economic modernization of the Ottoman empire.

On the other hand, one indicator of the spread of Islamic high culture and its legal conceptions is the *madrasa*, the Islamic colleges and lesser schools of learning. Although we have no comparative study of *madrasas* in the Balkans, in Spain, sub-Saharan Africa, India and so on such evidence as we have shown that *madrasas* dedicated to the 'Islamic sciences' did indeed spread along with Islamic culture throughout the Islamic lands, though at a very uneven rate. Over the centuries these institutions grew stronger and more widespread. This form of religious education – studying the Qur'an, *hadith*, Islamic law, Arabic and Arab history and some arithmetic – became the norm throughout the Islamic domains. As in the Middle East and North Africa, the development of Western-style universities and, above all, the study of the modern natural sciences, had to wait until the end of the nineteenth century (the earliest), and otherwise until the twentieth century before their emergence in the Islamic lands.[1] Thus the break-up of the cultural and political unity of the Islamic empire after the decline of the Abbasids did not result in a flowering of scientific creativity or development. Indeed, from the thirteenth century onwards, scientific culture in the Islamic lands continued to deteriorate – and this despite the formidable bureaucratic apparatus that the Ottomans assembled to govern their domains. The potential competition between, for example, the Ottoman lands, the Indian subcontinent, sub-Saharan Africa, and the various Malay states did not result in heightened scientific or technological creativity. Moreover, as Kuran shows in his study (and elsewhere), the competition between Europe and the Ottoman lands in the fifteenth century and thereafter did not result in enhanced economic development for the Ottomans, but in a general economic decline throughout the Ottoman lands. And in the realm of the intellect, there was at most an emulation of the prevailing Islamic religious studies model, while Cairo's great *madrasa*, al-Azhar, continued to be perceived as the locus of authentic Islamic authority. Yet as Muhammad Abduh (d. 1895) was to find out during his heroic efforts at the end of the nineteenth century, the al-Azhar scholars resisted every effort to modernize that school of higher learning (Livingston 1995).

As I pointed out some time ago, a major impediment to the development of modern science in the Muslim world was the lack of the concept of legal autonomy (Huff 1993). Without this idea and its institutional embodiment, there was no place wherein all the forms of intellectual inquiry could be carried on unfettered by religious or political censors. For the Islamic colleges, *madrasas*, were 'pious endowments', restricted to teachings fully consistent with the spirit of Islam.

By way of contrast, Europe in the twelfth and thirteenth century produced legal reforms and innovations that led to the clear articulation of the idea of a legally autonomous entity, namely the 'corporation', or 'whole body', which carried with it a bundle of rights. Moreover, corporate governance carried with it the principle of election by consent (Huff 1993/2003, especially Chapter 4). Thus in Western Europe this organizational form was enjoyed by cities and towns, by both businesses and charitable organizations, as well as professional guilds, and most especially by universities. In these newly founded universities scholars embedded the teachings of Aristotle, especially his 'natural books', along with philosophy, logic, rhetoric and other 'secular' disciplines. This created a fertile ground for the flourishing of modern science. In contrast to this the Islamic colleges, *madrasas*, were pious endowments within which only studies that strictly conformed to the spirit of Islam could be pursued.

Law and Commerce

As Timur Kuran reiterates in his study, the juridical concept of the corporation was absent in Islamic law, and over the centuries up to the twentieth century, Islamic legal scholars were unable to break out of this religiously ensconced conceptual impasse. With a wealth of new detail Kuran points out the many defects of Islamic law and the difficulties of effectively modifying it in the Ottoman lands. He points out that the only available alternative – apart from straightforward business partnerships – was the concept of the unincorporated 'pious endowment' (*waqf*). Kuran mentions briefly that in the Ottoman empire no cities were legally autonomous, and this seems to have contributed to the different economic strategies pursued by Ottoman administrators. That is, since cities and towns in the empire were not autonomous, rulers did not have to adopt policies that would encourage merchants to attend fairs or settle nearby. In Europe on the other hand, the prevailing legal autonomy of cities and towns led to efforts by local political leaders to support and encourage locally held fairs that would attract more business and hence revenue to their domains. This did stimulate competition between merchants and between cities around Europe.

Not only was the Ottoman administrative apparatus 'shallow' in its supervision of economic activity according to Kuran, businessmen themselves, and especially the Muslim subjects, were deprived of the opportunity to use the corporate form of business organization, a form that both distributed liability and maintained far greater stability and longevity than partnerships. Islamic business partnerships would be dissolved if one of the partners withdrew or died. One can see therefore the greater risks attached to attempts to create three- and four-person partnerships (see Kuran 2001). It seems important to note that Ottoman policies inadvertently favoured non-Muslim subjects in that they – but not Muslims – could have a choice of legal venues. Thus various inducements designed to appeal to foreign or non-Muslim subjects disadvantaged local Muslim subjects.

In the end, the only legal vehicle available for amassing personal wealth, as Kuran explains, was the unincorporated pious trust, the *waqf*, the same legal vehicle used to create the *madrasas*. Kuran grants that this vehicle did serve to provide public goods such as bridges, schools, libraries, and lodgings for travellers, yet there were too many limitations inherent in the legal form to allow it to be flexibly used. In general the pious endowment was used to amass personal wealth, and in the process contributed to the withdrawal of funds from the public domain, from government supervision, as well as from ordinary business investment. At the same time, Kuran points out that the regulation of the Ottoman rulers was such that 'wealth acquired through official privilege generally could not be bequeathed to one's descendants' (Kuran p. 157). In this regard the Ottoman policies 'prevented the creation of large and durable accumulations of wealth'. Furthermore, Kuran points out that throughout the nineteenth century Islamic rules of inheritance prevailed throughout the empire, and this likewise resulted in the division of inheritance and the dilution of capital available to single investors.

As the years unfolded, the Ottoman rulers found themselves without adequate resources, for a variety of reasons. To remedy this situation they began to move to confiscate *waqf* properties, though this had to be done very delicately, and with a simultaneous campaign designed to remove the religious sanctity of the pious endowments. In the event this went hand in hand with efforts to modernize and Westernize state functions in Middle Eastern regimes.

If we shift our attention back to the potential economic competition between the various autonomous Muslim states (the Ottoman, Safavid, Mughal or Uzbeki), there seems to be little evidence that any of them could remedy the defects of Islamic law which would have opened the way to continuous economic development. Of course Ottoman and other state policies themselves contributed to the delayed modernization of Middle Eastern economic life. In short, this case study, like that of China, seems to show the very great importance of institutional arrangements, above legal structures. Although there are reasons for believing that the Islamic lands were divided up into potentially competitive rivals, the underlying institutional structure based on Islamic law negated the creative potential of a rivalrous context.

Notes

1. The first of the Western-style universities was Robert College, founded in 1863 in Istanbul by Americans, followed by the American University of Beirut founded in 1866, also by Americans. The American University in Cairo was founded in 1919, but the newly created University of Cairo had been founded in 1912.

References

Dale, Stephen F. (1996), 'The Islamic world in the age of European expansion', in Francis Robinson (ed.), *The Cambridge Illustrated History of the Islamic World*, Cambridge and New York: Cambridge University Press, pp. 62–89.

Hartner, Willy (1957), 'Quand et comment s'est arrêté l'essor de la culture scientific dans l'Islam?', in R. Brunschvig and G.E. von Grunebaum (eds), *Classisme et déclin culturel dans l'histoire de l'Islam*, Paris: G.-P. Maisonneuve Larose, pp. 319–37.

Hodgson, Marshall G.S. (1974), *The Venture of Islam,* 3 vols, Chicago, IL: University of Chicago Press.

Huff, Toby E. (1993), *The Rise of Early Modern Science: Islam, China and the West*, New York: Cambridge University Press, 2nd edn 2003.

Huff, Toby E. (2002), 'Attitudes towards dissection in the history of European and Arabic medicine', in Bennacer El Bouazzati (ed.) *Science: Locality and Universality*, University Muhammad, publications of the Faculty of Letters and Human Sciences (conferences and colloquia no. 98), Rabat, Morocco, pp. 61–88.

Kuran, Timur (2001), 'The Islamic commercial crisis: institutional roots of economic underdevelopment in the Middle East', unpublished paper, November, accessed at www.papers.ssrn.com.

Lawrence, Bruce, C. (1999), 'The eastward journey of Muslim kingship in South and Southeast Asia', in John Esposito (ed.), *The Oxford History of Islam*, New York: Oxford University Press, pp. 395–431.

Livingston, John (1995), 'Muhammad 'Abduh on science', *The Muslim World,* **85** (3–4), 215–34.

Saliba, George (1994), *A History of Arabic Astronomy*, New York: Columbia University Press.

Vesalius, Andreas (1543), *De humani corporis fabrica*, Basel.

COMMENT

R. Stephen Humphreys

Professor Kuran's chapter is, quite simply, a very fine one. He has read widely and well; he understands the issues (and the countless pitfalls) in Islamic and Ottoman history which are relevant to our topic; he is very skilled in framing hypotheses in a testable way; and he proposes an original way of exploring a long-debated but poorly resolved issue: the failure of the Ottoman empire to achieve an economic breakthrough (or even to maintain its earlier levels of prosperity) in the seventeenth and eighteenth centuries. Several points might be contested, and some issues (for example European naval supremacy after the 1580s, or the refusal of most European states to allow Muslim merchants to reside in their seaports, even in restricted quarters) seem to be overlooked. On the whole, however, it is a chapter which invites discussion and further reflection rather than efforts at refutation.

In his customary manner, Professor Cook has done a very elegant job of addressing the implications of Kuran's paper for the theses proposed by Jean Baechler, so I need not focus on those issues in my comments. I would only say that if you find that Professor Cook's remarks have merit, you should not be discouraged. Scholars throughout the social sciences find the Middle East extremely theory-resistant. That is of course a large part of its charm for historians.

Professor Kuran's key thesis is that the Ottoman 'failure to thrive' is primarily due to the rigidities of Islamic commercial law – that is the widely accepted doctrines imbedded in the *shari'a* of partnership, investment, contract, profit and so on. These doctrines almost compelled small-scale, transitory business organizations, in contrast to the great chartered mercantile companies which proliferated in Europe between the sixteenth and eighteenth centuries. The *shari'a* doctrines had emerged and become almost universally accepted between the eighth and eleventh centuries; regarded as expressions of God's will (or at least our best guess as to God's will), they could not be altered later on simply to suit current whims and fashions. Ottoman imperial authorities, Professor Kuran argues, may possibly have been aware of the disadvantages faced by their merchants, but they were largely indifferent, since Ottoman merchants (whether Muslim or non-Muslim) were politically weak, and since Ottoman material needs were being quite adequately met by French, Dutch and English merchants.

The argument is a good one overall, I think. However, it is weakened by the barely adolescent state of our knowledge about two critical topics. First, the concrete historical development of Islamic legal doctrine over the centuries. In general, modern scholarship on Islamic jurisprudence (*fiqh*) has long favoured theoretical over practical issues. But there are thousands of published and unpublished authoritative opinions on concrete cases (*fatwas* – not at all a sinister word), and these have hardly begun to be studied. More crucially for Professor Kuran's topics are the tens of thousands of court cases preserved in Ottoman archives all over the Balkans and the Near East. Some of these have been examined, but very rarely from the perspective of commercial practice. So in fact we literally do not know what Ottoman commercial law was or how it was applied in the real world. Until we do know these things, Professor Kuran's argument will remain merely an intriguing hypothesis.

Equally to the point, we know very little about the internal trade of the Ottoman empire, although the research by Raymond and Hanna on eighteenth-century Cairo, by Marcus on Aleppo in the same period, and by Suraiya Faroqhi on central entailment in the seventeenth century have opened up important avenues. What we do know is that the Ottoman empire was a vast, extremely variegated place, and its trade with Europe was only a fraction of its internal exchanges. Rather like the United States in the first two-thirds of the twentieth century, the Ottoman empire's foreign trade was a significant but not dominant element in its economy. In any case, there is an enormous amount still to be learned about the organization of manufacturing and commerce, the accumulation and investment of capital, and so on. There is some very inter-esting work on the amassing of agricultural properties in the seventeenth and eighteenth centuries by local notables who often bore official titles but were hardly controlled in any systematic way by the central government in Istanbul. Clearly these great holdings sometimes involved commercial agriculture, though I hesitate to follow the lead of some world-systems enthusiasts who regard this as capitalist production. But the point again is that we do not really know how the Ottoman economy worked; pending that knowledge, Professor Kuran has made a very plausible case, but it is no more than that.

Professor Kuran's chapter suggests a number of crucial issues without developing them, and it would be interesting to hear his comments on these. For example, some scholars have argued that the Ottomans were ignorant of many crucial trends in early modern Europe because Muslim merchants were forbidden to reside in European port cities, unlike their Western counterparts who had residence and commercial rights defined not only by treaty but by traditional Islamic jurisprudence. The argument has merit, no doubt. However, the Ottoman empire was extraordinarily powerful relative to any European state except Spain in the sixteenth century, and still a more than equal oppo-nent in the seventeenth – precisely the time when the early 'capitulations' were being negotiated with France, England and Holland. Had the Ottomans desired to do so, they could certainly have coerced their European treaty partners to concede rights to Ottoman merchants. (Venice, in passing, did have a *fondaco dei turchi*, but this opening was not exploited.) Why then did they not do this?

Second, we could ask whether Ottoman Muslim merchants ever entered into partnerships with the Western Europeans. Partnerships between Muslim, Christian and Jewish merchants were commonplace in Fatimid Egypt in the eleventh and twelfth centuries, and there is no serious barrier to such arrangements in the *shari'a*. If not, what would be the reason? Would it be religious superiority and disdain, or administrative penalties imposed by Ottoman officials on Muslim merchants who stepped out of line? Or might it be the solid economic motive of comparative advantage: the Europeans were best equipped to dominate the Mediterranean sea lanes, while Ottoman merchants could best exploit the Empire's interior trade, which may well have been more lucrative in any case.

Another issue, perhaps related. We naturally tend to focus on Mediterranean commerce, but a great deal flowed across the Indian Ocean, the Persian Gulf and the Red Sea. Since India was one of the richest markets that one could imagine in the sixteenth and seventeenth centuries, perhaps we need to examine the role of Ottoman merchants in that commerce. There has of course been important work on the Indian Ocean trade, by Steensgaard and Chaudhuri among others; I cannot claim to be familiar with this literature, and possibly Professor Kuran could comment on this. We do know that Muslim shipping was an important element in this arena.

A final point on the Ottoman empire concerns the eighteenth century, when (as Professor Cook cleverly puts it) the empire became a crypto-federation – in principle still as always a unitary state with the sultan at its head, but in fact a loose agglomeration of provinces held together largely by history and the prestige of the Ottoman name. By the last decades of the century even that glue was dissolving, and not only in the restive Christian provinces of South-Eastern Europe. More importantly for our purposes, the Christian and more rarely the Jewish merchants were taking increasing advantage of the Capitulations to put themselves under European consular protection. They did so by becoming consular or sub-consular agents of the European trading companies; because they were Ottoman subjects, they could live and work almost anywhere (including some pretty godforsaken places), whereas their European employers were still largely restricted to the major port cities. In a way, this means that these non-Muslim Ottomans were leaving the Ottoman system. But it also means that European commerce was becoming a much more integral part of the Ottoman economy. Given enough time, could this change have brought about a significant structural transformation of the Ottoman economy? Recall that for most of the eighteenth century, European states still dealt with the Ottoman empire as a peer, not as a soft target for territorial expansion and exploitation.

Let me close by picking up a theme discussed both by Professor Kuran and Professor Cook. Both concur that political decentralization does not seem a very useful explanatory variable for the Islamic Middle East. There are (apparently) prosperous times, with a high degree of cultural dynamism and creativity, under both centralized and decentralized political systems. And of course one finds bad times and cultural stagnation in both cases. Perhaps the most useful way of thinking about the relationship between politics, economics and cultural dynamism is to assess the capacity of a given regime to assure order and stability without becoming predatory. The cause-and-effect relationship is of course often far from clear: should we ascribe the grandeur of ninth-century Baghdad or sixteenth-century Istanbul to the power of the Abbasid and Ottoman states, or should we say that these states owed their grandeur to an economic vitality which was quite independent of them? What is certain is that large states which spent themselves into fiscal crisis (as the Abbasids did) or which spun into fiscal crisis for reasons beyond their control (as with the later Mamluk empire in Egypt or the Ottomans at the turn of the seventeenth century) rapidly became predatory regimes, with disastrous economic (though not always cultural) results. The Ottomans worked through their crisis after a few decades of turmoil; the Abbasids and the Mamluks, not to mention their unfortunate subjects, were not so fortunate.

It would be intriguing, and in another venue very worthwhile, to look at the causes of the economic growth of the more successful Islamic regimes before the rise of the Ottomans. But as Professor Kuran has pointed out, those were different times, raising very different problems of comparison and analysis: Europe's financial and commercial institutions were no better than, and often markedly inferior to, their Muslim counterparts. But in early modern times Europe possessed the most innovative economic systems (along, of course, with many stagnant and backward ones). The Ottoman empire was certainly the Islamic world's best hope for keeping pace with these trends, and Professor Kuran is certainly right to have us focus on its successes and failures in this effort.

COMMENT

Erich Weede

Kuran wants to modify the hypothesis that political fragmentation promotes competition between polities and forces them to promote market-augmenting policies. Whereas the usual culprit in explanations of economic stagnation in Asia is political unity, in Kuran's account it is jurisdictional homogeneity and an extremely slow evolution of law. Although there are differences between the usual account and Kuran's account, I want to underline that the approaches are closely related. Obviously, political fragmentation is one background condition for legal fragmentation and evolution. Even when and where applicable in the Muslim world – for example, in between the Abbasid and Ottoman empires – political fragmentation could not lead to the usual results because the revealed divine law represented the unchanging will of God.

Of course, the impact of political fragmentation on economic development is indirect. Secure property rights are an important intervening variable. On the one hand, Kuran (p. 157) writes that 'the Ottoman judicial system regularly enforced the property rights of individuals'. A few lines later, however, one learns that 'traders who achieved affluence were liable to see their assets confiscated'. Although this sounds somewhat contradictory to me, I take this message to admit that property rights were not secure under Ottoman rule. So there seems to be agreement on the positive effects of property rights which actually are respected by the authorities.

Kuran insists that the value of law depends not only on its predictable application, but on its contents. Surely this is an important general point. Specifically, Kuran points to two characteristics of Islamic law which were harmful from an economic perspective: first, the egalitarian inheritance system which slowed the growth of enterprises and capital formation; second, the non-recognition of corporate actors as legal personalities in Islamic law. While this looks plausible and interesting to me, I insist that kleptocracy is the more fundamental problem. Successful capital formation by merchants and recognition of corporations is obviously of little use where governments regard everyone as fair prey.

In my view, inspired by Weber (1922/1964), the lack of safe property rights in the Ottoman empire is related to 'sultanism', a concept which Kuran (p. 150) mentions only to abandon without much discussion. In Weber's typology, sultanism is a subtype of patrimonial rule which together with feudalism is a subtype of traditional rule. Whereas patrimonial rulers are assisted by a dependent staff, feudal rulers rely on vassals who command resources of their own, including land, weapons and troops. Therefore patrimonialism permits much more arbitrary government than feudalism with its more even balance of power between kings and their armed vassals.

Weber chose the term 'sultanism' to describe the most extreme version of patrimonialism. Under sultanism the ruler's staff is recruited from foreigners and/or slaves. Such members of the ruling class enjoy their privileges only at the mercy of their ruler. They are always at risk. Therefore they are ideal tools of arbitrary government. According to my interpretation of Muslim and Ottoman history (for example Hodgson 1974), Weber is right in suggesting that sultanism was more frequent in the Muslim world than elsewhere. In contrast to Kuran I would add sultanism as another determinant of insecure property rights, or of the absence of market augmentation, in the Muslim world.

I find Kuran's observations on the *Shari'a* and on traditionalism quite persuasive, but I would like to add something. In my view, the *Shari'a* and traditionalism are inescapably linked. Why? The idea of a God-given sacred law handed down to mankind by a long-dead prophet must promote a backward orientation. A faithful Muslim jurist must ask himself, how would the prophet have evaluated the case. A forward-looking orientation might amount to framing the question in the following terms: what are the likely economic consequences of this ruling, or of an alternative ruling? Putting even the question in these terms is close to apostasy for which the proper or traditional penalty in Islam is death. So there are three reasons for the legal stagnation in Muslim civilization: first, the weakness of legal competition; second, the common roots of Muslim Law in the *Shari'a* further mitigated legal competition; and third, the traditionalism inescapably linked to the ideas of God as law-giver, the Prophet as the mouthpiece of God, and the closing of the gates of interpretation about the turn from the first to the second millennium.

References

Hodgson, Marshall G.S. (1974), *The Venture of Islam*, 3 vols, Chicago, IL: Chicago University Press.
Weber, Max (1922), *Wirtschaft und Gesellschaft*, reprinted 1964, Köln: Kiepenheuer and Witsch.

Index

Abbasid
  caliphs 195, 202
  empire 13, 24, 151, 171, 214
absolutism of Islamic state 150, 177
Abu al-Baqa of Ronda 188
Abu Yusuf 180
Age of Antiquity, Japan 8, 100, 102, 109
agrarian civilization 98–9, 131, 138–9
agricultural
  economy, Granada 191
  Sudra castes, India 129, 135,
  tax , Muslim 1704
agriculture, Japan 104, 106, 109, 116
al-Azhar, Cairo (*madrasa*) 207
Albert, Michel 103, 111
alcohol consumption 172
Aleppo's cloth dyers 154, 156, 161, 162,
  164
Alfonso VI of Castile 187
Almohads 12, 184, 186–8, 190–92
Almoravids 12, 184, 186–8, 190–92
al-Nahal, Galal H. 180
al-Waathiq 205–6
Andalusian
  astronomers 188
  merchant-scholars 190
Andreski, Stanislav 148
Arab
  astronomy 85
  civilizations, zenith 12, 191
  horses in Muslim Spain 189
  Middle East 159–60, 167
Arabian-Islamic culture and science 12,
  191–2, 206
architecture 40, 51
Arieti, S. 46, 54
Aristotle, teachings of 208
Armajani, Yahya 4, 16, 51, 54
Aryan settlement 130–33
Asakawa, Kanichi 119, 123
Ashoka, South India 134, 135
assassinations, Arab 151

astronomy
  Arabic 186,188, 205, 206
  China 82, 84
autarchic villages, India 133–4
autocracy in China 70–75, 86

Baechler, Jean 18–38, 68, 88, 197, 211
Barbir, Karl K 180
Barkan, Ömar Lütfi 180
basilica, Constantinople and Rome 25,
  26
Beasley, W.G. 111
Benson, Bruce 180
Berber tribes 184, 187
Berman, Harold J. 15, 86, 87, 140
Bernholz, Peter 11, 12, 184–92
Bhagwati, Jagdish 37, 38
Bodde, Derk 86, 87
Boyd, R. 137, 140
Brahmins (priestly caste) 10, 43, 131,
  134, 135
Braudel, F. 117
Bretton Woods, monetary system 104,
  109
Buddhism 40, 48, 59, 76, 78, 133, 148
  monks 49, 143
Bushidan (warriors) 121

Cahen, Claude 185, 188, 192
Caldwellö, J.A.M. 180
calligraphy as art, China 78
Candolle, A. de 41, 42, 54
capitalism 11, 15, 28, 113, 114
Carringer, D.C. 54
caste system 10, 11, 24, 130–35, 142–3,
  146–8
Castile, kingdom of 12, 188, 190
cavalry warfare, India 143, 144
centralization and decentralization 114,
  130
  Japan 96, 97, 103, 105, 107, 109
  political 213–214
  see also decentralization